SPECIAL NEEDS IN ORDINARY SCHOOLS

Series editor: Peter Mittler

Associate editors: Mel Ainscow, Brahm Norwich, Peter Pumfrey
and Sheila Wolfendale

Special Needs and Early Years Provision

Currently available in the Special Needs in Ordinary Schools series:

Special Needs and Early Years Provision

Hannah Mortimer

CONTINUUM
London and New York

Continuum

The Tower Building
11 York Road
London SE1 7NX

370 Lexington Avenue
New York
NY 10017-6503

First published 2001

British Library Cataloguing-in-Publication Data
A catalogue record for this book is available from the British Library.

ISBN 0-8264-5456-9 (hardback)
      0-8264-5455-0 (paperback)

Typeset by Kenneth Burnley in Wirral, Cheshire.
Printed and bound in Great Britain by TJ International Ltd, Padstow, Cornwall.

Contents

Editor's foreword

I am delighted to welcome this book as the final one in the series *Special Needs in Ordinary Schools*.

The series has spanned over fifteen years, which is a long period of time for a series of textbooks. It has encompassed a wide range of special needs and disabilities and has sought to showcase good practice, in teaching and learning. The series, true to its basic tenets, has consistently promoted integrated/inclusive educational and social practice.

This final book in the series focuses on special needs and early years and its inclusive ethos reflects that of the series. Hannah Mortimer is a very experienced practitioner – an ex-teacher and practising educational psychologist – who has built up an impressive portfolio of practical work, assessment and intervention strategies for working with young children, their parents/carers, teachers, and others who work with and care for them.

The timing of the publication of this book is most fortuitous; during 2001 there will be new special needs and disability rights legislation and a revised special educational needs Code of Practice will come into force, later in the year, to which all schools and early years settings must have due regard. Hannah has been able to include, in the book, reference to the likely contents of the revised Code of Practice, where it affects practice and procedures in the early years.

This book describes and celebrates the considerable achievements and developments in early years/special needs in recent years, notably in national and local policies and procedures, inclusion, partnership with carers and colleagues, consulting young children, practice in assessment, identification and intervention with young children.

The style of the book is interactive, whereby the reader is often invited to think about and reappraise his/her own practice in the various areas and at the end of each chapter is asked to consider ways of reframing ideas and practice.

Although this is a textbook, packed with information, illustrative case studies, references and resources, it reflects partnership with readers, acknowledging their expertise. This is an inspirational book, which fittingly concludes an impressive series, and which reflects evolving practice in a fresh and encouraging way.

PROFESSOR SHEILA WOLFENDALE
Psychology Department
University of East London

Acknowledgements

Sheila Wolfendale, Peter Mittler and Tiny Arora.

Mel Ainscow, Ann Chambers, Ann Condon, Cate Crallan, Martin Desforges, Mary Jane Drummond, Gill Edelman and I CAN, Ann Henderson and the Preschool Learning Alliance, Sharon Lissaman, Jane Morgan and Scholastic Ltd, Northallerton Primary Schools Cluster Group, Mike Pomerantz, Helen Robinson, Sue Roffey, David Thompson, Julie Vaggers, Judy Waters, Mollie White, Marion Wood, children of Brompton County Primary School (for illustrating the 'Welcome Profile'), the STAR Centre.

Also Garry, James and Beth for their patience and support.

Introduction: setting the scene

THE NEW LOOK IN EARLY YEARS

If you are reading this book you probably have a particular interest in the education of young children or in meeting their special educational needs. You might be working in an early years setting, you might be training in childcare and early education, you might be a parent, a support professional or a member of an Early Years Development and Childcare Partnership. We live in exciting times. Never before have there been so many substantial changes in 'early years' and in 'meeting special educational needs' and never before have the two areas begun to merge into a new field of interest: how to meet the individual educational needs of all very young children and how to do so inclusively. This book is an attempt to introduce the reader to some of these changes and describe the revolution that is taking place in the way we view special educational needs and the way we provide early years education.

This aims to be an inclusive book and therefore accessible to all readers, whatever their particular role, experience or training. By providing a balance of information, description of practice and practical advice it is hoped that the reader will gain a taste of some of the major issues which are current. Research findings and theoretical models are brought in wherever helpful, returning always to emphasize the practical implications for the key players.

There are bound to be limitations in writing a book in such a rapidly changing field, and it is hoped that this book will provide a snapshot of what is current and, through tracing how thinking and practice have developed, provide the reader with some sense of the wider picture and the direction of change. Why did we think in the way we did? How did this influence the way we worked with children? What changes are happening, and what is this likely to mean for us in the future? In other words, where have we been and where are we going to?

It seems that we are moving towards greater emphasis on partnerships and joint working: with parents, other professionals and other agencies. The Early Years and Childcare Partnerships have brought us together and provided us with a framework for planning and ensuring more equable provision for children and families. There are changes in the way early years provision is funded, from central funding to more chequered funding linked to making bids and setting clear and accountable targets. We are seeing moves from segregated and specialist provision for children with special educational needs (SEN) towards inclusive education for all children. We find that our training backgrounds vary widely from sometimes very little training and expertise in SEN and early years to recent trends towards increased and more uniform training requirements and provision. We can recall the time when many early years practitioners had little experience and confidence in meeting SEN, leaving the task to the 'specialists out there', yet accept that we now have new responsibilities and duties to identify and meet the SEN of children in our settings. Some of these major policy changes are described in Chapter 1.

As early years practitioners, we are still at very different stages of translating the various policy changes into new professional practice and new found confidence. This book aims to add to that confidence; instead of 'not knowing what it is you don't know', this book should provide you with a basic knowledge of the issues you might wish to explore further. The reference list and the list of useful contacts and resources at the back of the book allow you to go into much further detail than the scope of this book allows for.

THE CHALLENGE OF INCLUDING CHILDREN WITH SPECIAL EDUCATIONAL NEEDS IN THE NEW-STYLE PROVISION

Some would argue that the whole field of special education could be redefined usefully in terms of inclusion and exclusion (Booth and Ainscow, 1998). One can almost define 'special educational need' as representing that population of children who have been segregated in some way through the process of describing them or educating them differently from their peers. In the past, the definition of 'special educational needs' has involved the identification and remediation of children's deficits and defects. We (and this book is included) continue to describe children as '*having* special educational needs' or 'learning difficulties' and even this can be a stumbling block for children and their families, easily perpetuating the notion of 'us' and 'them'.

If we focus on a young child's disabilities or deficits, there is a tendency to 'lose sight of what is most important for learning and development during the early childhood years – that is, opportunities to engage successfully in a variety of playful interactions with people and objects in one's environment' (Wilson, 1998, p. 1). The traditional notion in special education that simply identifying them and 'fixing them' in some way can resolve educational difficulties has not borne fruit.

By focusing on a child's competencies and strengths, it becomes possible to remove barriers young children with SEN often experience in their attempts to play and interact. Environments can be adapted and activities developed which improve the child's competencies in play, social interaction and exploration. It is this competency model which is developed in this book; instead of chapters on different disabilities and needs, the book focuses on the key players (Part 2) and on methods of assessment and intervention of the individual needs of all children, including those who are emotionally vulnerable (Part 3).

As the philosophy of providing education inclusively begins to permeate, we are likely to see more emphasis on adjusting approaches to suit children, rather than placing children in different settings depending on whether or not they can 'cope'. Already we are seeing the dawn of new policies for inclusion which, in turn, are developing into more inclusive practice in the nursery or classroom. This change is happening from 'coalface up' as well as 'top down', as early years educators themselves begin to reflect on their practice and translate their own philosophies of inclusion into good practice with their children. We are still in the early stages of evolution and this book aims to provide some support for practitioners along their own personal journey towards working inclusively.

COMPARISONS WORLDWIDE

A recent review of inclusive practice in eight countries (Booth and Ainscow, 1998) suggested that countries differ widely in their perspective of inclusion and exclusion, and that these differences occur along certain dimensions. The very terms are defined rather differently in different countries, sometimes as unending processes and sometimes as black or white states in which one is 'inside' or 'outside' the mainstream. Some countries respond to learning difficulties as if they are defects or impairments that are within the child; others view learning difficulties as arising because the relationship between the child and the environment is not working successfully. Philosophies vary widely; some celebrate diversity of need rather than see it as a problem to be overcome. Some see mainstream education as a right rather than a product of professional decision-making. Some place an emphasis on a common curriculum for all and others on a special curriculum for certain 'special' children. It is recognized that inclusion pervades all levels, though in some countries it is more a matter of individual practice than national philosophy and policy.

When one looks at the dimensions along which different countries' perspectives on 'inclusion' change, it becomes clear how firmly they are embedded in the traditional views of special education and the medical model of deficit or defect. We attempt our own definition of 'inclusion' in Chapter 2 and examine how new-style inclusive early years provision might look and feel for the child, the family and the early years practitioner.

Though this book is primarily concerned with the development of early years and SEN practice in England, the approaches and examples given will be relevant to those in other countries, and there are references in particular to practice in Wales, Scotland and Northern Ireland.

HOW THIS BOOK IS ORGANIZED

The book is divided into four main parts. Part 1 describes these times of partnership and change. Chapter 1 traces the development of policy and legislation over the past twenty years or so, with pen pictures of children, their needs and the placement decisions made for them. Chapter 2 discusses 'inclusion' and ends with practical pointers for developing inclusive practice within early years settings.

Part 2 describes the key players in meeting SEN in early years partnership settings. Chapter 3 introduces the first educators, parents, and examines new trends in parent partnership and education, issues relating to working with parents and pointers for good practice in developing effective links between setting and home. Chapter 4 introduces the children. This book covers the needs of children in the foundation stage of their learning. This starts when children reach the age of 3 and continues until the end of their reception year at school. This book also covers a range of special and individual needs which represent a continuum of need from major disability through to minor and temporary difficulty, in line with the SEN Code of Practice (DfEE, 2000a). We discuss ways of providing child-centred provision and involving children as fully as possible in the planning and delivery of their early education.

In Chapter 5, we meet the early years settings which these children attend. The word 'setting' has been chosen as a description of all the establishments in which children aged 3 and 4 can be found. Over half of the three- to four-year-olds using services in England attend local education authority (LEA) nursery schools or classes (often half-day), or are already in the reception class of their local school. Over half of two- to four-year-olds attend a preschool or playgroup (part time) (percentages taken from National Children's Bureau, 1997). Others are in combined nursery or community centres run jointly by LEAs and social services departments. Some nought to four-year-olds will be attending social services day nurseries or family centres. A small percentage will be at independent schools and pre-preparatory departments. Some will be attending private nurseries, and this figure is increasing. About one in eight children between nought and eight years will be attending a childminder. We discuss the training needs of early years practitioners and examine some methods to enable them to develop reflective practice. Throughout the book, 'early years practitioner' is used to describe all those who work with children in early years settings, regardless of professional training and experience.

Chapter 6 looks at working across boundaries in a 'joined up' way. We examine ways in which multidisciplinary teams work together and ensure collaboration. We are also introduced to the new 'SURE START' and 'Centres of Excellence' initiatives to encourage cross-agency work. Pointers are given for developing effective teamwork in early years.

In Part 3, we look at assessment and intervention in the early years. Chapter 7 examines identification of special needs and the current gateways into various services. Chapter 8 redefines assessment as a dynamic and constructive process, and describes various issues and approaches that can be examined and used in early years settings. Once identification has been made and assessment carried out, interventions can then be planned to improve the child's competencies and adapt the environment to suit their needs better; this is introduced in Chapter 9. Chapter 10 looks at the monitoring of a child's SEN from the perspective of the revised SEN Code of Practice (DfEE, 2000a), translating this into practical implications for the key players. Chapter 11 addresses the needs of children vulnerable to emotional and behavioural difficulties, exploring issues about 'attachment', and looking at environments which inspire children's confidence and positive self-esteem.

Part 4 takes us into the future with visions and possible directions for change. What will future early years provision look like; is it possible to hazard a guess in these times of change and development? Readers might like to read the whole book as an overview, or focus on particular chapters which might meet their own needs in planning to include any child with very individual needs within a setting.

THE AUTHOR'S PERSPECTIVE

As the author, it is appropriate at this stage to say where I am coming from. My own interest in early years and in children who have special educational needs has developed over the past 30 years. I began to become fascinated in the potential of young children to learn when reading Experimental Psychology at Oxford University during the 'Child Development' module with Peter Bryant. I qualified as a nursery and infant teacher at Durham University and spent some time administering provision in two LEAs and also in nursery teaching. I was fortunate to do my Master's year in Educational and Child Psychology at Nottingham University with John and Elizabeth Newson where there was a strong emphasis on early years and on child development.

From there, I worked both as a generic educational psychologist and then as a specialist for early development. I found myself working in various multidisciplinary teams, in developing assessment models for identifying children's needs early and in developing home visiting and Portage services. With parenthood came a greater involvement with playgroups, toddler groups and parenting groups. The 'Music Maker' groups which were developed over these years have now been refined into a training approach for early years educators in a range of early years settings. The approach has been evaluated as my research doctorate at the University of Sheffield.

I now combine work as an educational psychologist for an LEA with work as a child psychologist for the National Health Service (NHS) advising families on managing their children's behaviour in the early years. I also write books and articles for early years magazines and journals, and do freelance training and lecturing. I am lucky that this brings me into first-hand contact with many different early years providers and children, and acknowledge all that I have learned from you all. I am also indebted to two very special principal educational psychologists who supported and encouraged me in developing my early years specialism: Mike Woods and Allan Milburn, both sadly missed from this life.

—Part One

Times of Partnership and Change

Recent developments in early years policy and partnership

It's not enough to mind if children with special needs are in your nursery, you must mind if they're not. (Headteacher of a Community Centre for Childhood)

I feel totally overwhelmed – planning the curriculum, preparing for Inspection, managing all the finance – and now you ask me to take on board 'Special Needs' as well. (Anonymous quote from an early years training evaluation form)

HOW HAVE POLICIES DEVELOPED RECENTLY?

Perhaps the contrasting quotes above do not seem quite so surprising when we consider just how many changes in policy and practice early years providers have seen recently. Not only is early years provision expanding, but the status of SEN within the early years is rising too. Over the past 30 years we have seen a continuum of provision from exclusive, through integration to inclusive. This chapter explores the evolution of special needs and early years legislation over this time. There are several dimensions to this change. You will see a move from central sources of funding to more chequered funding involving making bids, setting targets and evaluating value for money. You will also see how various responsibilities have gradually been devolved upon the settings themselves, with new requirements for managing their funds, assessing and monitoring SEN, and being accountable for quality early years provision and care.

To understand how the different strands in legislation come together, we need to trace how SEN guidance and legislation have developed, the evolution of the Early Years and Childcare Partnerships themselves, and how these weave into other developments such as Children's Services Plans, the early years curriculum, requirements for inspection, quality assurance, present funding arrangements and baseline assessment. Roffey (1999, ch. 2) provides a useful summary of this.

The pen pictures throughout the chapter give snapshots of three children who have received special educational help at different times over the past three decades. Whilst each cannot be representative in itself, they are taken from real examples which seem to have characteristics unique or typical of their time.

Pen picture: Nazia

Nazia is four years old and has Down's syndrome. She lives in a large hospital for the mentally handicapped in the middle of the countryside. She has lived there since soon after she was born. There are about 200 other 'patients' of all ages and level of disability. Nazia has been 'ascertained' by the Education Department as being severely educationally subnormal. There is a school-room in the hospital and Nazia spends her day there along with a small group of other young patients aged 2 to 9 taught by a teacher. Some of the children in her group have disturbed behaviour patterns and attend the 'behaviour modification unit', which is down a path to one side of the hospital, for a session each day. Nazia is fit and well, though can be withdrawn and tends to suck her fists and rock a lot. It is not expected that she will learn to read and write though she has a few single words now. (From a visit and observation, 1977)

WHAT CHANGES HAVE THERE BEEN IN THE WAY WE MEET SEN IN THE EARLY YEARS?

The status of SEN in early years has risen considerably over recent years (Wolfendale, 1997; 2000a). Until 1972, there was a population of children considered to be 'severely subnormal' who were not considered to be 'educable' in schools and were placed within Junior Training Centres. The 1970s saw all term-time provision for school-aged children coming within the remit of the LEAs. The Warnock Report (Warnock, 1978) gave under-5s and special needs a higher profile than before by recommending it as a priority area for teacher training and for proven early intervention programmes. There was a growth in Portage home-visiting schemes (Chapter 3) and a new emphasis on 'preventing' as well as 'remediating' children's difficulties in learning and development. The closure of the large mental handicap hospitals in the 1980s with a renewed emphasis on 'care within the community' emphasized the importance of supporting children and families in their homes and local communities and settings.

This paved the way for new legislation and the 1981 Education Act (which came into effect in April 1983) gave local education and health authorities new duties to identify and assess young children who might have SEN, following 'formal assessment procedures'. Children were now seen as having 'needs' which required 'support', rather than as having within-child 'handicaps' which needed 'treatment'. In time, the 1981 Education Act developed into the 1993 Education Act which, in turn, was subsumed into the consolidated 1996 Education Act.

With the 1988 Education Reform Act came new guidance on under-5s with special needs. Schools also had to take note of the Disability Discrimination Act of 1995, which required them to report on admission procedures for disabled pupils. Each school or nursery school had to make proposals as to how they were going to prevent discrimination, and also what arrangements they would make for ensuring that all children could access both the building and the curriculum.

Part Three of the 1993 Education Act referred exclusively to SEN and made the process of formal (or 'statutory') assessments clearer. It strengthened parental rights and required schools to develop 'special needs policies'. A 'special educational need' was defined as a learning difficulty, which called for SEN provision to be made. This Act soon led to the publication of the *Code of Practice for the Identification and Assessment of Special Educational Needs* (DFE) in 1994 in England and Wales, to be revised in 2001.

With the 'Code of Practice' came procedures for a staged assessment of children with SEN leading to planned intervention either at a within-class level (Stage 1), within-school (Stage 2), with outside support (Stage 3), during a statutory multidisciplinary assessment (Stage 4) or via a statement of SEN (Stage 5). Local education authorities and schools were required to 'have due regard' to the Code when planning and delivering services. There was a whole section on 'assessments and statements for under fives' which stressed the importance of LEAs, child health and social services working together to meet the needs of children under 5 with SEN.

The Nursery Education and Grant Maintained Schools Act 1996 brought with it a new duty on all institutions who redeemed nursery vouchers for four-year-olds to have regard to the SEN Code of Practice. Guidance was given to providers (DfEE, 1996a) but this went unnoticed by some (Mortimer, 1997a). The challenges of meeting the Code of Practice in early years settings are explored further in Chapter 10.

Pen picture: Jon

Jon is now three years old. He was referred to the Child Development Centre soon after birth because he was a floppy baby with poor muscle control and developmental delay. He was diagnosed with cerebral palsy when he was a few months old and attended the centre regularly for physiotherapy. He also saw the speech and language therapist and occupational therapist from time to time. He was referred to the Portage service as soon as his difficulties were recognized and received regular weekly home visits. The home visitor was able to link her teaching to the therapy targets through regular liaison meetings. When he was two years old, he was formally assessed by an educational psychologist, doctor and preschool teacher and it was arranged for him to attend a local school catering for children with severe learning difficulties for three sessions a week. From there, he was integrated into a nursery on a site next door, accompanied by one of the classroom assistants from his special school. He enjoys his time in both settings, though it is expected that his periods of integration may need to be reduced once he is five years old as he might not 'cope' with the academic demands of 'the 3 Rs'.* (From case history, 1987)

* reading, writing and 'rithmetic.

A revised SEN Code of Practice comes into effect from September 2001 and includes guidance that reflects recent policy developments (DfEE, 2000a). It follows the DfEE Green Paper *Excellence for All* (DfEE, 1997a), and will relate to the new era of Early Years and Childcare Partnerships. The Green Paper stressed the importance of early diagnosis and appropriate intervention in improving the prospects of children with SEN. It could reduce the need for expensive interventions later on or even prevent the development of SEN in some cases. The government's 'Programme for Action' (DfEE, 1998a) cross-refers various initiatives such as Early Years Development and Childcare Plans (below) and 'SURE START' (see below).

Partnerships must produce regular 'plans' showing how they will cater for the needs of children with SEN within both childcare and early education (DfEE, 1998b). Also, accredited Baseline Assessment Schemes (QCA, 1998), which came into force for children on entry to school in England and Wales from September 1998, must be sensitive to SEN. The revised code sets SEN within the framework of the Early Learning Goals (QCA, 1999) and shows how early years children with

SEN can be identified, assessed and monitored either with action taken within the setting, or with additional action from outside professionals or external resources.

So far, we have explored the development of SEN policy in England and Wales. There is related legislation in Scotland (SOEID, 1996) and Northern Ireland (DENI, 1998) though the detail is rather different. For example, the 'statement' of SEN in England and Wales is called a 'record' in Scotland. The procedures for opening and monitoring a 'Record of Needs' are outlined in The Scottish Office Education and Industry Department Circular 4/96 and include eight steps rather than the five stages defined in the 1994 SEN Code of Practice in England and Wales. These steps are identification of learning difficulties by the teacher, referral to a learning support co-ordinator within the setting, referral to outside support services, consideration of needs by an educational psychologist, consideration to opening a Record of Needs, medical examination and psychological assessment, meeting to discuss the opening of a Record of Needs, and the final step of opening such a record. The procedure in Northern Ireland is very similar to that in England and Wales (DFE, 1994) though there are minor changes in terminology.

WHAT INFLUENCE DID THE CHILDREN ACT 1989 HAVE ON SEN PRACTICE IN THE EARLY YEARS?

The Children Act 1989 (Department of Health, 1991) had an enormous influence on the planning of children's services and the regulation and monitoring of childcare and preschool services. Social services authorities were now required to identify children 'in need' and to maintain a register of disabled children, liaising with the health service and the LEA. The priority was to develop services that would enable families to care for and bring up children in need in their own homes and communities and to enable these children to live as normal a life as possible. They were required to publish information about such services and to listen to the views of children and parents when planning for and meeting their needs. A child is deemed to be 'in need' if their mental and/or physical health or development is likely to be adversely affected if provision for them or their families were not made.

An Order under section 17(4) of the Children Act 1989 made 'Children's Service Plans' mandatory for social services departments from April 1996. These plans were to involve close collaboration with LEAs, health commissions and trusts, and other agencies concerned with childcare. There was an emphasis on developing services for children in need under eight years old, including day care, holiday care and after-school care. Within the service, a child who has an identified disability or special need should be offered an initial visit by a social worker and an assessment of the family's needs. This might lead on to family support, respite care, access to financial support, adaptations to the home through the occupational therapist, day care provision or advice, training and information.

HOW DID EARLY EDUCATION AND DAY CARE REGULATIONS AFFECT POLICY?

With the Schools Standards and Frameworks Act 1998 came the part-time funding of early years places for all four-year-old children whose parents wanted it. This is being extended to a gradual increase in the funded places for three-year-olds from 1999. At first, the funding was provided via the redemption of vouchers by parents of four-year-olds, and later through central reimbursement via the LEA-led Early Years Partnerships. Partnerships have the responsibility of ensuring that children are matched to places which best suit their needs and of registering provision.

The government's National Childcare Strategy (DfEE, 1998c) brought with it an increased responsibility for partnerships to ensure affordable, good quality childcare for children age 0 to 14. The 'Early Years Development Forums' set up with representatives from different agencies, voluntary organizations, elected members and parents, were soon to become the new-look 'Early Years Development and Childcare Partnerships'. These partnerships are required to produce regular plans showing how quality early years provision and childcare will be provided in their area.

By 1999, the stage was set for the Office for Standards in Education (OFSTED) to take over the reins of a new integrated regulation system, under national standards set by the Department for Education and Employment (DfEE), covering both childcare and early education provision. This heralded a change in role for Social Services Under Eights Officers who had previously been responsible for inspecting and regulating childcare under the Children Act 1989.

Partnership plans must state the provision that is available in the LEA to meet the SEN of preschool children, and it is expected that inclusive arrangements should be made wherever possible. All early years providers registered with the Partnership have to provide information on their SEN policies and their facilities available, the knowledge and skills that the staff have with regard to SEN, and the links with other organizations concerned with SEN. They should appoint one member of staff who is familiar with the SEN Code of Practice who can become a link person or 'SEN co-ordinator', supporting and informing other members of staff. Central funding became available for training and development.

Also, all providers registered with the Partnership were required to offer a range of activities which encourage children to work towards the Desirable Learning Outcomes (SCAA, 1996), later to become the Early Learning Goals (QCA, 1999), and to be subject to regular inspection (DfEE, 1996b). There had to be involvement of a qualified teacher in all settings, which led to the development of early years advisory teachers and early years support services in most Partnerships.

Pen picture: Sultan

Sultan's languages were late to develop, and this needed careful and ongoing assessment from the speech and language therapist and educational psychologist with help from the local centre for multicultural education. Sultan was statutorily assessed when he was four and now attends an inclusive nursery with some support assistance provided through the LEA and regular involvement of a speech and language therapist. Makaton sign language is used throughout the nursery and this has helped Sultan to develop confidence and to want to communicate more with the other children. His parents have been delighted with his progress and how he has settled. Sometimes they wish that more help might have been available without having to have a 'statement' and without being singled out for 'support' which they find stigmatizing. (From case history, 1997)

THE ARRIVAL OF THE QCA AND INSPECTION
REQUIREMENTS

The Desirable Learning Outcomes in 1996 introduced to early years providers the concept of six 'areas of learning': language and literacy, personal social and emotional development, mathematics, knowledge and understanding of the world, physical development and creative development. This paved the way for children's early learning to be followed through into baseline assessment measures on entry to school (from September 1998) and into National Curriculum assessment for school-age children. It was expected that the integration of these three would contribute to the earlier identification of children who were experiencing difficulties in making progress.

The government took the view that defining a set of learning outcomes by the time children enter compulsory schooling (the term after their fifth birthdays) was critical to ensuring that nursery education was 'of good quality and provided sound preparation for the National Curriculum'. In order 'to assure parents and taxpayers' that the nursery education was of good quality, institutions which participated in the Voucher Scheme had to have their educational provision inspected regularly. The nursery inspectors, appointed by OFSTED, would assess the quality of the early years educational provision, look at the clarity of roles and responsibilities within the setting, and be interested in plans for meeting the needs of individual children and developing improved partnership with parents and carers. The Preschool Learning Alliance gave practical guidance to its member settings for preparing for inspection (Bender and Henderson, 1996) and various other publications gave practical suggestions for planning and preparation (e.g. Kenyon, 1998).

Some authors argued strongly against the idea of dividing the early years curriculum into distinct 'areas of learning', since young children left to their own devices certainly did not separate their learning experiences in this way. Nutbrown (1999, p. 117) traced a curriculum for 'thinking children' based on their 'schemas' of thinking and behaviour, and contrasted this with the requirements of the Desirable Learning Outcomes. She introduced an alternative method of assessment which went far beyond the confines of a narrow curriculum and looked at the whole child's thinking and learning. According to the author, the best way to help children to get ready to be three-year-olds is to allow them to be three when they are three and four when they are four. This developmental perspective with an emphasis on 'learning through play' led to lively debate during the consultation phase on the Early Learning Goals.

In September 2000, the Desirable Learning Outcomes were replaced in England by Early Learning Goals (QCA, 1999) which most children are expected to achieve by the end of the 'foundation stage' to children's education, i.e. their early learning from age three until the end of the reception year. Trouble is taken to set these goals into context so that they are seen as an aid to planning ahead rather than as an early years curriculum to replace 'learning through play'. Effective early years education was seen as requiring both a relevant curriculum and practitioners who understand and are able to implement the curriculum requirements. To this end, practical examples of 'stepping stones' towards the goals were provided and detailed curriculum guidance issued (QCA, 2000).

In Scotland, there is also curriculum framework for three- to five-year-olds (SCCC, 1999). This is:

> based on the fundamental principle of equality of opportunity. All education systems of quality must recognize that no individual or group should be disadvantaged on the grounds of race, gender, culture, disability, class, belief, lifestyle or family circumstances. Effective learning and teaching can only take place in an atmosphere of mutual trust, respect and security. An inclusive approach is therefore essential to the provision of high quality learning experiences for all children. (Ibid., p. iii)

Here, there are five key aspects of learning: emotional, personal and social development (including religious and moral development), knowledge and understanding of the world (including environmental studies and mathematics), communication and language, expressive and aesthetic development, and physical development and movement.

The greater emphasis on play and early experience (rather than a narrow band predominately based on *skills*) is also reflected in the early years curricula for Wales and Northern Ireland. In Wales (ACCAC, 1996) there are six areas of learning: language, literacy and communication skills, personal and social development, mathematical development, knowledge and understanding of the world, physical development and creative development. In Northern Ireland (NICCEA, 1997), the seven areas of learning are personal, social and emotional development, physical development, creative/aesthetic development, language development, early mathematical experiences, early experiences in science and technology, and knowledge and understanding of the environment.

HOW ARE SEN TO BE MET WITHIN THE EARLY YEARS FRAMEWORK?

The DfEE produced a Self-Appraisal Schedule to help settings review their practice and prepare for inspection (DfEE, 1998d). Within this, providers are invited to state their current position and define areas for development relating to their policy for SEN and how this policy relates to the 1994 Code of Practice for SEN. They are asked to consider how the policy is known, agreed and implemented by all staff, what support is available for children with special needs and how the setting monitors the effectiveness of its arrangements for children with special needs. They are also asked to state what arrangements are made for liaising with agencies, and with others who care for children with special needs.

The *Early Learning Goals* document (QCA, 1999) gives a greater emphasis than previous documents to SEN and disabilities. Practitioners are expected to plan for each child's individual learning requirements, including those children who need additional support, or have particular needs or disabilities. The focus should be on removing barriers for children where these already exist, or preventing learning difficulties from developing. It is clearly stated that early years practitioners play a key role in identifying learning needs for all the children in their settings. It is not sufficient to consider that they are 'meeting SEN' if they welcome children already identified by someone else as having SEN into their settings. Now, they might find themselves in a position of needing to identify a child's SEN themselves, with all the challenges this has for assessment, making plans and liaising with parents. They are expected to respond quickly to difficulties and develop effective strategies for intervention (see Chapter 9). Wherever possible, joint working with other agencies should be developed (see Chapter 6).

Early years practitioners are expected to help children with SEN make the best possible progress through making provision for those who need help with communication, language and literacy skills (e.g. through the use of alternative and augmentative communication, using different format texts or making use of information and communication technology). They are also expected to make plans for ensuring that children with SEN have access to learning opportunities. These might include plans where necessary to develop a child's understanding, using all available senses and experiences (e.g. through the choice of sensory materials, running commentary and use of information technology) and plans to help a child participate fully in learning and in physical and practical activity (e.g. through providing additional adult support, adapting environments or using specialist aids and equipment). Early years practitioners are also expected to help children who have particular difficulties with behaviour to take part in learning effectively (e.g. by adapting activities or spaces, setting reasonable expectations, establishing clear boundaries, praising efforts, giving encouragement and developing self-respect).

As Early Years Partnerships came to embrace childcare and after-school care as well, they were given clear guidance on preparing their Early Years Development and Childcare Partnership Plans. For example, the planning guidance for 1999–2000 (DfEE, 1998b) tells partnerships that their plans should contain the following information relating to SEN (Annex 8, p. 30). They should detail the support which will be provided to ensure that all early years providers are able to identify and assess SEN. They should also provide information about childcare and early education provision available locally for children with SEN or with disabilities, including support services and the partnership's plans for making provision inclusive. There should be details of the specialist training available locally for childcare and early education staff working with children who have SEN or disabilities and details of information and advice available to parents and carers about childcare and early education for children with SEN or disabilities.

BASELINE ASSESSMENT AND ADDED VALUE

A Baseline Assessment Scheme is a scheme designed to enable pupils in a maintained primary school to be assessed for the purpose of assisting the future planning of their education and the measurement of their future educational achievements under the Education Bill 1996 (Part VI, ch. 1). There was no specific reference here to SEN or to children's diversity, although the historical root of baseline assessment lies in the early identification of SEN (Lindsay, 1998). It has been recognized for the past 30 years or so that early intervention is socially and educationally justifiable for vulnerable 'at risk' children and this has driven many early years initiatives (e.g. Wolfendale and Bryans, 1979). Teachers and LEA staff began to see how they could intervene early, rather than waiting until children had begun to 'fail' at age 7 or above. Various approaches for early intervention were developed and, as this approach began to move down the age range to children entering school, they became known as 'baseline assessment'.

From September 1998, all children entering school in England and Wales had to receive a baseline assessment within seven weeks of starting there. All Baseline Assessment Schemes had to be accredited with the Qualifications and Curriculum Authority (QCA). There was no explicit reference in the bill to assessing 'value added' as a school factor, though the words 'the measurement of their future educational achievements' do suggest this as one interpretation. In reality, this does seem to have been one of the purposes underlying baseline assessment. One way of comparing National Curriculum assessment scores across schools is to take into account the levels of skills of the children entering school and see which schools have 'added the most value' despite their catchment areas and populations of children.

There is much evidence for the usefulness of Baseline Assessment Schemes as part of a sequential approach to identifying learning needs and SEN, argues Lindsay (1998). He still sees the needs for strong quality assurance of these schemes with a need to check that they are reliable and valid measures (as they are in the Infant Index developed by Desforges and Lindsay, 1995). They also need to be used wisely to identify and teach children whose learning might be at an earlier level than their peers, for whatever reason, rather than to identify 'deficit' or 'failure'. Sensitive communication with parents is vital to achieve this, together with personalized feedback and positive recommendations for ways forward.

HAVE CHANGING PATTERNS OF FUNDING AFFECTED PRACTICE AND PLANNING IN EARLY YEARS?

With the changes in early years legislation, the pattern of funding became complex. 'Vouchers' which could be redeemed for a part-time place at a registered early years setting for a four-year-old were soon replaced by a system of central funding, though there were various other sources of funding as well. It became one of the responsibilities of the Early Years Development and Childcare Partnership to be aware of what these various sources of funding were, and how they could be obtained. Strategic planning enjoyed an ascendancy with 'those in the know' struggling to have bids in by a certain date and to duck and dive with the particular criteria of that grant.

In the late 1990s, funding to local authorities arrived via Revenue Support Grants based on the number of four-year-olds in LEA-maintained provision, and specific grants under the Nursery Education and Grant Maintained Schools Act 1996 on the basis of a termly headcount including all the providers in the plan outside the maintained sector. Because LEA-maintained providers could now claim funding for four-year-olds, many schools offered places to four-year-olds from their fourth birthdays with a consequent shift away from other preschool providers which particularly affected those in rural areas. This resulted in a fragmentation of services at the early stages of the partnerships, with a worrying trend towards a reduction in choice for parents rather than an increase in developmentally appropriate places for four-year-olds. The debate about what is 'developmentally appropriate' for a four-year-old continued, with revisions being made at the consultation stage of the *Early Learning Goals* document (QCA, 1999) leading to the *Curriculum Guidance for the Foundation Stage* (QCA, 2000) which re-emphasized the importance of play and interaction in early learning.

As well as the 'headcount' funding, there were various other sources of funding. Funding for training became available through the Standards Fund, and many partnerships have made use of this to strengthen their training in SEN, as required to do so under their plans. Childcare funding became available based on census records of children aged 0–14 in the partnership, with additional funding for disadvantaged areas. The New Opportunities Fund was set up under the National Lottery Act 1998 and was available to fund out-of-school childcare and integrated childcare and education projects.

Central funding to support the National Childcare Strategy became available to Early Excellence Centres which could illustrate good practice in providing a high quality, integrated multi-agency early years service. Many are featured as examples of good practice throughout this book. In addition, the SURE START initiative has been set up to provide support and guidance to more vulnerable families with babies and young children.

In SURE START schemes, parents (as 'first educators' of their children) are targeted to receive information, support and guidance to help them make the most of their young child's developmental, learning and social potential, and also to improve upon their parenting and child-rearing skills. The aim is to improve the life chances of young children in areas of 'risk', through improving their access to education, health services, family support and advice on nurturing. Typical SURE START schemes, based on existing innovative approaches designated 'Trailblazers', provide a range of services and provision. There might be outreach and home visiting, support to families, support for good quality play, quality learning and childcare experiences for young children, advice on child and family health and support for families who have a young child with SEN. Some examples are given in Chapter 6.

Add to these funding from the New Deal for the Unemployed, the New Deal for Lone Parents, the New Deal for Communities, the Single Regeneration Budget, the Rural Development Commission, Regional Development Agencies, the European Social Fund, the National Lottery, Millennium Awards and charitable trusts (DfEE, 1998b), and bidding for funding becomes a truly specialist area. The risk of losing sight of priorities and/or fragmented planning becomes great.

Childcare has traditionally suffered from underfunding and the need to be aware of various sources of funding is not new. However, it is one of the single most challenging responsibilities of any Early Years and Childcare Partnership to hold on to its 'vision' and pursue co-ordinated plans based on real partnership and collaboration, which are securely funded. Criteria for bids constantly change with new government priorities and timescales for grants may be short-lived. In the centre of this financial arena are families and children with real needs who may not happen to fit the criteria or 'designated area' of the time. To be of long-term benefit, such time-limited projects need full and controlled evaluation so that 'good practice' can influence future planning and financing. Later in the book we celebrate some examples of 'good practice' and help the reader reflect on how local practice can be made more effective. The challenge of providing equable, well co-ordinated and inclusive services is enormous. This is what we explore in the next chapter.

SUMMARY

Changes in policy affecting how SEN are met in the early years

Over the past 30 years, the rights of children with SEN to receive quality education and to have their SEN met have increased dramatically.

The status of SEN within the early years is rising, particularly with the implication of the Code of Practice for SEN and the legislation arising from the Children Act.

We have seen a move:

- from segregated care to integrated education, through to inclusion;
- towards meeting the needs of children and families in their own homes and communities;
- towards providing more early years places for children under 5;
- towards greater responsibilities on early years practitioners to identify and meet SEN of children in their settings;
- towards creating a Foundation Stage for early learning in which the needs of early years children are seen as qualitatively different from those of schoolchildren;
- towards parents and children having a greater say in SEN provision;
- towards professionals and agencies joining together more closely in their planning and their provision;
- towards a wider and exciting range of provision for young children and families with particular needs which is, as yet, still patchy and in need of evaluation.

—2————————————————————

Early learning for all:
issues in planning inclusive provisions

We've got to accept each child for what they are. They may not be
'tuned in' to us, but we should try to be 'tuned in' to them.
(Nursery teacher during an in-service training day)

THE PATHWAY TOWARDS INCLUSION

In this chapter, we examine what 'inclusion' might look like both at
the level of whole settings and at the level of working with an individual child. It would be helpful to start by defining some of the terms
used when describing where and how a child's SEN should be met,
and to trace the route along which SEN thinking has progressed.
Wilson (1998) offers the following definitions and suggests that confusion often arises when the terms are used too interchangeably.

In *mainstreaming*, a child with SEN is placed within a setting or a
programme designed for children who do not have SEN. It has usually
been seen as appropriate whenever the child can participate fully in
the curriculum on offer there. If major adaptations to the facilities or
curriculum would have to be made in order for the child to have their
needs met, then mainstreaming might not be recommended.

Where a *least restrictive environment* is recommended, the understanding is that children with SEN will be educated along with
children who do not have SEN to the maximum extent considered to
be appropriate. Separate (or 'special') schooling or classes only take
place when the nature or severity of the child's SEN is such that education in mainstream classes with the use of appropriate aids and
services cannot be achieved successfully. However, this term can mean
different things to different people. Under the original SEN Code of
Practice (DFE, 1994), LEAs were required to comply with parents'
preference for the school to be named on a statement of SEN:

unless the school is unsuitable to the child's age, ability, aptitude or SEN, or the placement would be incompatible with the efficient education of the other children with whom the child would be educated, or with the efficient use of resources. (Ibid., p. 90)

In practice, the 'efficient use of resources' often came to mean that the 'least restrictive environment' was more related to matching children's needs to provision already available, than to planning less restrictive and more inclusive provision. The emphasis of the new Code of Practice (DfEE, 2000a) has moved more in the direction of inclusion.

During *integration*, different groups of children who have been previously segregated are brought together. In the early days of 'integrated practices', classes for children with SEN were sometimes set up within a mainstream school, with opportunities for integrating all the children at break times or for less structured activities such as art or drama. There might have been an 'integrated nursery' within a mainstream school in which children of all needs were educated together before deciding whether a child with SEN needed more specialist provision at the age of 5. Or a child with SEN might attend a special school for some sessions each week, 'integrating' into a mainstream school or nursery for others.

This arrangement tended to give the child with SEN a 'visitor' status rather than to consider them as a 'full member' of the group. There was also research which made it clear that physical integration alone did not lead to children mixing and learning together. Instead, purposeful and careful support must be planned to ensure that genuine integration takes place. For example, Wolery and Wilbers (1994) found that many children with disabilities do not imitate their peers unless taught to do so. Also, many children with and without disabilities do not interact frequently unless supports are provided to encourage such exchanges. Acceptance and positive attitudes about children with disabilities do not necessarily result from integration; adults' behaviour can significantly affect the way children think and feel.

Inclusion is the practice of including all children together in a setting. All children participate fully in all the regular routines and activities of the classroom, though these might need to be modified to meet individual children's goals and objectives.

Most of this chapter is devoted to the benefits of inclusion with pointers for practice, though some would state that inclusion should be a 'given right' rather than something that has to be argued for. As one father of a child with disability said, 'Why must children "prove" that they are ready to be in regular classrooms? We do not ask that of any other members of our society' (Howard, Williams, Port and Lepper 1997, p. 9). Before discussing inclusion in more detail, it is only right to state that there are other points of view as well. Perhaps this is why there is such a diverse range of SEN provision in existence and why LEAs and settings are at many stages along the pathway from segregation towards inclusion.

Research on the topic of full inclusion is complex and, at times, arrives at different conclusions. This is not so surprising when we see how different countries see 'inclusion' as meaning different things and therefore provide many different variants of 'inclusive education'. Some research, for example, has argued that while children with SEN who achieve well will do better in inclusive settings, more disabled children tend to perform better in more segregated settings (e.g. Howard et al., 1997). Not all parents want their child with SEN to attend an inclusive setting, wishing for a more protective environment in order to prevent rejection from more able peers. Many still argue for placement decisions to be made on a case-by-case basis, depending on the individual needs and circumstances. Peterson (1987) suggested that these factors could be taken into account when deciding in which setting to place a child:

- Will the intervention actually increase the child's chances of functioning at a developmentally more age-appropriate level?
- Is the setting culturally compatible with the values and practices of the child's family and community?
- Is the setting equipped to provide the forms of stimulation and care that are age-appropriate for the child and consistent with the child's SEN? .

THINKING IN NEW WAYS ABOUT MEETING SEN IN EARLY YEARS SETTINGS

'When you consider how practice has evolved over the past 30 years, it is easier to understand how we have sometimes become 'set in our ways'. In the past, our efforts to 'integrate' children with SEN into mainstream settings imported practices that developed in the special education sector. Ainscow (1999) traces how special needs provision has changed over the years and how providers can be helped to provide more inclusively for all their children, with and without SEN. In time, providers soon found that highly structured individual programmes based on careful assessments and systematic interventions did not fit easily with how mainstream teachers plan and go about their work. The result is that any integration that depends on importing practices from 'special' education is almost certain to lead to difficulties. The message becomes one of 'special' children needing 'special' practices. Classroom assistants, sometimes untrained, unsupported and poorly informed, may be appointed to provide this 'special' input. When such support is withdrawn, teachers or early years practitioners feel they can no longer cope as they themselves lack the 'special' training. At the same time, settings are beginning to believe that more and more children require specialist individualized programmes, requiring ever more time and ever more resources. The proportion of children with statements of SEN has risen steadily as a result.   ·

There is now a gradual recognition that 'schools for all' will not be achieved by transplanting special education thinking and practice into mainstream contexts. What is needed are ways of making the learning more personal to each child rather than making the lesson more individual. An approach to inclusion is needed that involves 'a shift from seeing inclusion as about individual special educational planning and special pleading for individual students, to the development of a pedagogy of inclusion and a commitment to the rights of all to belong' (Booth and Ainscow, 1998, p. 244). This provides us with a neat view of 'inclusion' as a *process* pervading all areas of philosophy, policy and practice, rather than a set of actions that 'tinker with' and adjust provision already available. In this sense, 'inclusion' can be seen as a revolution in the way we think about children's special educational needs.   ʹ

One of the most significant international documents ever to appear in the special needs field was the Salamanca Statement on Principles, Policy and Practice in Special Needs Education, agreed by representatives of 92 governments and 25 international organizations in 1994 (UNESCO, 1994). It argues that regular educational settings with an inclusive orientation are 'the most effective means of combating discriminatory attitudes, building an inclusive society and achieving education for all'. It goes on to suggest that such settings can 'provide an effective education for the majority of children and improve the efficiency and ultimately the cost-effectiveness of the entire education system' (quoted in Ainscow, 1999, p. 74).   ʹ

The move towards inclusive education must progress at many different levels. In Chapter 1, we traced how recent policy developments have begun to bring the domains of 'special educational needs' and 'early years' more closely together. Until we have the one fully included within the other, we are not likely to see inclusion flourish. In the past, there have been two separate realms of specialization. Wolfendale (2000c) described some of the disparity that has existed between 'special educational needs' and 'early years', and also highlights some hopeful signs of realignment. For example, until recently, very few LEAs have had special needs policies which incorporated early years, and very few early years policies detailing special needs provision. At a national level, too, there has been an historical separation of powers, interests and responsibilities in the two.

Whereas the Desirable Learning Outcomes (DfEE, 1996b) referred to special educational needs only superficially, the *Curriculum Guidance for the Foundation Stage* (QCA, 2000) detailing the early learning goals, approaches special needs in more detail and more inclusively. The paving stones are now being laid for developing more inclusive practices for meeting individual needs in all educational settings. Perhaps 'early years' offers an exciting opportunity for 'getting it right from the start' as far as meeting SEN is concerned.

The move towards fully inclusive provision is progressing quickly, though currently exists more in 'philosophy' and 'policy' than in 'practice'. Some early years practitioners might be working within partnerships that have stated their clear aim to develop inclusion but where the settings themselves are still in various stages of development. Others may already be working in an inclusive setting such as the Cleves School illustrated on the next page. Others may wish to take time to examine their own practice and ensure that they are developing inclusive approaches when working with individual children. What factors might they consider?

WHAT FACTORS SUPPORT INCLUSIVE PRACTICES?

When various studies that have evaluated practice in inclusive education are brought together, there seem to be certain common features that promote inclusion. Sebba and Sachdev (1997) describe these as:

- careful joint planning, especially to make sure that any within-class support is used effectively;
- the use of educational labels rather than categories or medical labels (such as 'co-ordination difficulty' rather than 'dyspraxia', or even 'child who has SEN' rather than 'SEN child');
- teachers and adults who provide good role models for the children because of their positive expectations and the way they respect and value the children;

- the use of strategies which improve children's communication skills;
- the use of teaching strategies which enable *all* children to participate and to learn;
- individual approaches which draw on pupils' earlier experiences, set high expectations and encourage mutual peer support;
- the flexible use of support aimed to promote joining in and inclusion rather than to create barriers and exclusion.

What might a visitor to an inclusive school actually see? A visit to the Cleves School in Newham would provide such an insight.

INCLUSION IN ACTION: THE CLEVES SCHOOL (NEWHAM) EXPERIENCE

Cleves Primary School is in Newham, East London. Newham is a lively cosmopolitan area and its LEA has a clearly stated Inclusion Charter. This states that children with disabilities and other difficulties should be educated with everyone else because of the benefits for all the children and the community. The aims of the school are listed below and they are reviewed annually (Alderson, 1999).

Cleves Primary School, Newham: our shared aims

1 Access to learning
- to provide an environment where each child of every race, gender, class and learning need is truly recognized, accepted and valued;
- to create an environment where there is a place for everyone and there is a feeling of belonging;
- to develop high positive self-esteem in all children and adults;
- to enable children to be aware of their interdependency on each other.

2 Curriculum
- to have an approach to the curriculum that promotes high levels of achievement and which enables children to reach their potential;
- to enable children to have access to and experience of the whole curriculum (including the National Curriculum and religious education);
- to have a recording and assessment system that demonstrates children's achievement, their development and progression.

3 Process of learning
- to acknowledge that all children are decision-makers and to enable them to become active participants in their own learning;
- to enable learning to start from the child's needs;
- to ensure that all the experiences for the children are positive and rigorous;
- to provide a smooth transition from the early years to Year 6;
- to prepare the children for the transition from primary to secondary school successfully and confidently.

The whole-school approach at Cleves is based on the principles of an early years approach: self-motivation, fostering self-esteem and learning through doing. The idea is to build on the enjoyment young children have in learning that is fun and interesting, learning through play and making mistakes. Every child has an Individual Curriculum Plan which serves to keep parents informed about their child's schoolwork, and also to follow the guidelines of the SEN Code of Practice (DFE, 1994; DfEE, 2000a) but to do so *inclusively* for all children.

The first thing that a visitor to Cleves School might notice is the busy foyer area. The entrance is fully accessible for all disabled users and is welcoming to all. A large notice proclaims the fact that this is an inclusive school, and a 'welcome' is announced in all the children's languages. The building is used regularly for various community functions and, so, is a familiar place for families and friends.

The building branches into four wings, one of which contains the Foundation Stage children. Within each is a central activity area with four rooms leading off it covering different aspects of the curriculum. Children can be found in each area at any one time, relating to any one of the number of adults who work there. The children are busy, fully engaged, and actively planning and reviewing their activities. The adults help them achieve a spread of experience and draw out learning points, supporting and extending the children as they play and learn. There are children of many levels of need and ability, working together in small groups.

Plenty of space encourages movement and exploration and the children soon learn how to find and use the equipment they need. The flexible use of space encourages the children to work together harmoniously. The early years children have talked about simple rules to encourage this harmony: 'be happy, be friends, tidy up when you finish, look after the books, and don't throw things'.

Each wing has four base teachers responsible for up to 30 children each, and a fifth specializing in curriculum support. There are also about six learning support staff offering curriculum support for children with SEN, though all the children work with all the staff at various times. This helps to move away from the idea that 'special' children need 'special' support and that this support needs to be on a one-to-one basis, which could isolate the child. Assistants at Cleves School are seen as links rather than barriers, ensuring that disabled children have plenty of opportunities to play and work alongside the other children and staff.

Even the most profoundly disabled children are supported in a curriculum based on their own individual needs as well as their entitlement. Topics can be developed at a sensory level for those who would benefit. Visiting professionals are encouraged not to withdraw children for individual treatment but to work in the usual classroom setting, or with a group of other children too. Staff meet regularly to plan and review the curriculum and feel convinced that inclusion brings the best out of their children.

MAKING THE NURSERY OR PRESCHOOL AN INCLUSIVE SETTING

The National Early Years Network has produced a practical handbook for early years workers on how to create inclusive services for disabled children and their families (Dickins and Denziloe, 1998). The authors encourage making play and learning approaches accessible for *all* children wherever possible. Having 'special' activities for 'special' children and buying plenty of 'special needs' equipment does not help the development of inclusive services. So often, an activity can be changed in some way rather than excluding certain children from it because they cannot 'fit in' with it. Flexible approaches and adaptable timetables and routines make this easier.

For example, outdoor play areas need to contain quiet, sheltered spaces as well as busy active areas. Indoors, tables and equipment need to be at adjustable heights and floor spaces comfortable and safe to play on. Acoustics can be softened with soft surfaces, cushions, carpets and curtains, making it easier for everyone to hear clearly. Storytimes can be kept concrete by using props and visual aids. Communication can be enhanced by making sure that all adults are familiar with any language or communication system used by the children. Children can also have a communication book showing how they make their needs known. Making more use of colours, textures and smells can encourage different senses. The 'activity centre' at the Lydney Church of England School Nursery gives a good example of how this can be done.

An activity centre for everyone to enjoy

The activity centre designed at the Lydney C of E School in Gloucestershire is the product of a valuable collaboration between an 'A' level Design and Technology student, Victoria Deacon, and a local nursery/Opportunity Centre. The setting caters for 70 children, a third of whom have some kind of special educational need. The aim was to design and build an outdoor, sensory play activity centre that was safe, practical and stimulating. Many of the children had language and communication difficulties and it was hoped that the centre would encourage language and exploration. The equipment designed was based on the senses of sight, sound, touch and smell. There are drainpipes to be banged into position, mirrors to reflect light and distort images, 'smelly' and 'feely' boxes to explore. The staff have been surprised to see the children developing new links in their playing which they had not planned for, and have been pleased with the opportunities for extending topic work and language which the equipment has provided. (Griffey, 1999)

Early years practitioners can look for ways of making their tools and equipment easy to handle by all children. Dickins and Denziloe (1998) give practical examples such as foam padding wrapped around paintbrushes to make them easier to hold or non-slip dycem matting used to hold small toys in position. Throughout the curriculum, practitioners can look out for materials, pictures and books that portray positive images of disabled people and special needs.

MEETING INDIVIDUAL NEEDS INCLUSIVELY

In their publication *Inclusion in Pre-school Settings* (Chizea, Henderson and Jones, 1999), the authors start from the point of view of the parents of a child already identified as having SEN and give practical examples of what a 'good' inclusion setting might look like for their child. They argue that inclusion is not merely a matter of adjusting the provision or the setting; it is a process which has to run through the whole curriculum if it is to be genuine. For example, all children (and not just those with identified SEN) need to see images in preschool of a world in which people with and without disabilities have a contribution to make to one another. This should be reflected in the books, pictures, activities, attitudes and behaviours of staff and visitors. All children need to receive positive images of the group with which they might identify and this extends to issues of culture, ethnic group, age, gender, appearance and disability.

Under the headings of different kinds of disability, the book provides pen pictures of children with these kinds of difficulty and the interventions that the adults in the group are taking. The disability is explained with an indication of what this means for the child and what this means in terms of what the adults can do to ensure inclusion. Here is an example of the pen picture for 'Tracey' who has visual impairment.

Pen picture: Tracey

Tracey has been blind from birth. She is a lively and intelligent little girl and her parents want to keep her in mainstream education. They have therefore been looking at their local pre-schools. They want one with an inclusive approach, but they also want one which has a number of small rooms rather than one big one. Tracey will have to learn this new environment in order to move confidently in it, and her parents know from experience that she will orient herself more easily in smaller, more manageable spaces. Having found a group which can offer what they want, Tracey's parents then work with the staff and committee of the group to arrange that:

- The room layout will be the same whenever Tracey attends.
- Varied textures for items such as table covers provide information in a non-visual way.
- Notices and labels, including name labels, are in Braille as well as using conventional writing/pictures.
- Tracey's sessions in the group will begin with a guided 'feely' tour so that she can become familiar again with the resources on offer. Adults will then be alert to ensure that she is guided as appropriate to another activity/level of activity.
- At first, Tracey will be led by the hand from one room to another, counting the steps. Later, the accompanying adult will count without any physical contact. After a while, when Tracey feels confident enough, she will be able to go from room to room unaccompanied.
- The Early Years section of the local Partnership are approached for additional funding resource materials. Although the group already provides a rich environment, the pre-school staff and Tracey's parents feel that any

additional materials which are available will enhance the provision, not
only for Tracey herself but also for the other children. (Chizea, Henderson and Jones, 1999, p. 7)

Because inclusive practice pervades the whole curriculum, staff
and parents would also have gone on to discuss ways of enhancing
Tracey's learning, communication and self-confidence in the group.
They might also have looked for ways of helping her to identify voices
using their names and supporting her in making friendships and
playing socially in small groups.

In Italy, there is a method of meeting all children's needs very individually in the Reggio-Emilia approach. Because each child's way of
learning is valued and developed, a very inclusive approach becomes
possible. This inclusive approach is able to provide each child with a
sense of belonging to family, school and community and with a
positive view of their self-worth, whatever their needs. The next
boxed section is provided not so much as an example of 'what inclusion should look like' but as an example of how, were we to think
reflexively, we might reach an entirely new viewpoint of the value of
children in our society and our mutual contribution to learning and
development. The approach is discussed further on page 195 as one
vision for future early years education.

The Reggio-Emilia approach

Over the last 25 years, Reggio Emilia, a city in the Emilia-Romagna Region
of Northern Italy, has attracted worldwide attention and admiration for its early
childhood institutions and practice. The central concept is the 'rich' child; a
child rich in potential and competence and closely connected to the adults and
children around. The child is seen as autonomously capable of making
meaning from experience, and it is the adult's role to activate this in the child.
This philosophy leads to an inclusive and non-stigmatizing approach in which
all children are valued and parents are seen as having enormous importance
in their child's development too.

In Reggio Emilia there are a number of preschools and infant-toddler
centres serving the needs of children from three months to six years of age.
To the visitor, there is an ethos of calm, beauty, respect, co-operation and community. 'School' is seen as 'life' and not merely a preparation for 'life'. Activities
are built around the individual child's interests as they develop and reflect on
their ideas and what they have learned. Each adult holds respect for the

'hundred languages' the child is felt to have been born with and each child is provided with the opportunity to express themselves and learn in as many different media. There is a pedagogista who works with a small group of centres and helps staff reflect on their work, and an atelierista who supports the children's art and creative expression.

Through interest groups, exhibitions and visits, there is a growing interest in establishing and evaluating this approach in other areas of the world including the UK. An important initiative has been the *Quality in Diversity in Early Learning* document produced by members of the Early Childhood Education Forum and National Children's Bureau (1998). This paves the way for more child-centred and diverse approaches in which 'quality' in early years education is not compromised (see also page 196).

ENSURING EQUAL OPPORTUNITIES

Recent OFSTED reports continue to examine the issue of under-achievement in children from minority ethnic groups. It seems, not surprisingly, that progress in the early years only 'takes off' for some children when they have mastered the language of teaching. Siraj-Blatchford (1994) suggests various questions early years educators can ask themselves in order to ensure they are creating multilingual support and, therefore, including the needs of all children whatever their ethnic origin or language.

* *Induction.* How are children and their families introduced into your setting? What will their first impressions be? Will the children hear their first language spoken, at least whilst they are settling in?
* *Understanding.* Do all the early years staff understand why children just beginning to understand English may be silent or may make mistakes? Will the children feel 'safe' in trying to speak and understand English, and be helped to gain in confidence? Will adults accept non-verbal responses too? Will there be opportunities to develop English language skills in small groups and during play?
* *Communicating with bilingual children.* What chances will the child have to communicate in both languages? Who will support their learning in each language? How can parents support this too, and how can effective partnership with parents be achieved across different languages?

PROFESSIONAL SUPPORT FOR INCLUSIVE EDUCATION

Supporting professionals also need to consider shifts in their role if they are to provide a more inclusive service delivery. Boxer (1999) writes of shifts that educational psychologists will need to consider following the Green Paper (DfEE, 1997a). Perhaps the shifts that he suggests could be as relevant for other professionals who support young children with SEN, their parents and their providers. There needs to be a move away from one-off assessment towards continuous intervention, a move from professional 'expertise' towards 'empowerment' of others. Instead of a 'reactive' response to difficulty or 'when things are going wrong', there needs to be a shift towards proactive work in which interventions are improved and children's failure reduced. Finally, instead of following set 'procedures', professionals should be seeking to 'transform' practice, creating real and positive change for children, parents and providers.

Perhaps the logical way of allocating outside professional support inclusively, is to delegate budget and resources to the schools and settings themselves. There has been a tendency in recent government policy to delegate expenditure to schools for meeting and supporting SEN. However this has caused some difficulties since LEAs still retain the legal duty to ensure that pupils' needs are met, yet have had little power to guide schools in their priorities when individual pupils' needs have been at risk (Gray, 1999). In this context, until there is a stronger commitment from schools to include all pupils, LEAs have no choice but centrally to retain reasonable levels of support. This is used to support schools and ensure reasonable levels of access for all pupils to a mainstream curriculum, reducing exclusion and calls for specialist placement. Therefore the compromise position has been to support inclusive schooling by co-ordinating both internal and external support at a local or 'cluster' level, and many early years settings are now being supported in this way.

INCLUSION AT CURRICULUM PLANNING LEVEL: THE MUSIC MAKERS PROJECT

The Music Makers project (Mortimer, 2000a) trained early years educators to deliver an inclusive curriculum via a regular music 'circle time'. It was argued that, in order for early years workers to feel confident in providing an inclusive curriculum to all children in their setting, with and without SEN, they would need to learn about, to practise and then take on board a practical example of one such approach. 'How to do it' training was required, but delivered in a way which inspired confidence and engendered reflection about practice. The training method used (Mortimer, 2001j) was evaluated to see whether it could indeed be used to engender reflective practice in early years workers.

Each setting received four weekly visits from the author, and they were helped, week by week, to understand more about their duties to meet special educational needs under the Code of Practice, and to plan and run suitable activities within a regular half-hour music session. In return, they were asked for an undertaking to continue to run the regular sessions once the course was over. They were also asked to be available and welcoming for parents of other children with SEN in their local area (not yet in preschool) to join them with their child for the music sessions.

Each musical activity modelled on the approach was linked both to an individual teaching target for a child with SEN, using a specially designed checklist, and to the Early Learning Goals, thereby providing an inclusive approach for all the children. This simple approach gave practitioners a clearer understanding of how they could deliver practically an inclusive curriculum with confidence. The results of an evaluation study also suggested some interesting ways in which children and adults learn and gain confidence together, and these are discussed on page 76.

POINTS TO CONSIDER WHEN DRAWING UP AN INCLUSIVE SPECIAL NEEDS POLICY

The following checklist might be a useful prompt for seeing how inclusive is the special needs policy of an early years setting. The core information that a special needs policy should contain is shown on page 158. The checklist can be used as a topic for discussion between colleagues within an early years setting and is most usefully shared with local parents and carers.

Testing the special needs policy; how inclusive is your setting?

1 Does your setting make it clear that it is inclusive and that it welcomes all children whatever their individual needs? Is this clearly stated in any parents' handbooks?
2 Does your setting meet the requirements of the SEN Code of Practice?
3 Do staff members have the opportunities to take up training in both special needs and early years practice?

4   Is your curriculum planning suitable for all children? Are there opportunities for all children to have positive outcomes from each learning opportunity?
5   Do you share observations and planning with parents?
6   Do you use methods of communication which include everyone, and which can be used between children (such as including sign language and using more than one language within the setting)?
7   Are you prepared to be flexible and change what you are doing in order to meet a particular child's needs?
8   Are you happy to involve professionals from outside agencies and to include them in your planning?
9   Will all your staff work and plan together to meet any special educational needs?
10 Can you provide families with the names and contact details of relevant support services? (Adapted from Grenier, 1999)

SUMMARY

Planning inclusive provision

In this chapter, we have defined some of the terms used when deciding where and how a child with SEN should be educated, and have focused on what it means to provide 'inclusive' education in the early years.

The historical pathway along which thinking has travelled was traced, in order to reach an understanding of the present revolution in how we meet SEN.

We looked at some of the disparities that exist in 'special needs' and in 'early years', and explored how thinking in these two areas might be combined.

We reached the conclusion that 'inclusion' has to work at all levels; it has to arise out of a philosophy and become translated into policy and practice.

Examples were given of what inclusion might 'look like' at the level of a whole school or at the level of working with an individual child in an early years setting.

Finally, pointers were given for developing more inclusive policies and practices within settings.

—Part Two

Meeting Special Needs in Partnership Settings: the Key Players

The first educators:
parental influences and partnerships

We have found no better way to raise a child than to reinforce the abilities of parents to do so. (Court Report, DHSS, 1976)

INTRODUCTION

In this chapter, we explore features common to effective parent partnership and make practical suggestions for links between early years setting and home. We also explore some projects aimed at helping parents to become more effective educators of their children, and look at issues relating to positive communication between parents and settings. We start by looking at some of the new initiatives which will influence the support that parents and families will receive over the next few years as part of the government's attempts 'to create joined up solutions to joined up problems' (Pugh, 1999, p. 7).

The Green Paper *Supporting Families* (Home Office, 1998) recognized that the interests of children are paramount, that children need stability and security, and that parents should be supported in supporting their children. There were proposals that all families should have access to advice and support. This would be done in many ways including the £540m SURE START scheme discussed on page 94. There would be plans for a national parenting helpline, an enhanced role for health visitors, additional support for parents to learn with their children through family literacy and mentoring schemes, introduction of education for parenthood as part of the school curriculum, support for grandparents and improved adoption legislation, and a National Family and Parenting Institute.

There were also moves to provide better financial support for families through initiatives such as benefits and tax allowances. The National Childcare Strategy aims to help families balance work and home, and links with a move towards more family-friendly employment rights. There were proposals for strengthening marriage with more mediation services for family breakdown, especially where children are involved. Finally, there were plans to provide better support for serious family problems, such as the parenting orders that are imposed on parents when their child has been convicted of an offence under the 1998 Crime and Disorder Act.

Whilst the spirit of all these proposals is to be commended, there is still a need to make sure that we move in the direction of what has been proven to work with children and families. With the burgeoning of new initiatives to support parenting and family life, there are golden opportunities for evaluating provision and proving effectiveness that we must not miss. There is also a real attempt to provide parents with the status they deserve as primary caregivers and first educators of their children.

PARENTING EDUCATION AND SUPPORT

These proposals have led to the development of various community and parenting education programmes throughout the country. There has been a tendency in Britain to develop 'top down' parent *training* courses in which professionals determine what they feel parents should know. One example of this is the provision in the Crime and Disorder Act (Home Office, 1998) to order 'parenting classes' for parents of offending youngsters. There is now also a trend towards more 'bottom up' parent *education* which is broader, has more of an open access and is based on what parents want to know. 'Parenting education' has tended to develop in the voluntary sector in response to consumer demand. Before designing any parent education or training, be it determined from 'above' or from the 'coalface', it would seem sensible to ask what works for whom and how.

One parent training programme which has been carefully evaluated is the service offered by Newham Borough in London.

Parent education and support in Newham

The London borough of Newham has an urban community and culturally diverse population. In 1992, its Education Committee adopted a policy on 'Parents as Partners in Education', arising from wide-ranging consultation in the area. The aims were to raise achievement in young people, in parents and in the community. Various developments followed, including the 'Learning Community Strategy' which promoted lifelong learning for all. As part of this, a series of programmes were developed to help parents become more aware of their children's needs, and to grow in confidence and self-esteem as a result of their new parenting skills.

At first, these programmes were based on existing training packages such as 'Parent Link' (from the Parent Network) and Caring Start (the High/Scope training approach for parents), see pages 203 and 204. In time, these were added to and adapted so that they were tailor-made for the Newham community. The demand for parenting programmes grew rapidly, and family members were asking for courses in their own community languages. The borough now runs regular programmes in English, Urdu, Punjabi, Somali and Bengali.

Courses typically run for five or six weeks during school term time, and there are crèche facilities available. Evaluation was done week by week and also by a focus group of participating parents at the end of the programme. From analysis of the weekly evaluations from dozens of such courses over three years, responses from parents tended to fall into these themes (reported in Wolfendale, 1999, p. 50):

- general value for parents in their role of parents;
- value in their role as behaviour manager;
- specific skill gains;
- learning practical strategies;
- confirmation that they are not alone, in having parental anxieties and lack of confidence;
- having a greater understanding of the parental role;
- general gains in confidence in being a parent;
- having realistic expectations.

As the evaluation sheets were collected, week by week, it became clear how parents were progressing towards increased self-confidence and a reappraisal of their methods of child-rearing and behaviour management (Samra, 1999).

So far, we have looked at what parents value from training and education programmes. What do they feel works for them in terms of professional support? Wolfendale (1999, p. 51) summarizes what the various data she has explored tell us about parent's needs for support services:

> Parents want accessible information about accessible services and the availability of support. Depending upon the focus, parents also need periodic respite from or support with stressful responsibilities. They do need to feel that professionals can engage,

temporarily but fully, with their (parental) problems. They do want to be treated with respect on a basis of equality, and on the premise that they too have much to contribute to the development and education of their children. They do wish to play a part in decision making over provision.

PARENT PARTNERSHIP

The involvement of parents at all stages is a basic principle of the SEN Code of Practice (DfEE, 2000a). This 'Partnership with Parents' is likely to be strengthened as further legislation is promised to set up special partnership schemes between parents and schools, with families being provided with an independent supporter, and the creation of a conciliation service resolving disputes between education authorities and parents. Other changes in hand will require local education authorities to comply with orders of SEN tribunals (Queen's Speech at the opening of Parliament, November 1999).

There have been many educational and social strategies that involve parents in the raising of pupil achievement. These include the National Literacy Strategy and family literacy, the National Numeracy Strategy and family numeracy, SURE START (page 94), parenting programmes, education action zones (which encourage partnerships between schools and local communities), the involvement of parents in baseline assessment and, from September 1999, the introduction of home–school agreements. There is a useful summary in Wolfendale (2000b).

Home–school agreements were a provision of the 1998 Education (School Standards and Framework) Act and were introduced in September 1999 (DfEE, 1998e). They mark a significant shift in educational democracy and provide a vehicle for parents to express their views on their children's education. A home–school agreement is a statement which explains what the school's aims and values are, what its duties towards the pupils are, the responsibilities of parents and what the school expects of its pupils. As part of the process of developing these agreements, schools have to review their existing home–school policy and consult with the parents.

However, 'partnership' is far more than a list of different forms of collaboration which can exist between parents and professionals when meeting SEN or raising achievement; it lies in the *quality of the interaction* which takes place day by day. The concept of partnership is based on the recognition that both parents and professionals have complementary contributions to make to children's education (Beveridge, 1997).

There are certain features common to effective partnership. The parents' fundamental role in their child's education is fully acknowledged by the staff. They develop a partnership based on shared responsibility, understanding, mutual respect and dialogue. There is recognition of the parents' role already played in the early education of their child and that their continued involvement is crucial to successful learning. Parents are made to feel welcome and opportunities are made for collaboration among parents, staff and children. Parents are given access to information at all stages and are fully informed of their child's progress and achievements. Admission procedures are flexible to allow time for discussion with parents and for children to feel secure in a new setting.

The relationship between parents of children with SEN and the setting which their child attends has a crucial bearing on the child's educational progress. To be successful, the partnership needs to be a two-way process with opportunities for knowledge, expertise and information to flow between all those involved. Reinforcement of opportunities for learning in the setting within the home, and vice versa, are important features of successful intervention programmes. Experiences initiated within the home are sometimes useful stimuli for learning within the early years setting, and vice versa.

The identification of a child's SEN may be an alarming time for parents. In some instances, parents might consider that their early concerns were not given enough attention. Early years practitioners need to develop the sensitivity not to interpret a failure to participate as indicating a parental lack of interest or willingness to support their child. We discuss this practically on page 42. Every effort should be made to develop the right ethos for partnership from the start.

Practitioners also need to be sensitive about how they communicate with parents. Some parents may have a difficulty in understanding written information or in communicating with an early years setting because English is their second language or because of their own literacy difficulties. The early years practitioner should take steps to ensure that communication can both be received and sent between home and school by using the home language or making use of interpreters, centres for multicultural education, taped or videoed information. These can help families see the ways in which their child is being supported in the setting, help them to keep in touch, to share their concerns or hopes and to negotiate how they can help at home.

It might be helpful at this stage to define the terms 'parent' and 'parental responsibility'.

Definition of 'parent'

Section 114 (1D) of the Education Act 1944, as amended by the Children Act 1989:

> Unless the context otherwise requires, a 'parent' in relation to a child or young person includes any person:
>
> - who is not a natural parent of a child but who has parental responsibility for him or her, or
> - who has care of the child.

Definition of 'parental responsibility'

Section 2 of the Children Act 1989:

> Parental responsibility falls upon:
>
> - all mothers and fathers who were married to each other at or after the time of the child's conception (including those who have since separated or divorced),
> - mothers who were not married to the father at the time of the child's conception, and
> - fathers who were not married to the mother at the time of the child's conception, but who have obtained parental responsibility either by agreement under the Children Act or through a court order.

All those with parental responsibility for a child have rights and responsibilities towards the child. If a child is subject to a care order, this is shared with the local authority. A setting should involve all those with parental responsibility as much as possible in the child's education. However, if this is not possible or practical, the setting may discharge its responsibilities by dealing with the parent who has day-to-day care of the child, such as the foster parents of a child 'looked after' by the local authority. The setting should ensure that all parents have information regarding the SEN policy and the arrangement for their child's SEN.

HOW CAN EARLY YEARS SETTINGS SHARE INFORMATION EFFECTIVELY WITH PARENTS?

When a child first starts in a new setting, it is a sensitive time for all parents. Add to this the particular concerns and mixed emotions which parents of a child with SEN might have, and you can understand that sensitive handling will be vital for effective partnership with parents.

Early years educators should invest time before a child joins their setting gathering information and establishing a relationship with child and parents. Asking positive, open-ended questions can provide information about the child's strengths and about the kind of help that they need. Parents soon feel discouraged if they find themselves listing all the things their child *cannot* do. Neutrally phrased questions allow the parents to feel able to answer either way, e.g. 'How much help does she need when going to the toilet?' (rather than, 'Is she toilet-trained yet?') or 'How have things been at home with his behaviour?' or 'What do *you* find helpful when he loses his temper?' (rather than, 'We think James has a behaviour problem').

It is helpful if time is taken to ask parents what they would like the setting to do to help, taking care they are not left feeling that they have failed in some way. Taking trouble to share the 'good news' from the start, helps any 'bad news' to fall more into context. Above all, settings can show that they care and are trying to work alongside parents to help the child.

HANDLING FEELINGS WITH SENSITIVITY

How do parents feel when they discover that their child might have special educational needs or disability? It is helpful if practitioners can reflect on some of the emotions which parents might have experienced, or might still be coming to terms with. There is a very powerful short piece of writing 'Welcome to Holland' by Emily Perl Kingsley (quoted in Roffey, 1999, p. 8) which is well worth reading and portrays this through a clever metaphor. All children can arouse incredibly strong, surprising and mixed emotions in their parents; 'I never knew I *had* a temper until I had Shari' or 'He gets right under my skin . . . ' Given this, it is not surprising that the parents of a child who has been diagnosed as having a disability or SEN go through many mixed and complicated emotions.

MacKeith, in Newson and Hipgrave (1982, pp. 100–1), listed these emotions. Parents often experienced a biological reaction towards a 'protection of the helpless' and, almost paradoxically, a deep 'revulsion of the abnormal' and, with this negative feeling, enormous guilt. There were also feelings of inadequacy; in their own reproductive system and in their child-rearing. Reaching the end of a pregnancy and meeting the 'loss' of the expected 'normal' child and the arrival of the 'unknown' brought with it feelings of bereavement: of anger, of grief and of adjustment. To this can be added denial and helplessness. There were also feelings of shock, of guilt and of embarrassment. Quite often, many of these emotions were experienced together with an overwhelming feeling of confusion and helplessness.

How professionals 'tell the news' of disability can have long-term consequences. If parents feel that they were informed insensitively or 'kept in the dark' unnecessarily, much of the anger, as in any grieving process, can become 'stuck' in a legacy of blame, suspicion and resentment. Professionals need to be as honest in telling what they do not know as what they do, and to develop a working partnership with parents from the first. Many of these confusing emotions may still be very raw at the time that a child joins an early years setting. Sometimes it is at this stage of the child's life that parental grief or insecurity surfaces again, as a parent has to share the care of a much loved child for the first time with another set of adults.

TALKING WITH PARENTS ABOUT SPECIAL NEEDS

It helps if early years practitioners can try to 'tune in' to some of these emotional reactions which they might be picking up from a parent. Remember the stages of reaction which parents may be going through in coming to terms with the fact that their child has long-term and significant special educational needs. There may be feelings of guilt ('What did I do wrong?', 'Are *they* telling me I'm doing things wrong?'). There may be an inclination to apportion blame ('What are *they* doing wrong?', 'All he needs is a good . . . !'). Another common strand is a strong feeling of wishing to 'protect the helpless' ('Can they cope like I've been coping?').

There may be very natural feelings of anger ('Who does she think she is telling me there's a problem here . . . ?', or one parent to the other, 'There's no problem at all; *you* tell them'). Grief is an almost universal reaction ('If we stop to talk about this, I'm afraid I might cry. Best to avoid it'). Most parents feel helpless ('Can I cope with the fact that I've now got to share my child's care with someone else at preschool?', 'Can I bear to lose control?'). There is a tendency at first to deny what is happening ('I'll rush off before anyone has a chance to talk to me', 'It will all be all right', 'He's just like Uncle Frank was', 'It's just the way she is'). It is also with a mixture of deep shame that some families might find themselves in a state of revulsion that their child is 'different' in some way ('I don't want to be the sort of person who has this sort of child. So I'll act as if it's not happening', 'I'm not willing to label him', 'I don't want her to be treated any differently from the rest').

So what can early years practitioners do about it? They could try to understand why a parent might be saying something. What does this tell them about the stage of acceptance parents might be at and how the setting might help? If there is still anger and grief, practitioners could contact the health visitor or find time to really talk through things with the family and become a listener for a while. *Someone needs to do a lot of talking and listening.* They should avoid using responses such as 'I know how you feel' (as they never can), using 'I think I understand' instead.

If there is avoidance of the issue, practitioners should take time to share the good news of progress before they need to share the challenges. Curriculum profile maps or clear information about the setting's expectations can be used in order to *inform* parents about what practitioners hope to achieve at each age and stage. There is an example of a part of a profile map in Figure 3.1. These are developed from the *Curriculum Guidance for the Foundation Stage* (QCA, 2000) by adding earlier 'stepping stones' (in this example called 'setting out') which act as 'catch-all' statements for all the children in your setting, whatever their developmental stage. Some settings also add sections for extension, linking into National Curriculum goals and baseline assessment. This will lead on to what they and parents are going to plan together for those areas that are showing any weakness.

It is helpful if parents and carers are involved in the early years sessions wherever possible so they can *see* what the setting is trying to achieve. As well as sharing the activities, practitioners can share the reasoning behind them and an idea of how children typically progress. They can also share some of their enthusiasm and excitement about the way children play and learn, and try to pass on skills.

Helpless or troubled parents need practical workable advice, but not the impression that the professionals are the successful ones and they, the parents, are failing. Parents with low self-esteem and high stress are quick to pick up the fact that they are 'not doing it right'. This leads to resentfulness and avoidance. Instead, home–school activities should be negotiated (see the 'play chart' on page 48) and suggestions, encouraging and warm. 'What seems to keep his

Setting Out	Stepping Stones 1	Stepping Stones 1	Stepping Stones 3	Early Learning Goal
• Looks around from parent's knee • Reaches out for offered toy • Is happy to come into setting with carer	• Shows curiosity • Has a strong exploratory impulse • Has a positive approach to new experiences	• Shows increasing independence in selecting and carrying out activities • Shows confidence in linking up with others for support and guidance	• Displays high levels of involvement in activities • Persists for extended periods of time at an activity of his/her choosing • Takes risks and explores within the environment	• Continues to be interested, excited and motivated to learn • Is confident to try new activities, initiate ideas and speak in a familiar group • Maintains attention, concentration, and sits quietly when appropriate
• Shows emotions of happiness and sadness • Responds to comfort from main carer • Plays alongside main carer at home • Plays close by main carer in the setting • Happy to play in the setting so long as main carer is in sight	• Separates from main carer with support	• Separates from main carer with confidence • Has a sense of belonging • Shows care and concern for self • Talks freely about home and community	• Has a sense of self as a member of different communities • Expresses needs and feelings in appropriate ways • Initiates interactions with other people	• Responds to significant experiences, showing a range of feelings when appropriate • Has a developing awareness of his/her own needs, views and feelings, and is sensitive to those of others • Has a developing respect for their own culture and beliefs, and those of others

Figure 3.1: Example of part of a curriculum profile map: area of learning – personal, social and emotional development
Source: Adapted from QCA (2000)

attention at home?' 'What toys would be good for teaching this activity?' 'What help do you need from us?'

If a parent denies there is anything wrong, practitioners should start with where parents are 'at' in terms of their understanding, but make it clear what might happen next:

> I'm glad you're not worried about him. But we must teach him to sit and listen at nursery, even if he's fine at home, because he needs to be able to learn in a group by the time he starts school. So perhaps we can talk about what seems to work at home and we'll put together a plan to teach him to concentrate here. As you say, he may settle very quickly. If not, we'll talk again next term and plan what to do next.

Once a plan has been agreed, they should be firm, stick to their plan, and continue to involve parents with every sign of progress or need, making it clear that they are doing this in order to keep them in touch.

If a parent cannot or will not stop to talk, practitioners might negotiate a home visit to meet on their home territory. They could start by establishing *parents'* views and feelings; this gives important information about their value judgements, which will help the practitioner decide how to introduce their own concerns. Listen first, talk later, find the common ground last. The common ground is usually the mutual attachment to and willingness to help the child who is 'special' to both.

Sometimes professionals might feel tempted to see parents as 'overanxious'. Parents' views should always be taken seriously, and point by point reassurance can be given with concrete evidence that all is well. Parents of children with SEN often say that they need a 'job to do'; the 'play charts' (below) are one starting point. Meeting together to negotiate the Individual Education Programme (page 161) should also bring parents firmly and practically on board with the plans for their child.

Sometimes parents might realize there is a problem, but refuse any kind of outside help, even though the providers are convinced that things have come to that stage:

> I know you are keen for us to address his needs here in preschool and you do not want anyone else involved at this stage. What we'll need to do is plan our approaches with you for the next term or so. We will set some targets between us that will show whether or not we are being successful. If we are not, then we *will* need further advice. We need to talk again on . . .

If you feel really 'stuck', practitioners sometimes ask the health visitor for advice; she or he might be able to visit the home or check the child's development as part of the routine child health surveillance.

What if adults are discriminating? 'If that child continues to attend, I'll take mine away . . .' or 'I can't work with that child; he shouldn't be here'. This is a direct challenge to a setting's special needs policy and cannot be fudged, though the fears or state of misinformation involved might be very understandable. Practitioners should explain that it is their policy to welcome all children regardless of special need. They should state clearly what steps they are taking (in general terms rather than personal details) to make sure the other children's needs are not compromised (e.g. in the case of a child with severe behaviour problems). Perhaps a session for everyone on 'managing difficult behaviour' would be constructive; usually every parent has his or her challenging moments at some stage. Henderson et al. (1991) have practical approaches for encouraging inclusion, eliminating discrimination (on any grounds) and encouraging equality in preschools with a number of 'What if . . . ?' scenarios.

PARENT PARTNERSHIP SERVICES

Parent partnership schemes have been in place since the 1994 Code of Practice (DFE), as part of the 1993 Education Act. Most LEAs appoint parent partnership officers to offer advice and support parents at any stage of the assessment process. They work alongside educational psychologists, support teachers, education social workers and office support staff but are also able to give independent advice. They can listen to parents' worries and concerns and explain the statutory assessment processes to them. They can also help parents to say what they think their child's needs are and help the child's views to be represented. If there are difficulties or misunderstandings between parents and LEAs, then the parent partnership officer will try to resolve them. Visits to prospective schools and support sessions might also be arranged as part of this service.

All LEAs must make arrangements for parent partnership services under the revised SEN Code of Practice (DfEE, 2000a). The aim of these is to ensure that parents of children with additional needs have access to information and guidance relating to the educational needs of their children. This will enable them to make appropriate, informed decisions. The service should be available to parents of all children who have SEN, and not just those who have been statemented. Parent partnership services can also put parents in touch with an 'independent parental supporter' (IPS) to offer them independent advice and support and put parents in touch with voluntary organizations or parent support groups. The national developments in parent partnership schemes (now called parent partnership services) were evaluated by Wolfendale and Cook (1997) for the DfEE.

DEVELOPING A PRACTICAL PARTNERSHIP WITHIN AN EARLY YEARS SETTING

Parents often ask how they can help at home when areas of concern are expressed by the early years setting. They might also approach the setting with their own concerns that they need the staff to address with them. Parents are the primary educators of their children and should be included as an essential part of the whole-group approach to meeting a child's needs from the start. They have expert knowledge of their own child, and the setting will need to create an ethos which shows how much this information is valued and made use of. Information-sharing is important and is a two-way process. Here are some practical ways of involving parents in meeting their child's needs.

Settings may need to take active steps to make a personal invitation to parents. For various reasons, parents do not always call into the setting on a daily basis. It is often helpful to invite parents into the setting to share information about their child's achievements, in an informal way, or to arrange a home visit if possible. Draw the parent's attention to a specific display, where examples of their child's work can be seen. Show parents what their child has already achieved and improvements made within the setting. Ask the child to show his or her parents what he or she can do or has learnt. Ask parents for their opinions, by allowing opportunities for them to contribute information and share experiences. It is often helpful to set a regular time aside when other demands will not intrude. Thank parents for their support and continue to celebrate success; this will ensure an ongoing positive partnership.

Where regular contact with parents is not possible, it can be useful to have a notebook between home and setting. A two-way system of sharing information about a child's success, experiences and opportunities can help in supporting the child. Home–setting diaries only work effectively if they are truly a two-way process: each participant making time to show that they have read what is written, and using questioning to encourage a shared response.

Play charts have been developed in many settings as one simple means of sharing activities between home and early years setting.

'Play charts' are activity sheets which early years settings and parents can negotiate together and which parents complete with their child at home, reporting back on progress week by week. They are one way of keeping parents informed about what their child is doing in the setting. They are a positive step towards helping the child to progress and achieve particular skills. Play charts can also reassure parents about their child's skills and progress, and offer parents practical suggestions about how to help their child. They offer opportunities for parents to share information from home within the setting. Finally, and importantly, they are fun and encourage a positive relationship between parent and child.

These examples feature 'Jonathan' who has a moderate hearing loss. He is introduced on page 162 where you will also find his Individual Education Programme.

Play chart for Jonathan

Play helps Jonathan to talk about opposites

Getting started: When describing objects such as 'big one', 'long one', offer a comparison: 'Here's a long pencil and there's a short one.'

Games to play:
1   Miming game. Mime the opposite of 'I'm cold. You are . . . '('hot').
2   Playing cars. Build a ramp to see whose car is fast and whose is slow.
3   When shopping, talk about whether you need more potatoes or less, or a lot of biscuits or just a few (etc.).

Ways to help: Learning about opposite words isn't easy. Give plenty of praise and encouragement.

(This section was completed by Jane, the playleader)

How did Jonathan get on?
*   Jonathan was very keen on the weather topic and we talked a lot about hot and cold weather and what we would wear.
*   Jonathan was struggling with the 'longest'. When I was ironing we looked at his trousers and his Dad's to find the longest pair. It seemed to help.
*   We had a new board game where you collect tokens to win. Jonathan thought it was great to win and for him to have 'more' tokens than me!

Comments:
Jonathan is due to start his school visits soon and I am worried how he will cope. When is the Teacher for Hearing Impaired coming in again?

(This section was completed by Mandy, Jonathan's mother)

GOOD PRACTICE IN LINKS BETWEEN HOME AND EARLY YEARS SETTING

Schools and early years settings have developed many different ways of developing their partnership with parents, the best being a direct response to identified local needs (e.g. Blamires, Robertson and Blamires, 1997). Here are some examples of local initiatives to improve links.

- The setting up of a toy and resource library for children and parents to borrow from.
- Early years curriculum workshops for parents and professionals to share.
- A bookshelf with useful pamphlets for parents on many topics including SEN.
- An 'open door' policy for parents to call in to talk with approachable staff at mutually convenient times.
- Multicultural story sessions by parents and extended family members.
- 'Borrowing' specialist skills from parents to share with the children: musicians, artists, industrialists, actors, footballers, craftworkers.
- A refreshment and social room/corner for parents and younger family members.
- Within-setting Portage parenting groups.
- Discussion groups for talking about areas of common interest (such as child behaviour) in order to share ideas and strategies.
- Regular parent education programmes tailor-made to the needs of the community and the cultures (page 36).
- Regular use of monitoring questionnaires and feedback forms.
- Multilingual parents' notice-boards and newsletters.
- Music-maker groups to welcome in parents and younger children with SEN in the locality (page 29).
- Action research within the setting designed by both professionals and parents.

THE INFLUENCE OF PORTAGE

The Portage model of home-teaching recognizes the primary role of the parent or carer and the importance of the home environment in the early education of young children with special educational needs. Within Portage, parents are partners in designing the education programme, teaching their young child with special educational needs and reviewing their progress. Moreover, it is an inextricable part of the Portage model that parents are represented on the Portage multi-disciplinary management teams.

Portage was first introduced to this country in the late 1970s at a time when parents would have traditionally been taking their child along to a 'centre of excellence' for assessment, therapy and 'expert advice'. Parents found themselves having to relate to many different professionals, and often felt that quality input had to be specialist and professional if it was to have the best effect. Their own intimate knowledge of their child's needs was underused or undervalued and their role in teaching and supporting their children deskilled.

The approach was developed initially in Portage, Wisconsin, USA, and it was adapted in the early 1970s for use in the UK. It brought together parents, professionals and families in an active partnership in the education of the young child with special needs. There are now Portage home-teaching services throughout the UK and beyond. Registration and validation of training are co-ordinated by the National Portage Association (page 204). Many services were set up with Education Support Grant funding, with the idea that local agencies (most often the LEA) would take on the longer-term funding.

The key elements of a Portage service are described by White (1997) in this way. There is a regular, usually weekly, visit to the home by a trained home visitor. A shared assessment framework, usually the Portage checklist, is used which draws on the child's development to establish a profile of strengths and needs. There is a shared design, delivery and recording of a programme of teaching activities tailored to the needs of the individual child. There follows positive monitoring of the child's progress with regular review. A positive management framework draws on professionals from all relevant disciplines to support the delivery of teaching programmes and to resolve problems raised by families/members of the home-visiting team. There is regular evaluation of service delivery based on changes in the child's developmental profile together with parents' satisfaction with the service received. Management and advisory support for the service is provided by a team composed of representatives from all the contributing agencies and parents.

Evaluation studies (White, 1997) have shown that parents welcomed the genuine partnership that developed in 'getting on with the job of teaching'. They also valued the fact that assessment and 'evidence' gathering under the Code of Practice for SEN was a positive and ongoing procedure and that they are celebrating and sharing their child's progress with a regular professional visitor. As one Portage home visitor put it, 'As we enjoy the privilege of extended contact with the family, we share with the parents and carers a specialism in the child; his developmental progress, strengths and interests, personality and behaviours' (Mortimer, 1997c). Because observations and records are kept over many months, there is a genuine 'ongoing assessment' to report as part of any statutory assessment procedure, overcoming the limitations of brief 'one-off' assessment by unfamiliar professional visitors (or, perhaps more threatening, centre-based one-off assessments). Moreover, this ongoing assessment is carried out as a partnership between parents and professional, using a scale of reference which arises from the child's own strengths and abilities rather than a set of criteria which might be irrelevant to that particular child and serve only to pinpoint weaknesses. Parents are therefore strengthened in their role as educators and evaluators.

There are many other schemes that have developed to support and strengthen the role of parents in educating their young children. One set of materials aimed at families of younger preschool children is the 'Playsense' pack.

Playsense

The 'Playsense' materials are a guide and resource for parents and main carers who are interested in watching and developing the play of their babies and young children under 3 (Barnard and Melidis, 2000). They are published by the National Association of Toy and Leisure Libraries (see page 204 for their address). A series of attractive colour-coded cards are organized into four broad areas of play and development: thinking and imaginative play, belonging and connecting, language play and movement play. Within each area, there are eight stepping stones representing common pathways of learning between birth and around 36 months of age. Each stepping stone card has a section 'have you noticed?' suggesting typical behaviour and ways of playing which parents might notice around each stage, though it is pointed out that each child has their own unique way of learning and growing. There are also suggestions for building on and encouraging play at around that stage. This approach fits well with the aims of the association, since parents are encouraged to use and borrow toys and playthings at various stages to support them in their role as early years educators.

BOOKSTART

Another project focused on helping parents to become effective educators of their own children that has mushroomed in the last decade is the 'Bookstart' scheme. This started in Birmingham in 1992 and there are now similar projects all over the UK including the nationwide BBC campaign 'Babies need books'. Babies at around the nine-months-old stage were each given a book when they were taken along to their local health centres for routine hearing checks. The book came in a bag along with posters and information leaflets for parents explaining the importance of sharing books with their babies and talking about the pictures. This simple idea was evaluated by Wade and Moore (1993) who found that Bookstart parents were using a wider range of strategies with their children for promoting early literacy skills, and their children were more responsive to books and pictures.

The families were followed through later using a controlled study and it was found that the children performed better than other children in their baseline assessment of literacy and even numeracy skills on entry to school (Wade and Moore, 2000). It seemed as though the early start with books had provided a reciprocal interaction between parents and child, a chance to experiment and enjoy, and the practice needed in order to lead to learning. This reaffirms the central role which parents and carers play in the education of preschool children. It also exciting in that it is a properly evaluated intervention that has the potential for *preventing* disadvantage and SEN for many children. Perhaps, too, the regular sharing of books encouraged attention and concentration in a pleasurable way. 'Bookstart' is now set to become a national programme with Book Trust and sponsorship support.

PARENT VOICES

It would be consistent with the spirit of partnership for the last voice to go to a group of parents of children with SEN quoted by Russell (1997):

- Please accept and value our children (and ourselves as families) as we are.
- Please celebrate difference!
- Please try and accept our children as children first. Don't attach labels to them unless you mean to *do* something.
- Please recognize your power over our lives. We live with the consequences of your opinions and decisions.
- Please understand the stress many families live under. The cancelled appointment, the waiting list no one gets to the top of, all the discussions about resources – it's *our* lives you are talking about!
- Don't push fashionable fads and treatments on to us unless you are going to be bound to see them through! And don't forget families have many members, many responsibilities. Sometimes we can't please everyone.
- Do recognize that sometimes we are right! Please believe us and listen to what we know we and our child need.
- Sometimes we are sad, tired and depressed. Please value us as caring and committed families and try to go on working with us.

SUMMARY

The first educators: parental influences and partnerships

In this chapter, we looked at some of the new initiatives which are raising the status, confidence and skills of parents as co-educators of their children.

We looked at the concept of lifelong learning for children, parents and communities and the development of parents training and education programmes.

We also looked at parents' needs for professional support and the 'why and how' of parent partnership within early years and SEN.

We explored ways of developing good communication and positive partnership between setting and home, and explored some examples of good practice.

We also tried to understand some of the particular pressures that parents of children who have SEN tell us that they feel.

We discussed some programmes which have been influential in developing the role of parents as educators, including 'Portage' and 'Bookstart'.

—4

The child, central to all

Why do children go to school/nursery?

Well, it's for working and you have your lunch here. (Five-year-old quoted in Sherman, 1997)

I like playing with the train track and I like making a spinner with a battery, crocodile clips and a motor and paper. I like writing abcdefghijklmnopqrstuvwxyz and BMW and making 'Who's that tripping-trapping over my bridge?' books. (Four-year-old quoted in Hutchin, 1999)

INTRODUCTION

So often, the opinions of young children have been overtaken by the 'more authoritative' values of other stakeholders in the education debate, yet careful examination of their remarks (e.g. Sherman, 1997) provides us with a remarkable reflection of what it is we appear to be providing them with. Their opinion must be considered valid if we are to include the opinions of everybody in the educational system in a more democratic and inclusive way. Wolfendale (2000a) argues that the rationale and justification for the inclusion of children's views and consulting them is threefold: on equal opportunities grounds, on educational grounds (so we can better match task and learner) and on psychological grounds (active involvement in learning increases success). In this chapter, we explore some of the guiding principles and practical ways forward to involving children with SEN in their own assessment and planning of provision.

GUIDING PRINCIPLES

In their book *Making Assessment Work* (Drummond, Rouse and Pugh, 1992), the authors endeavour to help the reader develop both principles and practice in assessing and working with young children who have special educational needs. Their overriding principles are these.

1   The principle of respect. Assessment should be carried out with a proper respect for the children themselves and their parents or carers and for their educators too. We must respect their culture, their ethnicity, their language, their religion, their age and their gender. The methods we choose for assessment and intervention must be respectful of all children regardless of their gifts, abilities or specific learning needs.

2   The principle that care and education of young children are not two separate, discrete activities. In our work as educators we both care and educate; quality care is educational and quality education is caring. As a consequence, when we work with young children, we will attend to their whole development and lives and not to certain aspects of it. This principle is a timely justification for the 'new look' early education and childcare partnerships.

3   The principle of the 'loving use of power'. Early years educators inevitably have power; this needs to be acknowledged and used lovingly, wisely and well.

4   The principle that the interests of the child are paramount. Assessment and intervention must enhance their lives, their learning and their development. It must 'work' for the child.

Hillary Rodham Clinton, President's wife and First Lady in the USA, chose an old African proverb as the title for her book in 1996, *It Takes a Village*. She chose this title 'because it offers a timeless reminder that children will thrive only if their families thrive and if the whole of society cares enough to provide for them' (Clinton, 1996, p. 12). Though 'parents bear the first and primary responsibility for their sons and daughters . . . children exist in the world as well as in the family' (*ibid.*).

This chapter also explores ways in which we can hold the child's individual interests as paramount. How can we safeguard their rights, involve them actively in assessment, and ensure that our approaches and interventions are child centred and enriching?

CHILDREN'S RIGHTS AND NEEDS

> The well being of children requires political action at the highest level. We are determined to take that action. We ourselves make a solemn commitment to give high priority to the rights of children.

This was the declaration made at the World Summit for Children held at the United Nations in 1990, setting the international scene for raising the political profile of children's rights. We had already seen the United Nations Convention on the Rights of the Child, adopted in 1989 and later ratified by 147 nations (excluding the USA, Cook Islands, Oman, Somalia, Switzerland and the United Arab Emirates) by September 1993. Newell (1991) describes what ratification actually means for children's rights in the UK and makes the case that all rights under the Convention must be available to all children without any discrimination whatsoever.

Article 23 states that the mentally or physically disabled child has the right to a full and decent life in conditions which ensure dignity, promote self-reliance, and facilitate the child's active participation in the community. Each child should also have access to education, training, care, rehabilitation, preparation for employment and recreation, where possible free of charge. Such an education (Article 29) should aim to:

- develop the child's personality, talents, and mental and physical abilities to their fullest potential;
- develop respect for the child's parents, his or her own cultural identity, language and values, for the national values of the country in which the child is living, the country from which he or she might originate, and the civilizations different from his or her own;
- prepare the child for a responsible life in a free society, in the spirit of understanding, peace, tolerance, equality and friendship among all people;
- develop respect for the natural environment.

Article 12 of the Convention is directly relevant to the involvement of children in children's statutory procedures:

States Parties shall assure to the child who is capable of forming his or her own views the right to express those views freely in all matters affecting the child, the views of the child being given due weight in accordance with the age and maturity of the child. For this purpose the child shall in particular be provided the opportunity to be heard in any judicial and administrative proceedings affecting the child, either directly or through a representative or an appropriate body, in a manner consistent with the procedural rules of national law.

Since the Children Act (1989), children in Britain do have a legal right to be consulted on decisions affecting their futures and placement in public care. Leach (1994) argues that the level of consultation is still extremely variable. Children are often excluded from case conferences or other professional consultations in the name of this being 'in the best interests of the child'. Direct participation in planning, policy-making or administration is rarely offered in any country to children under the age of puberty. However, some professionals have actively explored ways in which student reports can be a useful tool in shaping their schools, curricula and decisions about their futures (e.g. Gersch, Holgate and Sigston, 1993).

The *Code of Practice on the Identification and Assessment of Special Educational Needs* (DFE, 1994) at last gave legal weight (if only as guidance) to involving children directly in their own education planning and statutory assessments. In section 2:34 to 2:37, we were clearly told that:

The involvement and interest of the child or young person concerned will influence the effectiveness of any assessment and intervention.
   The benefits are:
- practical: children have important and relevant information. Their support is crucial to the effective implementation of any individual education programme.
- principle: children have a right to be heard. They should be encouraged to participate in decision-making about provision to meet their special educational needs.
   Schools should consider how they:
- involve pupils in decision-making processes.
- determine the pupil's level of participation, taking into account approaches to assessment and intervention which are suitable for his or her age, ability and past experiences.
- record pupil's views in identifying their difficulties, setting

    goals, and agreeing a development strategy, monitoring and
    reviewing progress.
  • involve pupils in implementing individual education plans.

Schools are asked to make every effort to identify the ascertainable
views and wishes of the child or young person about his or her current
and future education. Positive pupil involvement may not happen
spontaneously and careful attention, guidance and encouragement
will be required to help pupils respond relevantly and fully. Young
people are more likely to respond positively to intervention programmes if they fully understand the rationale for their involvement
and if they are given some personal responsibility for their own
progress.

Schools could, for example, discuss the purpose of a particular
assessment arrangement with the child, invite comments from the
child, and consider the use of pupil reports and systematic feedback
to the child concerned. Many children with special educational needs
have little self-confidence and low self-esteem. Involving children in
tracking their own progress within a programme designed to meet
their particular learning or behavioural difficulty can contribute to an
improved self-image and greater self-confidence.

All this sounded most encouraging but practitioners still had to
envisage and put into practice what involvement of the very young
child would actually 'look like'. Miller (1996) explored this practically
in her handbook for early years workers on how young children could
be involved in decision-making. What approaches to assessment and
intervention are appropriate to a developmentally young child,
perhaps with no experiences of school-life whatsoever and certainly
no concrete grasp of what the various options for the 'special educational support' might be? How can we develop practical approaches
which translate 'pupils' to 'young children' and 'schools' to 'early
years partnership settings', still maintaining these principles?

TALKING TO CHILDREN ABOUT THEIR SEN

For an older child, we can make a point of asking them what they are
thinking. We know that their reply may be shaded by what they feel
we wish to know, who is listening, what they understand to be the situation and what they feel able to voice. But at least we have a starting
point for asking them what they feel about their education plan,
whether they feel comfortable with it, and how they would like to
contribute.

Here is a set of approaches for taking steps to establish what very young children are thinking, using a personal construct approach. These were described by Dalton (1989) and to these I have added the 'talk-through' approaches developed by the author in her work with carers and parents of early years children, together with some of the methods for using play as a means of assessment. We explore early years assessment in more detail in Chapter 8.

Observation and interpretation

For younger children, our approaches may need to be less direct. We can take steps to stand back and observe what the child is doing in clear, objective terms: the level and range of play, the situations which encourage most interest or co-operation, signs of pleasure and distress. With such an observation, it might become possible to interpret what is maintaining a pattern of behaviour or play in a child, and to draw up a hypothesis for what is on the child's own agenda. This approach is described more fully in Mortimer (2000b).

Pen picture: James

James was four years old. He was referred to the educational psychologist because his behaviour at preschool was difficult to manage. His helpers described him as very aggressive (he would kick, hit and scratch other children), and claimed that, whenever there was a disturbance or fight during a session, James would be found at the root of it. His parents were rather surprised that he was presenting as such a 'behaviour problem' in the group, but recognized that advice was clearly needed on how to handle his behaviour more effectively.

As a first step, the psychologist arranged to go into the group and spend a session observing James and his peers in the situation where the 'problems' were occurring. She made a 'fly on the wall' observation (page 121).

The first useful fact was the amount of time James was able to spend on a particular activity which had caught his interest. Far from 'flitting from activity to activity looking for trouble' (as he had been described), he played constructively for a full twenty minutes creating the most elaborate and imaginative treble-deckered train with the construction bricks. Whilst this was happening, the helpers were focusing their attention on a group activity in another area of the room, and James's endeavours were passing unnoted. Two boys then approached. One of them tripped accidentally over the train, knocking a section of it over. James looked up, apparently made a judgement that this had been accidental, and repaired the damage quickly and quietly.

The second boy appeared to see an opportunity to make the situation more interesting, and with deliberation and direct looks in James's direction, aimed and kicked at the train. James again appeared to weigh the situation very rapidly, and lunged at the boy bringing him down. Within seconds, the adult helpers were on the scene, separating the children and remarking that they were relieved that the psychologist (for once!) was actually witnessing the disruptive behaviour that was so typical.

The observation had served a useful purpose in defining the strengths (level of interest and concentration for construction activities, level of social judgement in deciding to how to react to provocation), defining the 'problem' (quick loss of temper when provoked, risk of frequent provocation because of the reaction it provoked), and identifying behaviours in the carers which would need to be changed in order to reach a solution (giving positive attention when James was behaving appropriately, looking more closely at the antecedents to his behaviour in order to intervene earlier). This interpretation was more likely to provide an assessment and a plan for change which met James's own agenda as well as that of his carers.

Play with models

Sometimes we can observe the way children play with 'models' of their world and interpret how they are thinking about it. Over the years, psychologists, and particularly those of the psychoanalytical tradition, have developed ways of interpreting children's play and the readiness with which they absorb themselves in 'miniature worlds'. The wealth of observations that can come out of this type of play have led to both complex methods of presenting and interpreting, and also the development of intuitive insight from psychologists experienced in using this approach (e.g. Bowyer, 1970; Newson and Newson, 1979). We can observe the older brother or sister playing with the dolls, acting out considerable feelings of love, anger or fantasy after the arrival of the new baby. It seems that children can usually keep this behaviour distinct and separate from real life and can use it to deal with strong emotions without developing the behaviour at home. O'Connor (1991) describes how the various theories and techniques of interpreting children's play can be combined into a method of play therapy. Because these approaches have evolved following careful research and understanding of how young children behave and develop, they should not be used to interpret children's play too loosely.

Using children's drawings

Children's drawings, too, have been used extensively in assessing children's developmental levels (e.g. Self, 1977), emotional states (e.g. Dalton, 1989), records of achievement (e.g. Hutchin, 1999) and personal experiences (e.g. Bacon, 1991; Malchiodi, 1998). They form part of the dialogue we are able to share with them, and therefore form a springboard for further talking and thinking together. In a similar way, we can use drawings and illustrations as a stimulus for children's own comments and interpretations. This, too, will give us a glimpse of the way they understand their worlds.

Storytime

This leads on to the use of stories and picture books as a means of introducing situations and encouraging dialogue. Early years settings have built up useful collections of stimulus books for covering a range of new situations the child might meet: going to hospital, having a new baby in the family, living with one parent; why not 'My Statutory Assessment' or 'Ali's Special Needs'?

Talk-through approaches

The story as a stimulus for dialogue can be taken a step further into the realms of the Code of Practice through the use of talk-through approaches. The idea of scripting a structured conversation or 'talk-through approach' arose at a time when the author was considering ways of working consultatively with other professionals and carers (Hanko, 1985). A social worker asked for advice on helping a six-year-old to prepare her for the imminent death of her only parent. A mother asked for advice on preparing her physically disabled four-year-old for the curious questions he would meet from other children as he started school. A behaviour support teacher asked for consultation as she worked with the family of a five-year-old sister whose profoundly handicapped little brother had just been voluntarily admitted into care.

In each situation, the professional concerned wanted a developmentally appropriate starting point for her work with the child concerned. She needed a framework and a context in which to raise delicate and emotional issues so that the child would be able to make sense of the situation and genuinely understand and be involved in the life change. Each talk-through approach started with the statement 'Everyone is different, each one is special' and moved out from talking about the child himself or herself to considerations of the other familiar people in his or her life and their own states and circumstances. The scripts were in concrete, practical terms and led the child's understanding session by session towards answering all the as yet unspoken doubts and concerns that were present.

The *Starting Out* booklet described the approach for preparing a child with special needs for joining a new school or nursery (Mortimer, 2000d), and combines an adaptable script with activities to bring the points home. In each of the above cases, it was the professional or carer most close to the child who worked with the approach, leaning on the psychologist's support just for consultation and a developmental framework.

Pen picture: Sula

Sula was four years old and about to leave her small rural playgroup to attend a large primary school in the nearby town. She had been born with a rare genetic disorder that meant that she had unusual fingers and thumbs, was very small in height, and had unusually pigmented skin. Her development had been followed through at the local Child Development Centre and was progressing normally. She had learned to use her hands to do all the fine motor tasks that any four-year-old would tackle, finding new and innovative ways of getting round any practical problems. She was a familiar and popular figure at playgroup and, apart from needing a special stand to reach the sinks and toilet, needed no special support there.

Her parents were concerned that when she started primary school she would develop self-consciousness about her condition that she had not been aware of before. For the first time she would meet children who were not familiar with her and who would ask curious questions. They were keen to help her develop the words she would need to answer these questions, and to develop 'coping strategies' if she felt teased or singled out in any way. They asked the preschool to help. Her playleader used the 'Starting Out' approach (Mortimer, 2000d) to talk through all the things she had learned to do and the times of day when she needed help. Together with her parents, they agreed words to describe what her special needs were. They also talked together of how some children might be kinder than others; if she felt teased, who would she talk to? All their thinking and talking together was recorded in the booklet so that her teacher could share this too.

CHILD-CENTRED CHECKLISTS AND QUESTIONNAIRES

In a similar way, 'Welcome Profiles' can be adapted and developed in order to gather information about the child's view on entry into school (page 130). Open-ended questioning such as 'Tell me a favourite toy / activity / family outing / memory . . . ', 'Is there anything which makes your child particularly frightened?', 'How much help does she need when going to the toilet?', or 'How does he let you know when he is cross / happy / upset?' allows you to gather honest information about all children regardless of special need. These questions do not beg a certain reply and license the respondent to describe freely the amount of help which might be needed or to celebrate a newfound independence.

The ALL ABOUT ME materials developed by Wolfendale (1998) became influential in providing a practical framework for parents and professionals to involve children in their own assessments and planning. They started as a checklist that enabled parents to note down and record from time to time their child's development and progress. The record belonged to the parents and served as a useful basis for discussing ongoing progress with a teacher, playgroup leader or support professional. First it was trialled with over 130 children aged 2 to $6^1/_2$ from all over the country, and then revised on the basis of this feedback. It was notable at the time as being written in the first person, from the point of view of the child. The revised edition keeps the contents as before, but the 'Notes for Parents, Carers and their Children' have been revised, and there is a short new section entitled 'Guidance Notes for Early Years workers in using ALL ABOUT ME'. There are also new illustrations.

ALL ABOUT ME covers seven areas of the child's life and experience: language, playing and learning, doing things for myself, my physical development, my health and my habits, other people and how I behave, my moods and feelings. Though it started as a parent record, it was adopted by many schools and early years settings as part of the personal records and child profiling. It was also taken on board by many LEA parent partnership officers as a way of involving parents and children in the statutory assessment procedures, and as an aide-memoire to gathering information from parents.

INVOLVING YOUNG CHILDREN IN THEIR OWN ASSESSMENTS

We discuss methods of early years assessment in Chapter 8 but how can we make sure that we involve children as fully as possible in these procedures? We are encouraged in the SEN Code of Practice (DFE, 1994; DfEE, 2000a) to involve children directly in their own assessments and education planning. How can we do this with very young children at the earliest stages of their educational careers?

In many senses, early years carers have been exploring ways of making their assessments meaningful and child centred for a long time. We look for ways of 'starting where the child is at', 'going with the child', developing home-based services, and sharpening our skills in using play and observation as an assessment tool (e.g. Newson and Newson, 1979).

The use of play-based approaches for assessing and helping children has long-standing theoretical roots. Play was first incorporated into therapy of children in 1919 when Hug-Hellmuth (1921) used it as an essential part of child analysis. Anna Freud (1928) and Melanie Klein (1932) wrote extensively on how they adapted traditional psychoanalytic technique for use with children by incorporating play into their sessions. Their primary goal was to help children work through difficulties, life changes or trauma by helping them to gain insight. Whereas Anna Freud used play to build up a strong, positive relationship between child and therapist, Melanie Klein considered play to be the child's natural medium for expression, and a substitute for verbalization in therapy.

How can early years carers, parents and professionals contribute to child-centred assessments? How can we judge the child's agenda? How can we involve young children in planning and change? How can we place our teaching and assessment in a developmentally appropriate context? And how can we use play to make the whole process as non-threatening, even enjoyable, as possible for a very young child?

An extension of the talk-through approaches described above is to lead children through their own statutory assessments of special educational needs: why it is all happening; who they will meet; what will happen next; what they enjoy or wish for in a receiving school; what words they use to describe their special needs; and what the actual implications of these needs for the child are. The *Taking Part* booklet (Mortimer, 2000e) provided a practical format for a parent or carer to lead a young child through the process of assessment, thinking through the answers to certain questions all of which are related to concrete experiences in the child. A shared language is developed for describing the 'special needs' concerned and, through this, the child becomes an active participant in the agenda of the assessment. The approach can be followed with only minor adaptations for a verbal child, amending wording and example according to the particular child, culture and situation. For a preverbal child, the approach can be used to suggest ways in which a parent or carer can think through the assessment from the child's point of view, thereby serving as an advocate for their view, ensuring that any recommendations also fit the child's own agenda. The end product is a completed questionnaire which can be used to form a child contribution to the evidence of the statutory assessment.

CHILD-CENTRED APPROACHES TO ASSESSMENT AND INTERVENTION

As well as involving children in the process of assessment, we can make our very assessment tools as involving, pleasurable and positive for the child as we can. There are ways in which we can ensure the assessment arises naturally from a familiar situation in which the child is enabled to show of his/her best as well as of his/her level of need. This is most likely to happen at home.

The Portage home-teaching programme allows us to assess development over a period of time in a home setting which will be natural for the child (page 50). Moreover, the Portage assessment is a dynamic process, allowing different interventions to be tried and tested, providing a running record of the child's achievements in learning.

What of the young child with special needs who is attending an early years setting? Here, it may become difficult or inappropriate to withdraw a child for lengthy individual assessment and maintain the natural environment in which the child is usually learning and playing. The *Playladders* checklist (Mortimer, 2000c) was devised to take the process of play-based assessment into the group setting (page 124).

Using a combination of these play-based approaches, it should become possible to provide not only a child-centred assessment, but a child-involving one also. You have allowed them the right to be heard, gathered from them the essential and relevant information that they are in a position to share with you, and empowered them in the process of statutory assessment. These ideas are developed further in Chapter 8.

TALKING TO *ALL* CHILDREN ABOUT SEN

In the spirit of inclusion, it is helpful to make sure that the teaching materials and books within the early years setting reflect a wide range of ability, ethnicity and culture. Picture books which contain 'models' of differently abled children can act as talking points for diversity and difference. Most libraries have now developed specialist sections of books which relate to a wide range of special needs. As well as covering certain conditions, there are books which will appeal and be helpful to young children at certain stages of exploring and talking, such as 'multisensory' or 'interactive' books which can be enjoyed in many channels at once (see Useful contacts and resources).

INCLUDING *ALL* CHILDREN IN ENJOYABLE PLAY AND LEARNING

The curriculum has been described by Wilson (1998) in terms of 'the environment as he or she experiences it' and she goes on to emphasize that it is critical to ensure that any disabilities do not interfere with the young child's experiences of the early years environment. In order to ensure that *all* children have access to the learning environment, certain modifications may need to be made to the physical structure of the space, the approaches used or the routine followed. You need to think about the arrangement of furniture and fittings to ensure physical access, storing resources at child height for the child who cannot yet walk, or the use of soft furnishings, carpets and curtains to absorb sounds and facilitate floor play for the child with sensory or physical difficulties. Pictures to label storage spaces or photographs to signal coat hooks enable all children to identify where things go.

Colour-coded areas help with 'putting away' in the 'messy' area or 'home corner'. Symbols can be used to help children with communication difficulties to express choices or understand what comes next in a sequence of activities. 'Sandwiching' short structured activities with free play can make it easier for the child with attention difficulties to concentrate for longer, together with opportunities to think and play in quieter distraction-free areas. Specialist tools can be obtained for making computer equipment accessible to all children (see Useful contacts and resources). The opportunity to work in large and small groups, and sometimes individually, can again provide opportunities for *all* children to learn in a variety of situations. Various interventions are explored more fully in Chapter 9.

SUMMARY

Involving young children with SEN in early years assessment and intervention

In this chapter, we have explored how we can include young children's views and consult them about their education and needs.

This allows us to ensure they have equal opportunities, they feel involved and successful in their learning and play, and we match activities and interventions to suit their interests and strengths.

We discussed various approaches for including young children with SEN:

- observation and interpretation;
- talk-through approaches;
- play-based assessment and intervention;
- use of art-work, role play and stories;
- welcome profiles and personal records;
- increasing all children's awareness of SEN;
- developing inclusive and enjoyable approaches for all.

−5

Reflective practice in early years settings

I think the most important thing is that you've got to take the children as individuals so we try to do our planning to include all the children yet to have a little bit of individuality for all the children as well. (Early years practitioner reflecting on her practice in Mortimer, 2000a, interview 26)

ROLES AND RESPONSIBILITIES IN EARLY YEARS SETTINGS

We have looked at early years provision from the point of view of the parents and of the child. This chapter is devoted to the needs of the early years practitioner and, in particular, to their need for training and support when working with young children who have special educational needs. What can they do as early years educators to enhance the learning of *all* their children, including those who have very individual needs? How can they develop their practice reflectively in the light of new knowledge, new skills and new experiences?

The issue of marrying theory to practice is a challenging one for the trainer. How can training be designed to engender the 'reflective practitioner'? Reflective practice, suggests Schon (1995), takes the form of a reflective conversation with the situation. The best professionals know more than they can put into words. To meet the challenges of their work, they rely less on formulae and set approaches than on the kind of improvisation learned in practice. The professional recognizes that technical expertise is embedded in a context of meanings.

When an early years educator begins to think and act not as a technical expert but as a reflective practitioner, she or he tries to listen to children. What are they thinking? What do they already know? What are their needs and how do I meet them both individually and in the context of the group? Any training which aims to engender a reflective practitioner' must therefore go far beyond the teaching of technical skills and standard approaches. There must be an understanding of the 'why' and 'wherefore' of the approach, so that the trainee can present tailor-made activities for the particular child with special needs and the particular setting.

The greatest challenge to any trainer working with volunteers and early years educators in the non-maintained preschool sector is that each trainee will bring a unique combination of past experiences and training, ranging from none at all, through experiences of parenthood, to graduate or postgraduate teaching status. Who are these early years educators and what is the range of settings in which they work?

- *State nursery schools and classes.* Run by the local education authorities, these are mainly for three- and four-year-olds. Most children attend for morning or afternoon sessions during school terms. Nursery provision is staffed by qualified teachers assisted by trained nursery nurses.
- *Reception classes.* More four-year-olds are now going into the reception classes of primary schools, although children in the UK do not need to start full-time school until the term after their fifth birthdays. Some reception classes employ classroom assistants or trained nursery nurses to support the qualified teacher.
- *Special schools.* Some young children with SEN have already received a statement of SEN and are placed in special provision, sometimes on a part-time basis and attending their local provision as well. With the growth of inclusion, the number of such placements appears to be falling, though in many LEAs, children with profound and multiple disabilities are still felt to need the multidisciplinary support that a special placement can offer. The qualified teachers and special support assistants sometimes have additional SEN qualifications.
- *Combined nursery centres.* These are usually jointly funded and managed by the education authority and the social services department. They have developed in different ways around the country and most provide year-round day care. Some examples of these are given in the examples of 'early excellence centres' within this book. They are staffed by qualified teachers and nursery nurses.
- *Local authority day nurseries/family centres.* These are run by social service departments mainly for children felt to be 'at risk' in some way. They usually offer year-long day care. At the time of writing, half the staff must be qualified child-workers (see below).

- *Playgroups or preschools.* These are usually managed by parents within the voluntary sector and most offer morning or afternoon sessions, sometimes for only part of the week. Again, at least half the staff must have had some form of training in education and teaching. Those able to offer five sessions a week may be registered with the Early Years Development and Childcare Partnership.
- *Private nurseries and crèches.* These cover a wide range of settings from private nursery schools to private day nurseries and work-place crèches.
- *Childminders.* Childminders are usually self-employed. At the time of writing, a childminder may care for up to three children under the age of 5.
- *Portage services.* Portage is the home-teaching scheme for preschool children with special needs and their families. Portage home visitors usually visit a family weekly, negotiating and mod-elling how to teach 'next steps' in development and learning. Many schemes are now registered with the Early Years Develop-ment and Childcare Partnerships.

All provision which is registered with the Early Years Development and Childcare Partnerships for early years education and childcare will be subject to regular inspections under a new unified system delivered by OFSTED's 'Early Years Directorate'. The DfEE (2000c) issued a consultation pack proposing national standards by which this new branch of OFSTED will base its care inspections from September 2001. Among these are proposals that providers should be able to show that they can meet each child's individual care needs. The provider and staff will be required actively to promote equality of opportunity and anti-discriminatory practice for all children. The provider should also be aware that some children may have special needs and should ensure that appropriate action is taken when such a child is identified or admitted to the provision. Steps should be taken to promote that child's welfare and development, in consultation with the parents. Adults looking after children in the provision also need to be able to manage a wide range of children's behaviour in a way that promotes their welfare and development.

If we look at the provisions which children under 5 attend, a wide range of training qualifications is immediately apparent. In LEA nurs-eries and reception classes, there are teachers with education degrees or postgraduate certificates in education and nursery nurses with NNEB (Nursery Nurse Examination Board) qualifications or equivalent. At least half the staff in social services or private day nurseries must have some form of qualification; this is usually unspecified but is usually NNEB or NVQ (National Vocational Qualification). This is also true for preschool playgroups where the qualification is usually via the Preschool Learning Alliance or NVQ. Since registration with the Early Years and Childcare Partnerships, settings must also have input from a qualified teacher, and how this is achieved also varies widely. In the past, no qualifications were required of childminders apart from registration, though some follow NVQ-related courses (Pugh, 1998a). Portage workers attend a three-day basic training workshop followed by supervision as they work, though many may have other qualifications as well, or specific and relevant experience in SEN.

Traditionally, early years training has been delivered by 'a confusing tangle of courses and qualifications that have grown, somewhat chaotically, over the past years' (Pugh, 1998a, p. 1). Gillian Pugh argues that the confusion over training, the piecemeal way in which courses have developed, the low status that many of them carry, the lack of funding for the students enrolling on them, and the generally low level of qualification that besets the field, are but a symptom of a general malaise. The public attitude appears to have been that childcare and early years education have been seen as extensions of the mothering role, keeping status low and turnover high. The bringing together of childcare and early years education under the new partnerships is an ideal opportunity to begin to introduce national strategy and co-ordination in this training. Training in the early years is therefore set to change.

SEN INPUT TO EARLY YEARS TRAINING

What of the content of the training courses and, in particular, training in identifying and supporting early years children who have special educational needs? With such an array of early years training courses it is inevitable that the emphasis on 'special educational needs' varies enormously from course to course, qualification to qualification. Many initial and postgraduate teacher training courses still leave large gaps in the knowledge of newly trained teachers required to work within the SEN Code of Practice (DFE, 1994; DfEE, 2000a). Not surprisingly, most early years practitioners rely strongly on in-service training and continued professional development to cover what they need to know, and this 'need' might only become priority once a child with SEN is already attending. Early years magazines such as *Nursery*

World provide regular training publications which provide lists of early years courses and also courses aimed specifically at special educational needs (see Useful contacts and resources).

The National Early Years Network offers customized in-house training courses in early years learning including meeting SEN. The Preschool Learning Alliance in England and Wales covers an introduction to SEN in its Diploma in Preschool Practice training, with the opportunity to specialize in a further special needs certificate course. 'Children in Scotland' runs courses, seminars and workshops of interest to early years workers which includes SEN. The National Portage Association runs three- to four-day basic Portage workshops in home-based step-by-step teaching for young children with SEN. These courses are held in various parts of the country and are now validated by the association. National children's organizations such as the National Children's Bureau and the National Society for the Prevention of Cruelty to Children (NSPCC) run seminars on all aspects of childhood including many relevant to SEN and to child protection. There are professional development awards organized by the Council for Awards in Children's Care and Education (CACHE), and the National Association for Special Educational Needs (NASEN) are now extending their courses and resources to cater for early years settings as well as workers in schools.

There are many highly practical courses and training events run by voluntary organizations which provide information and support to parents and professionals on specific conditions. For example, the Royal National Institute for the Blind (RNIB) has education centres throughout the UK offering training for parents and workers with children who have visual impairment. The I CAN charity organizes courses for children with speech and language difficulties with many particularly aimed at the early years. The Sarah Duffen Centre at the University of Plymouth, supported by the Down's Syndrome Educational Trust, runs workshops and courses on the early development and education of children with Down's syndrome. Many other organizations publish resources and run training events, and their UK addresses are listed in the 'Contact a Family' or 'CaF' directory (see Useful contacts and resources).

HOW CAN EARLY YEARS PRACTITIONERS BE TRAINED TO DEVELOP REFLECTIVE PRACTICE?

In designing effective training for early years practitioners, it is important to consider how people learn and what factors contribute not only to their learning new skills and acquiring new knowledge and beliefs, but to their putting these into practice in the longer term. There appears to be no universally accepted theory as to how people learn, though several models are considered in this chapter. The Open University module 'The Effective Manager' (Open Business School, 1983) listed these characteristics of adult learning. People must *want* to learn and will only want to learn something if they see the need for it. They learn best by doing; they can learn by listening and watching, but they are likely to learn more effectively if they actively *do* something. *Skills* can only be learnt by doing. They will resist or reject new learning that does not fit easily with what they know already from experience. They also learn best in an informal environment and want guidance not grading. In other words, they need feedback to tell them how well they are doing, but they fear other people knowing if they are doing badly.

Perhaps the third point introduces the greatest challenge to any trainer working with volunteers and early years educators in the non-maintained preschool sector: each trainee will bring a unique combination of past experiences and training, ranging from none at all, through experiences of parenthood, to graduate teaching status.

Each will also bring their very own levels of confidence or uncertainty. Smith (1983) stressed the *emotional* aspects of adults learning; any learning process involves change, something is invariably added or taken away. Such 'unlearning' can lead to fear, anxiety and resistance on the part of the learner. This would suggest that adults learn best if the learning environment is kept informal and non-threatening, and that steps are actively taken to encourage the learner, inspire confidence and 'license' the learner to feel secure enough to 'have a go' with the new approaches. This informality of approach and the need for the trainer to inspire confidence in the learner are key features of the 'Music Makers' training package described on page 29.

The research evidence identifying the optimal conditions for effective work-related learning by adults have been described by Cline, Frederickson and Wright (1990). Traditionally, the held belief (William James, 1990, quoted in Cline, Frederickson and Wright, 1990) was that most people acquire all their new learning by the age of 25 after which the powers of assimilation have gone. However, such earlier studies relied on artificial rote learning that would be unrelated to aspects of working life relevant to the adult learner. The contemporary view (and current government policy) is that learning should be 'lifelong': learning extends far beyond school, and the home, family, work and community will be important centres for continuous learning.

The conditions for optimal learning appear to be the meaningfulness of the material to be learned. The more meaningful to the adult, the better was the learning and the less was forgotten over time. Recent practice is also important, with adults showing relatively better recall of knowledge and skills if they commonly have to apply them. Anxiety about performance is an important factor too. Adults in the workplace seem to have even more to lose in terms of status and self-esteem than children learning, if they feel that they are shown to be incompetent. Speed of performance appears to matter; adults achieve better performance if allowed to work at their own pace, on account of learning styles and approaches that they will have developed over a number of years. It also matters that the trainee feels motivated to learn and perceives the training material to be relevant. Mature adults are more likely than children to question the relevance of what they are learning or, indeed, to refuse to continue if the training is not useful to them.

McCarthy (1992) points out that people are a major resource in any organization and their development plays a major part in promoting its success. She defines five characteristics of a successful training approach. It arises from a perceived need that is identified and located within an overall planning process for the development of partici-pants. It addresses the difficulty of transferring theory into practice. There are built-in opportunities for learning by doing. It acknowl-edges that continuing support is required if participants are to implement what they have learned. It recognizes the political dimen-sion of change and that the structures and relationships of any organization may help or inhibit the transfer of learning into day-to-day practice.

WHAT DO EARLY YEARS EDUCATORS NEED TO KNOW ABOUT SEN?

In planning training for those early years educators who have minimal previous training or qualifications, there may be something we can learn from research with special needs assistants. Lorenz (1992) found that most training courses for special needs assistants sup-porting children with special needs in mainstream schools cover the basic teaching processes, e.g. hearing children read or managing chal-lenging behaviour (Balshaw, 1991; Clayton et al., 1989; OPTIS, 1988). These courses tend to be centre based and combine the teaching of skills with the welcome opportunity for ancillary staff to get together and share experiences. Her own courses in Leeds included five very practical modules covering SEN issues and the role of the special needs assistant, helping children with learning difficulties, managing children with behavioural problems, supporting children with sensory, language or physical difficulties and 'assertiveness and feeling good about yourself' (Lorenz, 1992).

WHAT DOES RESEARCH TELL US ABOUT THE MOST EFFECTIVE WAYS TO LEARN THIS?

So far, it is looking as if any effective training approach must introduce both new skills and the understanding to apply these in a reflective manner. Would theories of adult learning support this? In his Theory of Instruction (1964; 1966) Bruner suggested that there are three modes of learning: the symbolic, the iconic and the enactive. In symbolic learning, the trainee listens to a lecture or reads a book. During iconic learning, the trainee learns through watching others, and during enactive learning the trainee actually practises the skills being taught. Research studies have suggested that symbolic learning *per se* is insufficient if new skills are to be learned and maintained over time. Farrell (1985) found, when evaluating the long-term effectiveness of the EDY (Education of Developmentally Young) training course, that trainees maintained their practical skills long after they had forgotten the theoretical aspects of the course. Any training course in practical skills and approaches should therefore contain both theoretical and practical aspects if it is to be remembered and practised.

Looking at the training needs of social workers, Baskett (1983) described the kind of knowledge that they needed to acquire. This 'practice-based knowledge' related both to the work situation with its social constraints and culture, and also to the more organized theoretical knowledge within the field. It included knowledge about resources and how to get them, and knowledge about organizations and sub-cultures, their norms, values and how to deal with them. There was also knowledge of how to get knowledge, knowledge of oneself and how one learns, formal knowledge as found in books, articles and higher education courses, and coping knowledge – practical ways of coping with pressures and the contradictory demands of the work setting.

The evaluation of the EDY course (Farrell, 1985) showed how necessary it was for trainees, once they had acquired new skills, to move on to take the second part of the training course in which individual trainees devised their own training programmes using these skills, and were supervised through applying them over a number of weeks in their work setting. It seemed that, only then, did they maintain their new skills in the longer term.

How important is 'modelling' as a technique in skills training? Rosenthal (1978) sees it as working in four ways. Observational learning is most important at the early stages of learning relatively new patterns of behaviour. Modelling also helps give a particular interpretation of the situation to the trainee as being one in which certain types of his or her own behaviour are appropriate. Observing a behaviour in others gives discriminatory cues to help him or her organize their own behaviour. Finally, modelling helps the observer adopt the normative behaviour in others for that situation. In similar vein, social skills trainers would claim that the most important thing that social skills training achieves is the extension and refinement of behaviours already in the trainee's repertoire (e.g. McIntyre and Duthie, 1977).

AN EXAMPLE OF A PROJECT TO ENGENDER REFLECTIVE PRACTICE IN EARLY YEARS

The aim of the Music Makers project (which was introduced in another context on page 29) was to teach playleaders to run a regular music 'circle time' as part of their regular sessions. This could be used to improve the developmental skills of any children who have SEN in their settings. The training approach itself also aimed to develop their reflective practice. It was hoped that, following their training, they would be better placed to reflect on what it was they could do to enhance the children's learning within their setting.

Fifty-four early years educators attached to 29 settings were trained in the approach and used the methods they had learned to target 49 children with SEN. Questionnaire data were collected to evaluate how early years educators were developing their practice following training. A developmental checklist was designed and used to measure changes in the children's skills. Thirty early years educators were interviewed six months after training and the transcripts analysed using 'content analysis' and 'Grounded Theory' (Strauss and Corbin, 1990).

All settings continued to use the Music Makers approach twelve months after training. It was seen by them as increasing both their own and the children's confidence and in encouraging all the children to join in. Many reflected on the positive changes they had seen in all the children's motivation, behaviour and confidence, and how this was also generalizing to other learning situations.

A theoretical model describing the relationships that exist when adults and children learn together began to emerge (Figure 5.1).

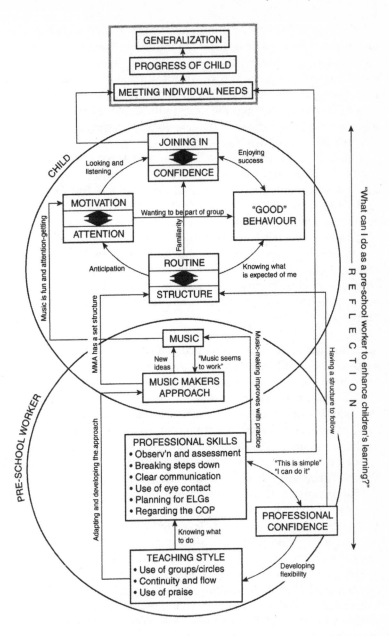

Figure 5.1: The relationships between reflective practice, the Music Makers approach and children's progress

When early years educators reflect carefully about their practice, they become better able to meet the individual needs of the children they are working with. This, in turn, enables them to see evidence of the children's progress and contribute further to encouraging and maintaining it. The more the children progress, the greater the confidence of the educator, and the more individually they become able to meet needs. The progress of the one affects the progress of the other as adult and child learn together.

Young children respond well to set structures and routines that enable them to anticipate and predict. This, in turn, seems to improve their confidence as learners, their ability to attend and their motivation to join in. With familiarity comes better attention, more appropriate behaviour and more opportunities to learn.

However, set structures and routines also help early years educators to develop their own skills and confidence, making them better able to deliver the curriculum with that level of flexibility and creativity needed to ensure that individual needs are met, moment by moment. Learning in both adults and children is therefore an ongoing process.

Practical 'how to do it' approaches enable early years educators to develop their skills and confidence. If such approaches 'work' in the sense that the children respond positively and make progress, then those approaches tend to be used long after the training period has ended. This enables further practice and development of skills that can then be generalized to new learning situations. It also allows any belief systems that have been strengthened by the approach (e.g. that 'inclusion works') to take root. Finally, it also allows the early years educator to develop the skills and confidence needed to help the children generalize their progress to new situations.

With practice and confidence comes the ability of early years educators to develop new teaching styles and approaches. They become able to 'take risks' in leaving their regular routines in order to 'go with the child', the opportunity and the moment. In fact, they have developed the ability to think reflectively about what it is they can do to enhance the children's learning and plan their next approaches in light of this, not only in their planning but 'on the hoof' as well.

The Music Makers approach was therefore seen as successful in encouraging early years practitioners to think reflectively about their practice and to develop their approaches so as best to enhance the children's learning and progress. This is despite many of them having little previous experience or training. The success of the approach may be because it supports the interaction between adults and children, developing the skills and confidences of both and enabling the success of one to foster the success of the other. It may also be because it allows the learning process to be extended over time and leads to generalization of skills from one area to another. Settings tend to continue to use the approach independently long after their training is completed.

It has also been shown to improve the developmental skills of children who have SEN, again perhaps because it uses routines and builds confidence over time. However, early years educators have found it to be an approach for *all* children (not just those with SEN), and it has therefore proved to be a practical way of delivering the early years curriculum inclusively.

THE 'QUALITY PLAY' TRAINING MATERIALS

Supported by a grant from the National Lottery charities board, the National Portage Association developed a set of 'Quality Play' training materials for early years practitioners 'in recognition of the rights of all children to enjoy and participate in the everyday experiences of childhood' (White and Parry, 1997). Again, this training follows what we know to be the best methods of engendering reflective practice; it helps those actually working with a child who has SEN to assess, plan and monitor in the setting, linking the approaches closely with family and home.

Through eight two-hour sessions, the materials help trainees to work closely with the family, observe the child whose development or behaviour is raising concern, and analyse starting points and strengths for providing play. They are helped to prepare an Individual Play Plan (an example of this is given on page 153) to meet the needs of the individual child and to analyse the adult's role in supporting the child's play. They learn how to monitor the child's progress, celebrate changes as the child progresses step-by-small-step, and examine strategies to manage behaviour and learning positively. The materials are accessible and the approach full of common sense and practicality, with the main examples being taken from playgroups. The skills and knowledge learned by the trainees, who practise new skills between training sessions, enables them to develop the kind of flow between assessment of starting points, through to individual planning and play which is shown on pages 152 to 153.

THE FUTURE SHAPE OF EARLY YEARS TRAINING?

Early years provision in the UK has traditionally been from services which are provided by different agencies, have different aims and objectives (some focusing on care and welfare and others on children's learning and cognitive development) and require different levels of staffing and qualification. The bringing together of childcare and early years education in England under the new partnerships is an ideal opportunity to begin to introduce national strategy and co-ordination in this training and Abbott and Pugh (1998) draw together the views of many early years educators in making a number of recommendations for what 'good practice' in early years training could look like.

Their hope is that one national body should be established to take overall responsibility for standards, training and qualifications in the early years. This will make training much simpler for the practitioner and ensure more equable quality of provision for young children. National targets should be set and adequate resources allocated for an appropriately trained early years workforce. The underpinning principles, content and approach of all early years courses should reflect key skills, knowledge and understanding (including play and learning, teamwork, working with parents and carers, leadership and management, children's rights, legal issues, equality of opportunity including for children with special educational needs, working with other professionals, assessment and the curriculum). They suggest that early years should become a specialist area within teacher training, of equal value as subject specialisms. Access to in-service training and continuous professional development should be the right of all early childhood workers so that reflective practice can be developed in post. All early years workers should have access to the support of early years advisers. In search of more equable training, the current differentials in pay and conditions of early years workers should be rationalized as part of the national early years strategy.

SUMMARY

Early years practitioners and their training needs

In this chapter, we looked at the various professionals and carers in early years and where they worked.

We concluded that early years practitioners brought with them a wide range of qualifications and experiences and looked forward to a national framework for co-ordinating qualifications and training.

We recognized that this variety of backgrounds made in-service training in Early Years Partnerships particularly challenging.

We discussed what early years practitioners needed to know about SEN and the most effective ways of delivering this training and encouraging reflective practice in their settings.

We also looked at two different training approaches that encouraged early years practitioners to think reflectively about how they could meet SEN within their settings.

—6—

Joining together: dovetailing the boundaries between agencies and disciplines

Can you get diaries under prescription? (Frustrated parent, tired with co-ordinating the visits of many various professionals to his door)

NEW OPPORTUNITIES FOR PARTNERSHIP AND FOR 'JOINING UP'

The establishment of the Early Years Development and Childcare Partnerships brings new opportunities for a coming together and collaboration of early years stakeholders from different settings, services, agencies and disciplines. Within the new framework, the importance of inter-agency working and joint planning of services was stressed from the beginning, and there have been various government initiatives to improve working across agencies and professional boundaries, some of which we will meet later in this chapter. The vernacular term for describing the current (Labour) government's drive to harmonize a number of policy areas between and within different departments and sectors is 'joined up' policies. There is a useful 'rich picture' of the various agencies that might be involved in, for example, family work in Wolfendale (2000b, p. 7). What guidelines are there for recommended practice when 'joining up' policies and practice in the area of special educational needs, both across the different agencies, and between the different members of a professional multidisciplinary team?

PLANNING ACROSS AGENCIES

Children who are identified as having special needs and disabilities early in their lives have usually received services through child health, education and social services. Nowadays, it is not uncommon for parents of children with disabilities to have at least five (sometimes ten or more) 'helping professionals' involved or visiting at any one time. Although each will be committed to helping the child as best they can, the sheer scale of numbers of different disciplines and agencies involved sets the scene for conflicting advice, duplication of services, confusing input to the family, and inter-professional rivalry (Dale, 1996). Dealing with the various agencies involved can be the most stressful aspect of caring for a child with disabilities.

Planning across agencies has both its challenges and its rewards, as illustrated by this example from social services. Social services involvement has increased since the Children Act 1989 and the arrival of Children's Services Plans in 1996, with more local services being developed for children with disabilities and their families. The Social Services Inspectorate (1998) identified common features for good collaboration in planning and developing services across agencies. Where practice was seen to be 'good', there was a shared understanding of the roles and responsibilities of each agency with clear information for families. There were also shared understandings of the legislation, guidance and priorities to which each agency works with opportunities for joint training. Databases and management information systems were co-ordinated with shared registers of children in need between agencies. A planning system was co-ordinated with key individuals from each agency on the planning groups. There were shared budget commitments with agreed priorities.

Above all, the inspectorate indicated the need for better communication at every level: clearer information about services, better listening and explaining with parents, and closer involvement of the children themselves. Good communication takes time and, when services are under pressure, 'time' might be the area that is sacrificed first.

MULTIDISCIPLINARY COMMUNITY TEAMS

Early years professionals have been exhorted to work more closely together for many years now. The National Children's Bureau was first established to promote co-operation in childcare and, through working parties and publications, came to foreshadow the influential Court Report (Court, 1976) and Warnock Report (Warnock, 1978). The Court Report led to the setting up of multidisciplinary teams to provide diagnosis, assessment, treatment and education for children with 'handicaps', as they were then termed. These teams were made up of paediatricians, nursing officers, social workers, psychologists and teachers who were based in Child Development Centres or District Handicap Teams. The Warnock Committee considered how the assessment could be most effective and suggested a continuous and staged model involving close collaboration between the professionals concerned. This staged model, with close multi-agency liaison and joint working, has been further developed in the Children Act (Department of Health, 1991) and the Code of Practice for the identification and assessment of SEN (DFE, 1994).

In the 1980s, there was a rapid growth of Child Development Centres and District Handicap Teams with a range of clinical functions. Children and families were offered diagnosis and multidisciplinary assessment of congenital and acquired handicapping conditions, with treatment and intervention. Medical treatment was available, as well as advice and provision on aids, adaptations and resources. Advice, counselling and support were generally available to parents and families, and information was available on statutory and voluntary services. The centres were also able to contribute towards advice on the children's special educational needs.

Since then, there has been a move towards supporting children and their families in their own homes and communities wherever possible, though the Child Development Centres have remained as 'gateways' into services and bases for professional teams, and for multidisciplinary assessment. How well these centres link together with other community and multi-agency provision (and vice versa) still varies considerably from area to area, though the trend is for closer 'joined-up' working, with the aim of providing seamless services for children and families.

CHILD DEVELOPMENT TEAM ROLES

Any family referred for the first time to their local Child Development Centre is likely to meet a confusing variety of professionals. Each will have their own questions, their own models of working, their own theoretical frameworks, their particular organizational culture and their own assessment tools. Who are these professionals, and what are their roles? The author was interested to look at how the various professional roles dovetail together in multidisciplinary teams that help early years children and their families (see Mortimer, 1997b, for a fuller description). In this study, professionals were asked what *they* felt their particular and perhaps unique role within the assessment team was. In other words, what are the distinct ingredients of 'Educational Psychology', or 'Occupational Therapy', or 'Paediatrics' that make each profession distinct and specific in the role it plays out in the discovery and helping of a young child's special needs? The descriptions below are taken from their own words.

The role of the preschool teacher
Teachers play a central role at the time of transfer into school, nursery or preschool. They have particular knowledge of the statutory assessment procedures, and are therefore well placed to talk families through the process, liaise with schools and education authorities, and set up any introductory visits. Because of their experience and knowledge of how children learn in a range of settings, they are well placed to complete the educational advice in any statutory assessment of a young child's special educational needs. Once a child is placed in a preschool setting, their parent liaison role usually continues, particularly if problems arise, or where nurseries need advice in setting individual teaching programmes. It is helpful to follow children through at six-monthly reviews, so that other professionals have the benefit of teaching advice from someone who had known the family and child over the preschool years. Sometimes they have specialist qualifications in teaching children with very particular needs. Some teachers are involved in directly teaching children individually or in small groups, in centres, mainstream settings, assessment nurseries or at home.

The roles of the paediatrician and community doctor
As a doctor, the paediatrician offers paediatric and neurological examination, with investigations and work with parents to identify cause and diagnosis. Early diagnosis, counselling and support, perhaps even before referral to the multidisciplinary team, are sometimes provided. Paediatricians also have a role in providing or arranging genetic counselling when necessary, and in tapping into in-patient facilities. Paediatricians also provide the service of monitoring medical condition and needs as the child grows older, and monitoring hearing and vision are an important part of this. Community doctors can also help to liaise with schools and education, and can assist with the statutory assessment of SEN.

The role of the speech and language therapist
Speech and language therapists offer assessment, treatment, advice and counselling to people of all ages with a speech, language or communication disorder and related eating and swallowing problems. They also offer support and advice to carers such as parents, teachers

and nursing staff to help them understand the nature of the problem and how they can help. Most speech and language therapists working in multidisciplinary assessment teams are involved in the assessment and treatment of speech, language and communication disorders, including preverbal skills. Advice is given on feeding, sucking, mouth and tongue movements, and textures of foods. Sometimes, advice on alternative and augmentative communication becomes necessary and training is given to other professionals, parents and carers on the use of communication aids and signing systems. Specialist advice is also available on articulatory, phonological and fluency problems in young children.

The role of the physiotherapist
Physiotherapists can elect to specialize in children's work. Their aim is to work towards helping the child reach his or her maximum potential. Following assessment and therapeutic diagnosis, the physiotherapist will work closely with parents or carers to establish appropriate goals for the child. This individually planned programme of physiotherapy might cover careful positioning and movement, advice and support, special handling skills, exercise regimes, walking practice, balance and co-ordination exercises, stretching of muscles, chest physiotherapy and special equipment. Most paediatric physiotherapists are involved in the assessment of gross motor skills, and treatment of motor delay. They work particularly with children with physical disabilities and delay, providing advice on handling and care, lifting, positioning, nasal suctioning, inhibiting abnormal reflexes and advising on splints, boots, braces, wheelchairs and buggies, sometimes with overlap with the occupational therapist. They contribute to team assessments by advising on goals and interventions for motor skills, and are often particularly involved in liaison with the special care baby unit. Sometimes, advice is given on the use of therapeutic electrical equipment. Physiotherapists provide stretching and direct physiotherapy and also give time to passing these ideas to the parents and carers for following through at home. Some physiotherapists also work to help parents relax and avoid the physiological effects of stress.

The role of the occupational therapist
Occupational therapists work with children of varying ages whose development is interrupted by physical, psychological or social impairment or disability. They aim to develop the child's maximum level of independence thereby improving practical life skills which

hopefully promotes a better quality of life. Work is carried out in conjunction with the child's family or carer in a variety of settings. They assess gross and fine motor skills, any dyspraxic difficulties, writing, independence skills, visual perception and body awareness, and the need for specialized equipment for home and preschool including seating, wheelchairs, toilet and bathing aids, and adaptive equipment to improve everyday skills. Sometimes they provide a specialist assessment of switches and information technology. They are also called upon to advise on handedness for a child beginning to write where this is still undetermined.

The role of the clinical psychologist
Some multidisciplinary assessment teams have considerable overlap between educational and clinical psychologist with caseload determined by age and stage, or even geographically. In other teams, these respective roles are determined by the availability of the particular psychologist. Clinical psychologists can offer, in particular, family support and counselling, family therapy, advice and intervention on attachment difficulties, cognitive and developmental assessment, advice on behaviour management, and specialist knowledge of certain conditions such as autism.

The role of the educational psychologist
Educational psychologists attempt to assist others to find solutions to difficulties or problems or needs. They help by clarifying and defining the problem, generating teaching and management approaches and evaluating the success of these. They express this help in the contexts of the relationships and environments that the child experiences, and to draw up advice. They can provide specialist assessment of cognitive or learning difficulties, provide assessment and advice based on the paradigms of child development and learning theory, and the use and interpretation of normative psychometric assessment. They are well placed to advise on the education system, the resources and provision available and the statutory assessment procedures. Educational psychologists aim to provide an objective, independent, or non-medical view and to see the child's needs in a wider context than the assessment clinic. Advice on behaviour management is often given. They are able to help colleagues and parents to focus their observations, and also to make useful interpretations of how the child was playing. Sometimes, specialist skills in bereavement counselling or conflict resolution are called upon.

Following the Green Paper *Excellence for All* (DfEE, 1997a), there have been recommendations that educational psychologists should be more actively involved in early identification and support of SEN, and spend less time completing statutory assessments. A picture of their present role with examples of good practice and creative recommendations for core functions in the future is given in the report of the working group to consider the developing role of educational psychologists (DfEE, 2000b).

The role of the social worker
Counselling and family support are offered, usually with the ability to visit the home, and assess or support the family situation and dynamics. They have access to social services provision, including day nurseries, respite care, shared caring, and preschool support schemes. Child protection procedures are also a crucial and specific role, with the possible conflict that this can raise for some families.

The role of the Portage worker
Portage is a home-teaching scheme for preschool children with special needs and their families (page 50). Home visitors call regularly to assess where a child has reached in each area of development, to negotiate what to teach next and to model how to teach it. Portage workers are able to work on a regular weekly basis with the family in a home setting. This provides them with particular knowledge of the family's needs, and a chance to acknowledge the parents' expertise and value their contribution. They are able to negotiate skills to be taught with the family, break these down into manageable next steps and, thereby, encourage the child's motivation and confidence. Moreover, they can highlight learning opportunities in the home, acknowledge the child's need for fun and relaxation, and allow family and child personal choices. Their ongoing and regular contact with the family places them in a good position to liaise with other members on the team, and to provide regular reports on progress.

Cunningham and Davis (1985) emphasize the point that it is also most important to ask how parents themselves construe professionals. This is bound to affect the kind of help they anticipate and, therefore, its perceived usefulness.

There is a useful description of the various roles and responsibilities of early years/SEN professionals in Roffey (1999) with helpful suggestions for joint planning and collaboration when assessing and supporting young children who have special needs. She emphasizes the importance of professionals, parents or carers and early years practitioners meeting together when a child with SEN transfers into an early years setting in order to help people think through the needs of individual children and how these might be met in the setting. An initial joint planning meeting in the early years setting can fulfil all of these purposes.

Purposes of the initial joint planning meeting in the early years setting

- Gathering and sharing all relevant information.
- Enabling good quality planning to take place.
- Handing over between professionals.
- Valuing the contributions that everyone makes.
- Establishing good communications.
- Establishing positive relationships.
- Promoting a positive 'can-do' ethos.
- Reassuring parents.
- Reassuring and supporting staff who will be in direct contact with the child.
- Addressing potential difficulties early on.
- Detailing the need for any specific resources from outside school/nursery. (Roffey, 1999, p. 73)

MODELS OF WORKING WITHIN MULTIDISCIPLINARY TEAMS

We have seen how teams have a wide range of different functions and membership. Another way of classifying team structures is with regard to the manner in which the team members work. Cunningham and Davis (1985) describe 'multidisciplinary' teams and 'interdisciplinary' teams. The first implies that the child and family might be seen by several specialists, each from different backgrounds and theoretical standpoints. Each might be working in a relatively isolated way from colleagues of other specialisms.

However, in an 'interdisciplinary' service, specialists work more closely together, exchanging knowledge with each other, co-ordinating their assessment and interventions, and sharing certain core skills such as counselling, family support and good communication across disciplines, with equal status. Interdisciplinary co-operation depends on team members respecting one another and establishing good working relationships in order to negotiate mutually acceptable goals and actions (Cunningham and Davis, 1985). The authors emphasize the value of an interdisciplinary team, where specialists work more closely together, specialist knowledge is shared across disciplines and each specialist is able to communicate about their work to the other members of the team. Moreover, each professional takes responsibility for co-ordinating their information and intervention with that of other members of the team and, since no single type of specialism is seen as having all the answers, each type is valued and all specialisms have equal status. Finally, all professionals share core skills, e.g. in counselling, family support work, communication skills and partnership methods.

A further model of working is shown in the 'transdisciplinary' team. Here, boundaries between disciplines are minimized and the emphasis is upon arena-style assessments where many professionals meet with the parents to view, discuss and assess the child. Here, there is consultation between members in order to plan approaches which integrate goals from all disciplines (e.g. Bagnato and Neisworth, 1991). In practice, this might be difficult to achieve (Mortimer, 1997b) with boundaries blurring and quality depending on particular charisma and style.

What are the most common barriers to effective teamworking in early years intervention services? These have been described by Wilson (1998) as staff, time and budget limitations with poor communication skills and competitiveness between team members. Sometimes there are narrow or self-serving interests and a lack of incentive to change. Teams lack training and skills in co-ordinating their efforts, and there is sometimes a preoccupation with administrative structure rather than with the function of the agency. Sometimes team members lack political awareness and sometimes there are other political issues or a general resistance to change. 'Turf' issues and territoriality can get in the way of collaboration, as can a lack of information about other agencies' mission and function. Perhaps the team processes are generally haphazard and poorly planned. Perhaps administrative support is questionable, discipline-specific jargon rife and practical problems occur in communicating and meeting due to a lack of shared language or to travel distances.

INTEGRATED SERVICES

Where professional teams work together collaboratively, they have usually worked out procedures for breaking down these barriers. The 'Honeylands' service was set up in the 1970s and was an early example of developing a service based on shared philosophies and aims across different professional disciplines. Above all, it aimed to develop an effective partnership with the families involved and to provide child-centred approaches at a time when these were relatively new concepts.

Honeylands

The Honeylands Family Support Unit in Exeter is an example of an integrated team service. A team of nurses, teachers, doctors, social worker, therapists and psychologists plan corporately with parents the programme that their child will follow. The programme is implemented, reviewed and modified regularly as the child's needs develop. A 'keyworker' provides continuity of professional contact for the family. The Honeylands model is to ensure that its staff:

- share the same philosophy and aims;
- share management decisions for the service provided;
- constantly review their policy and practice;
- work in a complementary, rather than competitive, way to other services.

STAR (St Helen's Advice and Resource) Children's Centre provides a contemporary example of a comprehensive, interdisciplinary, integrated service to early years children with SEN (see Figure 6.1). The service is housed in a council-owned building and is therefore more community based than Honeylands. Running costs are shared with the health authority. Bright colours and flexible-use rooms provide a range of services for the child and family. Photographs in the entrance hall show the range of professionals whom the child might meet, ranging from doctors, therapists and Portage staff to cleaning and administrative staff, and therapists. There is a comprehensive staff handbook for all those involved. Once a child has been referred to the service, an Action Plan and an individually designed assessment of the child's needs is drawn up. First contacts with the family are usually made through home visits. Intervention might include a whole range of services with additional specialist input from elsewhere being drawn in as needed. This service is described fully in Hamer (1997).

JOINT WORKING WITHIN THE COMMUNITY

The development of Early Years Development and Childcare Partnerships (Chapter 1) has provided a framework for working jointly across agencies and groups with all children in early years and those

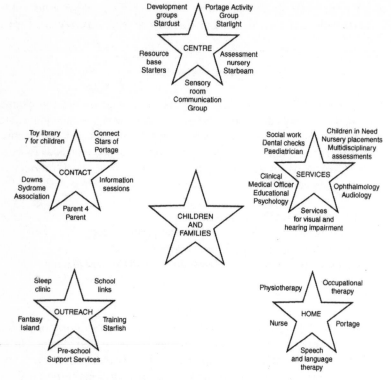

Figure 6.1: The Star Children's Centre service

receiving childcare. Where these are working effectively, there has been joint planning of provision, joint projects for inclusion and opportunities for joint training involving carers, communities and parents.

Some creative interventions become possible when professionals join together to work with parents and children. The box contains one example of actual practice where this author was keen to develop simple patterns of partnership on a local and low-cost basis (British Psychological Society, undated, issued 1999).

RUMPUS groups

An educational psychologist and a team of community health visitors hold regular 'RUMPUS' (ARe yoU Mas and Pas Under Stress?) groups in local health centres. The groups aim to support young parents and their early years children where there are particular difficulties in managing behaviour. A combination of approaches has been developed by the team to put parents at their ease, improve the attention skills of the children, encourage early language and lap play, build up family relationships and provide practical advice based on realistic expectations and week-by-week management of behaviour. Parents also make their own plans for encouraging positive behaviour in their children in a supportive atmosphere that aims to enable and empower rather than to prescribe.

Other positive examples of working together across boundaries and agencies are given in the various Centres of Excellence and SURE START programmes which have attracted government funding in the late 1990s and early 2000s.

CENTRES OF EXCELLENCE

At the same time that Early Years Development Plans were first being put together by LEAs in England, the government was inviting bids for the establishment of the first 25 pilot centres of excellence. These were expected to exemplify how early education and childcare can be combined with a number of other services designed to support families (such as the teaching of parenting skills, family learning, adult basic skills) and to stimulate good practice by other providers in the surrounding area.

Rowland Hill Centre for Childhood, Haringey

In 1998, councillors in Haringey voted to move the borough's only special needs nursery away from its hospital setting and into the local community. It merged with a local nursery to form the new, inclusive, 'Centre for Childhood'. The purpose of the centre is for 'all children and their families to make positive relationships, learn together, grow in confidence and self-respect and be happy'. It also aims to fulfil the expectations of a centre of excellence in providing children with the highest quality nursery curriculum and giving staff the opportunity of career development and satisfaction. It sets out to represent all that is best about multi-agency working so that health, education and social services together respond to local community needs.

Rowland Hill is an inclusive supportive nursery centre where all the staff members are fully committed to welcoming all children and believing that children have the right to learn and be together. The centre's philosophy is to adapt to children's needs rather than expecting them to 'fit in'. The curriculum is continuously developed and differentiated as each unique child develops and changes. All their children come from the local community and some will have profound and multiple disabilities, some may have behavioural difficulties whilst others may have severe language or communication delay.

There is a busy nursery, a toddler group, training facilities, a breakfast club and a four o'clock club, a family outreach service, a play therapist and regular sessions from a speech and language therapist. The facilities are easily accessible for children with disabilities and the staffing ratios available can support children with complex or severe needs. The philosophy is that support professionals are brought to the child rather than expecting the child to attend for therapies. The children learn through their play experiences and are free to choose their own activities, with staff working alongside them to support and introduce new ideas. Parents and staff together draw up Individual Education Plans for those children who have special educational needs. Parents are welcome to come and discuss their child's development at any time.

SURE START

SURE START is a cross-departmental government initiative aimed at children under three years old and their families in a small targeted area of disadvantage. It concentrates additional resources and additional services in this tightly defined area in order to achieve seamless provision of preventative services. It involves all aspects of their lives including their health, education, social and leisure time. It brings together many different agencies and organizations in the statutory, private and voluntary sectors aiming to break down barriers and ensure co-ordinated and 'joined-up' provision.

The SURE START initiative is based on what we know from current research. A review of research on prevention and early intervention which contributed to its creation (Pugh, 1998b) concluded that there were four groups of protective factors which helped children in adverse conditions achieve good outcomes:

- An adequate standard of living.
- Temperaments or dispositions that attract and encourage care-giving, lead to high self-esteem, sociability and autonomy, ability to solve problems, and an internal locus of control.
- Dependable caregivers: growing up in a family with one or two dependable adults whose child-rearing practices are positive and appropriate; a warm family and the absence of family discord.
- Networks of community support: living in a supportive and safe community; a peer group that is prosocial; and a school where children are valued and learning is encouraged. (Pugh, 1999, p. 11)

SURE START is therefore grounded in evidence from child develop-ment and attachment theory (see page 180), as well as what works in supporting parents and young children within local communities.

The Howgill Family Centre, Whitehaven

The Howgill Family Centre in Whitehaven was one of the first voluntary-led services to achieve both 'SURE START' and 'centre of excellence' status and funding. Set in a remarkable Georgian building at the heart of this reviving community, it has offered a range of centre-based and outreach provision since 1977. There is open access to a family centre with playrooms, training rooms, counselling services and resources. Trained volunteers offer family support in local homes which aims to be preventative as well as supportive in times of need.

Their Early Support Programme identifies children in need at an early age, introducing them to the Howgill preschool playgroup and developing parenting skills whilst carers play alongside their children. Trained in Portage home-teaching, the volunteers also offer special home support to families who have a young child with special educational needs, with additional funding through joint finance. The 'Howgill Hippopotabus' is well equipped and visits commu-nity parent and toddler groups. Carers and toddlers can also visit the centre for play sessions and there are also twins and triplets groups when needed.

'Shadow' is a group that helps those living under some form of shadow in their lives, with independent counsellors offering sensitive support and grief counselling. Another independent (though closely linked) service operates in the basement, offering art and craft activities for fun, for therapeutic help and for those of all ages with special needs. Finally, the centre runs training for carers, volunteers and professionals, and an equipment loan service.

The official targets for SURE START are:

- improving the social and emotional well-being of children through improving parenting skills;
- improving health, particularly the numbers of low birth-weight babies and a decrease in infant mortality;
- achieving speech and developmental levels that are 90 per cent within the normal range, and improving readiness to learn;
- strengthening families and 'natural' communities;
- increasing the productivity of operations and targeting the money effectively.

The emphasis is on empowering local communities to speak for themselves and develop their own initiatives and projects for decreasing child poverty and deprivation. In putting together successful bids, professionals have had to make sure that what *they* felt the local community needed matched what local people wanted to see. Projects have included home-visiting schemes by trained parents, carers and toddler facilities, training opportunities with crèche facilities and parenting classes. One of the omissions in the earlier bids was for projects including improved and affordable childcare to break the poverty cycle. In the early stages of SURE START, there was still much joined-up thinking and planning to be done on how SURE START would link with other early years initiatives such as the Early Years and Childcare Partnerships, funded places for three-year-olds or the National Childcare Strategy.

BUILDING EFFECTIVE TEAMS

Looking back upon what we have learned about 'joined-up' working, what might effective teamworking look like? These suggestions would be as relevant for a team of professionals working in an early years setting as for those working with young children who have SEN in a child development setting or integrated community service.

Have a clear set of aims and visions for your service, agreed with the families and community you serve. Make sure you are all clear about your roles and responsibilities within the team. Set up regular team meetings at mutually convenient times and make these a priority for everyone. Nominate a keyworker for each child who will take lead responsibility for liaising with other professionals and with the family.

Set up regular means of communication with each other: regular telephone contact times for team members, a shared message book, regular memoing about cases with whoever is keyworker for a child, shared centre bases to allow for 'quick words in passing'. Set up a regular shared system of decision-making both for administrative/management tasks and for casework. Establish regular six-monthly reviews so that team members can jointly review a child's progress and agree an individualized programme for the future.

Provide clear and up-to-date information for each other and for the families about the different agencies, services and personnel in your area by liaising with the Early Years and Childcare Partnership. Develop listening skills and peer support skills so that you can show respect and value each team member's contribution. No individual team member should be seen as holding the 'expert' view. Make sure each team member has contributed to the child's individualized targets and that everyone is acquainted with the plan of action to be taken. Regard parents as equal and essential members of the multidisciplinary team. Consider ways of involving children in the decision-making and planning that affects them.

SUMMARY

Joining together: dovetailing the boundaries between agencies and disciplines

In this chapter, we looked at some of the challenges facing agencies and departments in providing 'joined-up' services for children with SEN and their families.

We looked at the roles of various professionals who might be working with the family and at patterns of working together in teams, first at Child Development Centres and then in other community teams.

Some examples of centres of excellence and SURE START projects were introduced and a call made for full evaluation of their effectiveness so that these could feed into good practice and service development on a wider scale.

On a personal level, we looked at some of the ways in which effective team-working can be promoted between professionals within any setting.

—Part Three ──────────

Assessment and Intervention in the Early Years

Early identification:
gateways into early years action

> I think everybody learns that they are just normal children – just developing. (Early years practitioner reflecting on her SEN practice, Mortimer, 2000a, interview 12)

THE IMPORTANCE OF EARLY IDENTIFICATION OF SPECIAL NEEDS

In this chapter, we look at the identification of special educational needs; Ruth Wilson appropriately terms this process 'Child Find' (Wilson, 1998). Unless children with special educational needs are identified and assessed, their particular needs may not be understood or attended to.

It might be that a child's special educational needs have already been identified before they join a setting, in which case we will look at how early years practitioners can make best use of gathering information in the early stages of that child's placement. It might also be that it is the early years practitioners themselves who, in partnership with parents, are identifying a child's needs for the first time within the setting or responding to parental concerns. In an inclusive setting, such identification can arise seamlessly from the early years provision itself and we will look at ways in which this might be done later in the chapter. We will look also at how early years practitioners and parents or carers can work together to identify and assess special educational needs and how the early years curriculum might provide a useful framework for doing this.

In the Code of Practice for SEN (DFE, 1994), the importance of early identification is highlighted:

> The importance of early identification, assessment and provision for any child who may have special educational needs cannot be

over-emphasized. The earlier action is taken, the more responsive the child is likely to be, and the more readily can intervention be made without undue disruption to the organization of the school, including the delivery of the curriculum for that particular child. If a difficulty proves transient the child will subsequently be able to learn and progress normally. If the child's difficulties prove less responsive to provision made by the school, then an early start can be made in considering the additional provision that may be needed to support the child's progress. (Ibid., p. 10)

Identifying children with special educational needs is often a complex and elusive task. The Green Paper (DfEE, 1997a, p. 12) remarks that 'whether or not a child has SEN will therefore depend both on the individual and on local circumstances. It may be entirely consistent with the law for a child to be said to have SEN in one school, but not in another'. In early years, the challenge is even greater as many of the tools and approaches that might be used with older children are not appropriate or practicable. In Chapter 8, we look at some of the methods of assessment appropriate for children in the early years, and in Chapter 10, explore what the SEN Code of Practice (DFE, 1994; DfEE, 2000a) has to say about the identification, assessment and monitoring of special educational needs.

IDENTIFYING SPECIFIC CONDITIONS OR SPECIAL NEEDS?

There are some books on 'inclusion' (such as Chizea, Henderson and Jones, 1999, and the series by Mortimer, 2001 to 2002) which focus on particular kinds of SEN or disability and show how these needs can be supported in an inclusive setting. This has been the traditional approach in the past and is still an approach welcomed by early years practitioners in many settings (e.g. regular reader surveys conducted by the publishers, Scholastic). Early years practitioners have commented that this is a particularly helpful and practical approach for them, particularly where contacts and support organizations are given and readers can obtain further information about each condition and what it means. Some of these contacts are given on page 203.

In the present book, the author has chosen to approach 'conditions and disabilities' from the other end; from the perspective of *all* children's individual needs. This is partly because, in a truly inclusive approach, 'child' will come first and 'condition' second. A 'child who has SEN' has a different ring about it to 'an SEN child' (or 'an epileptic' and 'an autistic').

It is also because each child is a unique individual whose needs may not fall neatly into given categories or 'conditions'. This can be heart-breaking for a family struggling to come to terms with their child's special educational needs and desperate for a 'label' to bring some sense of identity to the whole situation. Nevertheless, it is a fact that the vast majority of special educational needs in the early years will have no set 'cause' or 'label'. There is sometimes a concern that, without the 'label', an early years practitioner cannot set out to under-stand the condition and therefore meet the needs. And because they are not 'experts' in identifying the label, they cannot make steps towards meeting the needs.

However, it is knowledge of the *needs* which leads to *action*. It becomes more pragmatic and constructive to speak of 'needs' than of 'conditions'. Suddenly this allows the early years practitioner a way forward. They are already experienced in how children learn in the early stages of development and the *Curriculum Guidance for the Foundation Stage* (QCA, 2000) can provide a framework both for providing the early years curriculum and identifying needs and planning action within it (page 112).

Because general areas of need (for example, 'learning difficulties', 'speech and language difficulties', 'autistic difficulties', 'attention dif-ficulties') do play a role in the assessment and identification of many children's special educational needs, there are boxed sections throughout Chapters 9 and 11 with practical pointers for identifying and intervening with children who have certain clusters of difficul-ties. The suggestions are kept general so that the reader can visualize a practical and concrete way for 'getting started' at a time when it might seem that nothing can be done until the 'experts out there' have 'proclaimed'.

GETTING TO KNOW THE CHILD

Many very young children who have significant and long-term needs or disabilities will already have had these identified through their local Child Development Centre or Child and Family Service. They and their families will therefore have become known to some of the local support professionals. As a result of this, there should already be a certain amount of information making sense of a child's needs when he or she joins an early years setting. The first task of the early years practitioner becomes one of asking relevant questions, translat-ing assessment information into what it means for the child and for the setting, and making the entry into the setting go as smoothly and happily as possible for the child and for the family. It is through 'getting to know' the child that the practitioner can 'get to know' their special educational needs and translate this knowledge into the action involved in meeting those needs.

Suppose that a young child already known to have special educational needs is about to join an early years setting. The first thing the early years practitioner will need is a lot more information. If we are going to tighten up our assessment, our multidisciplinary 'networking' and our planning of objectives, then it is helpful for the child that information arrives in a form that makes practical sense for the receiving practitioner. A joint planning meeting held in the setting and involving outside professionals and parents or carers can be a useful start (page 89). The first few days are so important in establishing confidences in child, family and teacher, and setting the whole ethos of the inclusion. Without careful planning, early mistakes and misunderstandings can colour the whole success of the placement, and leave parents feeling distrustful and teachers feeling deskilled.

Once the practitioner has gathered information on what the *practical implications* of the special needs are (as opposed to the theoretical descriptions), then this can be interpreted in terms of existing teaching skills and previous experiences. Suddenly, perhaps, the needs are no different from those that the practitioner will have met time and time again. There may be more of these needs, there might be a need for even more help or special equipment to meet them, but with the right information, support and resources, the mystique in catering for the 'special' child disappears. Early years educators do not have to be experts in special education in order to meet these needs; they are already specialists in how individual children learn and develop.

The next source of information in preparing for the first few days will be gained from continuing the dialogue with the parents or carers. For the child who has a statement of SEN (page 169), there might well be a representation from the parents which will provide a view of their own feelings about and hopes for their child's needs. We need to have starting points in our discussions and to know which questions to ask first. Parents are inevitably experts on their own children but it is up to professionals to draw out the considerable information they will have in a structured way that makes practical sense to the class and the teaching. Again, adopting a practical emphasis to this communication makes a positive and helpful starting point which places parent and professional within a shared agenda.

Parents welcome the chance to talk about what their child *can* do as well as where the difficulties lie. Professionals need to choose their

language carefully and to learn to ask unbiased and interest
tions. Information is best collected before the child actually sta
the class at a stage when the receiving practitioner is still in t
position of not knowing the child. At this stage, parents will be expecting the questions and will not be offended that the practitioner is
needing to ask them. They will be able to say freely what they feel their
child's particular needs are, and give their own views of why the child
will be joining that class and what the implications for the class will
be. Particular concerns they might have about the early days also need
to be tapped at this stage, as it is likely that these will be transmitted
to their child in some way.

Questions need to be asked in a way that does not beg a certain
reply. Direct questions such as 'Is she toilet-trained yet?' can immediately suggest to a parent that perhaps she ought to be and perhaps this
will affect whether or not the setting will cope. However, questions
phrased in terms of help, 'How much help does he need when going
to the toilet?', lead equally into whatever answer. They leave the
parent free to proudly claim that their child is now independent, or to
talk openly about the level of help required. This sort of open questioning can be used for many situations the child is likely to meet in
the new class. Moreover, it supplies unbiased and practical information which will give much clearer 'evidence' for additional support or
resources than those first impressions or concerns gathered from the
paper documentation alone.

It is important that early years educators are supported within their
settings in asking whatever questions they need to know, and this
would normally be done by involving the setting's special educational
needs co-ordinator or 'SENCO' (page 158). The child may have a particular condition that has not been experienced within the setting
before, and parents are likely to be a valuable source of information
and a good contact for national organizations and for local professionals likely to be available for advice in the future. Trust will be built
up by being honest about what is not known as well as what is. Questions can be interested and can demonstrate that the enquirer has
really thought about the child. There will be many run-of-the-mill
questions that a parent has been asked over and over again so that
they lose their personal meaning. If a question is turned around so that
the parent has to pause to think for a moment, new and personalized
information may be gathered: 'Has she ever surprised you by doing
something you really felt she couldn't?'

It should be possible to think through the nursery or school day, and
frame questions that will provide all the information that is needed to

rst days until the child is better known. The
picture shows the questions that a receiving
gether to prepare for Caroline joining her class.

Pen picture: Caroline

Caroline was four years old and had been born with Down's syndrome. This had concerned her future teacher who had not taught a child with this syndrome before. So she put together these questions to collect more information from Caroline's parents.

- How has Caroline been when you have left her with other people in the past?
- How much help does she need with managing her coat/drinking/going to the toilet?
- How does she let you know if she is upset/cross/thirsty/needs the toilet?
- What does Caroline enjoy doing most?
- What are her favourite toys?
- What would you say her greatest difficulties in mixing with other children are?
- Is there anything I need to know about medication/special equipment/medical condition/things to watch out for?

Once she had asked her questions and shared the 'Portage' developmental checklist that plotted Caroline's progress, it occurred to her that Caroline had already learned most of the skills she had come to expect of her three-year-olds joining the class. Her parents were able to explain that they were hoping that Caroline would be able to benefit from the experience of sharing the language of the other children, and that she would also have the chance to generalize and share the play skills she had so far only developed as an individual. Her teacher was able to see a definite role for her class in meeting Caroline's needs, and could see in practical terms how this might be done. (From Mortimer, 1995)

Having gathered information and spoken with the parents, the next preparation to be made is for the early years practitioner to meet the child. All the paper information and answers to questions will fall into place when the practitioner has the opportunity to interact with the child. It is at this point that the child comes first in the impressions gathered, and the condition second.

The first time when practitioner and child meet and play alongside one another is a crucial stage in establishing hypotheses about how the child will respond to different approaches. As such it needs priority and time, and should take place apart from the hurly-burly of a busy classroom on the first day of term. The best introduction to both parents and child will come in the family's own setting, if they feel comfortable with this. During a home visit, the child sees his or her future teacher as a 'friend' of the family and sees the teacher as special on the first day; a familiar face and somebody with whom 'the ice has already been broken'. Fears can be allayed and appetites whetted with photographs of nursery activities and of the other children. Some reception classes link families together before the first days, particularly if a child with special needs is joining them from outside the immediate area.

Introductory visits to the setting can also serve as a gentle way in, perhaps starting with an informal visit at the end of a session when the children have gone home and when the child can map his or her surroundings and experience some of the activities quietly with a parent. On these visits, parents can also be invited to demonstrate how they cope practically with the implications of their child's condition: how much help they actually need to give with self-help skills, the level of language which the child can follow, particular signing that is used, how to operate the electric wheelchair, what to look out for during an epileptic episode, or how to tune the hearing aid. If practitioners still feel insecure about managing, then parents (if able and willing) might help the staff through the early days until they feel reassured or until a case has been made for any additional resourcing required. All staff need to be encouraged to play *with* the child on these visits as the 'hands on' experience will be far more informative and reassuring to them than that gained by watching alone.

Settings will need to plan how they can share information effectively in a multicultural world. Some partnerships or clusters of settings have access to bilingual co-workers or centres for multicultural education so that joint visits can be conducted in the home language and so that professionals can gain more insight into cultural contexts. In Newham, for example, there is a Bilingual Co-worker Scheme. Within the Speech and Language Therapy Service, these workers have been trained to carry out basic language assessment in the mother tongue. They can then contribute to the diagnosis of any difficulties and in the child's management plan. In Haringey, there is a Community Development Project that aims to provide links between community associations, health, education and social services.

The Community Development Project in Haringey

Three part-time community development workers are employed within the West African, Turkish, Kurdish and Asian communities and there are sessional workers from the Somali, Polish, Albanian and French-speaking African communities. By providing links across agencies, they aim to:

- ensure that families who have children with disabilities are identified and referred to appropriate services;
- ensure that relevant information is made available and accessible to families;
- encourage families to place their children on the Children with Disabilities Register;
- enable the social services home intervention scheme and the named worker project to offer a service which is responsive to the linguistic and cultural backgrounds of the families in these communities;
- empower parents to be part of the consultative process in planning for their children;
- set up support groups. (From Roffey, 1999, p. 67)

WHEN DO WE DECIDE THAT A CHILD MIGHT HAVE SPECIAL EDUCATIONAL NEEDS?

So far, we have talked about how children already known to have special educational needs can be welcomed into an early years setting. We have talked about gathering information, talking with parents and playing alongside the child as useful ways of identifying what the child's needs mean for a particular setting.

For other children, their needs might not become clear until they have started to attend an early years group. In any early years setting, there are likely to be children with many different ages and stages of development. Each child is a unique individual who brings his or her own experiences and particular pattern of developing and behaving. In time, it might become clear to those working with a child that there are special educational needs. How does the practitioner know when to be concerned if a child seems to be developing differently? What is the legal definition of a 'special educational need'?

Definition of special educational needs

A child has special educational needs if he or she has a learning difficulty which calls for special educational provision to be made for him or her.

A child has a learning difficulty if he or she:

(a) has a significantly greater difficulty in learning than the majority of children of the same age; or

(b) has a disability which prevents or hinders them from making use of educational facilities of a kind generally provided for children of the same age in schools within the area of the local education authority

(c) is under five and falls within the definition at (a) or (b) above or would do if special educational provision was not made for the child.

A child must not be regarded as having a learning difficulty solely because the language or medium of communication of the home is different from the language in which he or she is or will be taught.

Special educational provision means:

(a) for a child over two, educational provision which is additional to, or otherwise different from, the educational provision made generally for children of the child's age in maintained schools, other than special schools, in the area

(b) for a child under two, educational provision of any kind. (From Education Act 1996, Section 312)

The Act tells us that any difficulty must be *significant*, over and above what you would expect from the child's age, and affect the child's ability to access the play and learning activities which your setting provides. It is not sufficient for the child to be *different*. So, to speak a language different from the majority of the group, or to suffer a medical condition which does not affect day-to-day learning, will not represent a 'special educational need'.

Children might be described as having SEN for many different reasons; perhaps they have a physical disability, perhaps their development is delayed, perhaps they have a language and communication difficulty, or there are behaviour or emotional difficulties. Early years practitioners now have a duty to recognize and identify any special educational needs within their setting so that they can plan what action they can take to support and help the child.

The revised SEN Code of Practice (DfEE, 2000a) suggests that the triggers for intervention through 'Early Years Action Plus' (see page 166) could be a practitioner's concern about a child who, despite receiving appropriate early education experiences:

- makes little or no progress even when teaching approaches are particularly targeted to improve the child's identified area of weakness;
- continues working at levels significantly below those expected for children of a similar age in certain areas;
- presents persistent emotional and/or behavioural difficulties, which are not ameliorated by the behaviour management techniques usually employed in the setting;
- has sensory or physical problems, and continues to make little or no progress despite the provision of personal aids and equipment;
- has communication and/or interaction difficulties, and requires specific individual interventions in order to access learning. (DfEE, 2000a, p. 20)

WHAT EARLY WARNING SIGNS SHOULD I BE AWARE OF?

When identifying special needs for the first time, the following questions to early years educators and to parents might be helpful in establishing whether the child might have special educational needs. To make these sound more child centred, we shall give the children names.

The purpose of asking 'what helps?' along with 'are there any difficulties?' provides you with information about whether you need to make plans which go beyond the individual approaches which you would normally take for the range of individuals in your care. If you find that you need to target and monitor a child particularly closely in order for them to gain access to the early years curriculum, then this is tantamount, in the current terminology, to saying that the child has 'special educational needs'. The 'label' or 'condition' cannot be separated from what it is the practitioner needs to do about it; it is both together which provide you with information about whether or not a child has special needs:

1   *Hearing.* Has Ali had recurrent ear infections or colds with fluctuating hearing? Has he failed two successive hearing tests? Has he seen a hearing specialist or had grommets inserted? Have parents ever been worried that he is not hearing them? Does he have aids

and how do these help? Do adults need to communicate with him in a particular way?

2   *Vision.* Can Tara see clearly, as far as you know? Have parents ever been concerned about her vision? Perhaps the setting feels that Tara is not seeing clearly, or not making sense of what is seen (provide examples); have parents seen this kind of response at home? How does she compensate for any difficulty? What approaches seem to help?

3   *Speech and language.* Can Darren's spoken language only be understood by familiar adults in a familiar context? Is he mostly silent? Does he have difficulty in following a simple instruction in a familiar context? Does he find difficulty in socially interacting, even with an interested adult? Does he use only single words or learned phrases to express himself? Does he hardly ever respond to adult suggestion when playing? How does he make his needs known? What can adults do to help him understand more clearly? Does he receive help for a speech, language or communication difficulty? What approaches have helped?

4   *Behaviour.* Is Mara's behaviour extremely challenging both at home and in your setting? Once settled in, does she show no signs of responding to your group's routines and rules; is this similar at home? Does she seem to be very unhappy, quiet and withdrawn, even once she has had a chance to settle in with familiar adults and familiar children? Are parents concerned about her clinginess or withdrawal at home? What seems to help? Have there been major events in her life that she has had to cope with? Will she make a close attachment to a familiar adult in the setting?

5   *Cognitive development.* Is Rashid at least a year behind what you would expect for his age? Is this despite his having had all the usual experiences to learn and to play and despite your providing opportunities for learning and play familiar to his cultural context? You might like to use a developmental checklist (page 124) as a guide, making sure that it is appropriate to his cultural and linguistic background. What are his learning styles? What helps to maintain his concentration? What things motivate and stimulate him?

6   *Physical development.* Does Harriet have a physical difficulty or disability that prevents her joining in the activities with the other children? How does this affect her? What resources, aids or methods of support help? Can she dress/feed herself/go to the toilet (etc.) unassisted? Where is she most vulnerable? What helps?

All these questions are merely starting points in the common sense that can be applied to finding out more about individual children's needs and how to meet them. Roffey (1999, ch. 5) provides a useful list of questions to ask when carrying out joint identification and planning for children with special educational needs in early years settings. The 'Welcome Profile' on page 132 might be a helpful tool when gathering information about a child entering a new setting.

IDENTIFYING SEN WITHIN THE EARLY YEARS CURRICULUM GUIDANCE

The *Curriculum Guidance for the Foundation Stage* (QCA, 2000) provides a welcome framework for meeting children's needs in the early years. It links children's learning closely with practitioners' teaching and illustrates how the one is inextricably linked with the other. Even when children learn spontaneously, it is through the experiences and opportunities which others, both children and adults, provide. The extension and development of this learning often depends on the sensitivity of the adults in observing how and what the children are learning and how they can use the child's motivation, interest and success to take this further.

In the same way, a child's special educational needs might be identified within the six areas of learning through an inclusive process of observing where each child is 'at' in each stepping stone of learning, e.g. through using curriculum profile maps (page 44). By providing every opportunity for each child to make progress and by carefully monitoring those whose learning needs do not appear to be met, the practitioner will already have identified those who have special educational needs. For example, there may be children who remain around the very first stepping stone of learning despite the fact that the practitioner has provided all the same learning opportunities as for the others. These are the children for whom more detailed monitoring is necessary (Chapter 10) and for whom the practitioner will attempt to differentiate the curriculum and make it more accessible (page 148).

Most settings would allow a child to settle into their group and to benefit from their structure and opportunities for at least a term before assuming that the child's needs might be 'special'. Settings are also encouraged to have a flexible enough curriculum with an individual enough approach which allows them to move seamlessly into approaches which are going to foster and encourage the child's learning and development from their first days in the setting. The questions below provide a starting point of how learning progress within the six areas of learning might be used to identify and plan for a child's individual needs:

1 *Personal and social development.* Thinking of his self-help skills, have you been able to help him become independent on the toilet yet? Can he take off his anorak now, eat a biscuit, drink from a cup? Looking at the relationships she has formed in your setting, is she playing alongside other children now? Is she sharing, watching others, smiling? Is his behaviour quiet and with-drawn? Does he respond to 'no'? Can he accept rules with reminders?

2 *Language and literacy.* Can she understand single words and labels? Does she use single words? Can she point, follow simple direc-tions, listen within a group?

3 *Mathematics.* Does he understand 'big'/'small'? Can he count to three? Does he understand 'more' and 'all gone'?

4 *Knowledge and understanding of the world.* Is she aware of her sur-roundings? Can she follow the familiar routines of the group?

5 *Physical development.* Thinking of his gross motor skills, is he walking steadily? Can he jump, run, throw with an approximate aim and kick a ball? In his fine motor skills, is he scribbling with a pencil? Can he pour water, build blocks, turn pages?

6 *Creative development.* Does she join in during action rhyme sessions? Can she move independently to music? Does she enjoy paints?

Some early years settings are devising their own means of identi-fying children who might have SEN at an early stage. Staff from a combined nursery centre in Stockport (described in Rodger, 1999) have drawn up a 'worry list' of signs to look out for before alerting the special needs co-ordinator for support and advice. Once worries have been identified, steps are taken to plan interventions and monitor progress in line with the SEN Code of Practice. This is an important point, since a 'worry list' remains a list of a child's weak-nesses until complemented by a fuller assessment which also includes their strengths and 'starting points' (see page 151). Here is an example:

Worry list

Literacy
Poor listening skills
Poor communication – verbal/non-verbal
Speech delay/language delay
Problems with general recall
Poor manipulative skills/clumsy
Withdrawn/limited eye contact
Inability to follow simple instructions
Reluctance to draw or make marks
Hearing/sight problems
Lack of imaginative play
Uses language inappropriately

Numeracy
Lack of spatial awareness
Inability to sequence
Cannot sort or match
Unable to complete a simple jig-saw
Unable to differentiate. (Grennan, 1996)

The following box shows examples of how the *Curriculum Guidance for the Foundation Stage* (QCA, 2000) might be used to identify 'special educational needs'. Practitioners might like to develop similar examples based on their particular settings and the range of needs they meet there.

Identifying SEN: mathematical development

Does a four-year-old child show little interest in numbers and counting?
     Is this despite the fact that the practitioner has used number language (for example, 'one', 'two', 'three', 'lots', 'hundreds', 'how many?', and 'count') in a variety of situations over several weeks?

Is there no spontaneous use of number names and number language when the child is playing?
     Is this despite the practitioner encouraging the child to use numbers in play (for example asking for 'two biscuits please' in the cafe corner)?

Does the child have difficulty in joining in with number rhymes and songs?
Is this despite the practitioner using stories and rhymes regularly to develop an understanding of number? (Examples from QCA, 2000, pp. 74–5)

DUTIES OF LIAISING AND INFORMING BETWEEN AGENCIES

For a child with a clear medical diagnosis or condition, it will usually be the health service that offers the first point of support for parents. In Chapter 6, we looked at some of the ways in which multidisciplinary teams work together to identify and assess special educational needs in the early years. The health authority has a duty (DfEE, 2000a) to inform LEAs of any children who they think may have special educational needs. The health authority also has to ensure that there are systems in place to make sure that all schools have a contact for seeking medical advice on children who may have special educational needs and to play a role in statutory assessment (page 167). When a child under 5 is felt to have special educational needs, they should also give parents information on the full range of services which might be helpful and the names of voluntary organizations that might be of assistance.

Social services departments have similar duties under the Children Act 1989, and are required to provide information on their services to parents of children felt to be 'in need'. They should ensure that all schools in their area know how to contact the designated officer who has responsibilities for special educational needs. Early education settings are advised to seek advice from their local Early Years Development and Childcare Partnership about partnership arrangements in place and contacts for their area.

SUMMARY

Early identification: gateways into early years action

In this chapter, we looked at the importance of identifying special educational needs early.

We looked at the situation of a child already identified with SEN joining a setting and how the early years practitioner can gather information, working closely with parents.

We also looked at how early years practitioners themselves can identify a child's needs for the first time within the setting. We argued that, in an inclusive setting, such identification can arise seamlessly from the early years provision itself and we looked at ways in which this might be done.

We also argued that it was often meaningless to separate a child's specific conditions from their special needs; how 'needy' a child is depends on what steps the practitioner is able to take in order to meet or support those needs.

We discussed when a setting might decide that a child might have special educational needs and shared early warning signs and helpful questions. We examined how the early years curriculum guidance might provide a framework for the identification of individual needs within an inclusive setting.

Finally, we mentioned the duties that different agencies have of liaising and informing each other about any child felt to be in need, particularly in the new era of 'joined-up' practice.

—8—

Early years assessment:
a dynamic and constructive process

·

> Thank you for asking me what my child can do, and not what he can't. (Parent of a young child with special needs)

ASSESSMENT OF WHAT?

This rather obvious question lies at the heart of all assessment. If early years assessment is to be worth its salt, it should (as Wolfendale, 1993, points out) have a clear purpose, be ongoing, include parent(s), and reflect cultural and linguistic background.

By the 1980s, the term 'assessment' had come to suggest an objective, mechanical process of measurement. This was especially so with the implementation of the Education Act in 1981 as LEAs planned approaches and protocols for identifying needs, establishing priorities and defining criteria for access to statutory assessment procedures or resourcing. Many LEAs defined their criteria for placing children's names at different stages of the Special Needs Register (Chapter 9) in terms of the extent of a child's delay or the centile of the population at which their abilities and needs fell (e.g. 'the weakest 2 per cent'). Assessment had to be seen to be accountable and to lead to decision-making which was equable to all children and families. Such 'assessment' suggested checklists, incontrovertible facts and figures, and psychometric measures of skills and abilities.

In recent years, assessment has moved more into the arena of curriculum; if we wish to 'assess' the point which children have reached in their learning (it is argued), it makes sense to look at what we are aiming to teach in the first place. Some LEAs began to define 'special need' in terms of the stage the child had reached on the National Curriculum, defining level or 'stage' of need in terms of how the child performed on the teacher assessments and 'Standard Attainment Tasks' commonly known as 'SATs'. The Education Reform Act in 1988 set out to give parents choice in their child's school and, since this involved making comparisons between schools, 'league' tables could be drawn up comparing different schools' 'successes' or 'failures' on the SATs results. This brought with it controversy and new tensions for children with SEN, their parents, and the schools whose results might be 'lowered' by certain scores.

The 'Rumbold Report' (DES, 1990) reported on the quality of educational experiences offered to three- and four-year-olds and helped to make the issues more clear. The report reviews the characteristics that all young children have in common and paved the way for a more inclusive curriculum for all under 5s. 'We believe that . . . educators should guard against pressures which might lead them to over-concentrate on formal teaching and upon the attainment of a specific set of targets' (DES, 1990, para. 66). The report saw the need for collaborative planning based on systematic and regular observation-based assessment of children in all areas of their development, and record-keeping based on contributions from the educator, parent and child which would feed into learning and teaching.

In this context, 'assessment' comes to acquire a wider meaning. It ceases to be a means of measuring something inside the child's head: some elusive 'potential' or 'IQ'. It ceases to become a measure of where the child has reached on a set of teaching criteria. It becomes 'a process in which our understanding of children's learning, acquired through observation and reflection, can be made to work for the children's benefit' (Drummond, Rouse and Pugh, 1992). It involves, in other words, both adults interacting and children learning. It also becomes an inclusive process, pertaining to each and every child's individual or 'additional' needs.

IDENTIFYING STRENGTHS AND WEAKNESSES

The SEN Code of Practice (DFE, 1994; DfEE, 2000a) advised settings to adopt approaches for assessing and monitoring children's SEN that should both:

- 'identify children's areas of weakness which require extra attention', and
- 'assess children's performance, identifying strengths as well as weaknesses, using appropriate measures so that the rate of progress resulting from special educational provision can be assessed'. (DFE, 1994, Section 2:119)

Some LEAs (e.g. Hertfordshire County Council, undated) make sure that the child's strengths are always assessed alongside their weaknesses by recording 'strengths and interests' on the child's individual education plan (page 161) alongside the areas of difficulty or concern. That way, the strengths can be used when designing approaches and setting targets to help the child overcome their particular difficulties.

WHAT IS 'SPECIAL'?

Does an assessment of SEN need to be qualitatively different from the assessments used for all the children? Some settings have felt misled by the term 'special educational needs' and have seen the term as referring to a group of children whose needs have already been defined by other specialists. They have therefore seen 'assessment of SEN' as a specialist process that takes place in other places and by more knowledgeable professionals. Others have reserved the term for those 2 to 3 per cent of the total population of children who have 'statements' (page 169). The document *Excellence for All* (DfEE, 1997a) points out that these assumptions are far from the truth and that the majority of children's special educational needs should actually be identified as part and process of their education.

Some would argue that we should be devising inclusive assessment procedures that are as useful in identifying the needs of *all* children as they are for identifying SEN. There is a useful development of these arguments in Wolfendale (2000c). The fundamental principles and practices of early years assessment must apply to all children and 'the best assessment practices being identified in preschool provision are improving our ability to identify special needs' (Hinton, 1993, p. 52).

Therefore, each setting needs to develop approaches and tools which can be used to identify a child's needs in that setting. If an assessment is to work for the setting and for the child, then it has to be manageable and to be useful in planning. It also needs to be reliable and valid; in other words, not based on 'assumptions' but on real 'evidence' of what children actually do, and able to be observed by all who live, play and learn with the child.

The main assessments used in the early years have been described by Hutchin (1999) as talking to parents and carers, talking to the child, making an observation, listening to or participating in a conversation with a child, examining a sample of something the child has done, getting a child to perform a particular task and administering a test.

All these approaches are as relevant to the child with special educational needs as to any other child and, in an inclusive approach, 'special' assessment becomes an extension of the regular assessment used within the setting. When an early years educator or a parent has a particular concern, then all of these approaches will assist in identifying whether a child has learning difficulties.

IS THERE A ROLE FOR PSYCHOMETRICS?

You may well find that specialist 'testing' has a relevant role to play as a part of this assessment, but early years educators themselves have the key role in identifying if a child is learning or behaving in a way which requires special educational provision to be made. With the implementation of the Code of Practice for SEN (DFE, 1994), assessing SEN becomes part of a team effort and cannot be delegated to 'the specialists out there'.

Thus a child may well be 'tested' to establish if their hearing or vision is satisfactory. A speech and language therapist may be involved in establishing whether children can understand abstract vocabulary and how they are expressing themselves and communicating. In doing so, he or she will be using many of the methods of assessment we have listed (talking to parents and carers, talking to the child, making observations, listening to or participating in a conversation with a child, examining samples of the child's language, getting a child to perform a particular task) but this may be done in a 'standardized' way. Because the 'test' has been delivered using a standard approach that has been applied to very many children, the therapists will be able to state with confidence that 'most children at a stage of, say, two years tend to understand language at this level'. This kind of test is described as 'psychometric' since the scores can be linked statistically (at a given level of statistical 'confidence') to a large sample of children so that the tester can state the 'norm' for any age.

Another example of a psychometric test is the IQ test that originated at the beginning of the last century and played a large role in educational assessment and selection. The scores on the assessment are distributed in a 'normal distribution' (or bell-shaped curve when you plot score against numbers of children scoring at that level). The 'average' score for any age will be 100, with only around 2 per cent of the population scoring below 70 and above 130. So 'absolute' was the interpretation of these scores that educationalists would speak of 'education subnormality' in terms of children scoring an IQ lower than 70 on a single intellectual assessment. Traditionally, the Stanford Binet Tests, followed by the Wechsler Intelligence Scales and later the

British Ability Scales, were used regularly to diagnose and to make predictions about 'potential'.

There has been a growing discomfort among many psychologists about using these tests, or at least in using them in an isolated way. Critics of intelligence tests typically state that IQ tests label children inappropriately, do not offer information about curriculum planning, are culturally biased and are not as statistically reliable or valid as their developers claim (e.g. Gillham, 1978). Educators and parents some-times saw a child's 'IQ score' as a fixed and unchangeable measure that was part of a child's internal make-up, rather than a measure of performance on a certain test on a certain day.

Nevertheless, IQ tests are still widely used as measures of a child's 'ability'. This rather assumes that 'ability' is fixed and stable over time and, therefore, determines the child's future learning. We need to be wary that, if we believe this, we may in reality be discriminating against the child by having expectations which are fixed and which limit the child's opportunities to learn and to develop.

To counter some of these criticisms levelled against intelligence tests, methods of curriculum-based assessment, criterion-referenced tests and checklists of achievement have been developed. These approaches are usually derived from a series of learning objectives and aim to find out what the child already knows and what might be taught next. By breaking the 'next step' down (using the method of 'task analysis'), each step can be made achievable and successful for the child. The 'Portage' home-teaching approach (page 50) is one example of this.

Another approach has been to move away from 'static' measures of what a child is doing at a particular moment in time, and on to more continuous assessment approaches (linking assessment to teaching on a regular and frequent basis) or more 'dynamic' approaches. Some of these approaches are described below.

OBSERVATION

We gain information about children all the time we are with them. The observations we make affect what we provide for them. We might carry out a *'fly-on-the-wall' observation*, observing a child over a period of time (say 30 minutes) and writing down in clear, unambiguous terms what they are doing and how they are interacting. There is an example of this approach being used for 'James' on page 59. We might used a *timed observation* by noting what a child is doing, say, every five minutes regardless of what is happening in the nursery or group. We might involve the child in an activity and make a *participant observation* of what the child does and how they interact and learn. *'On-the-spot' observations* involve the adult noting down significant events or achievements after they happen.

In providing for the needs of children with SEN, the observations we make have to be reliable for our planning to be appropriate. More formal or structured methods of observation (which have been developed to be reliable and valid across observers and situations) can ensure that information gathered is accurate and this is why some settings use standardized checklists of observation to help their assessments and planning. Observational methods used may vary according to the information sought. *Selective observation*, for example, focuses on specific areas of the child's behaviour chosen by an adult. Here are some examples:

1   *Behavioural observation* using an 'ABC chart' can help to identify any factors that may be affecting the child's behaviour. By recording the 'Antecedent' (what happened before the behaviour took place), the 'Behaviour' (exactly what the child did) and the 'Consequence' (what happened as a result of the behaviour) a clearer view of the context of the behaviour can be gained.

What led up to it?	Behaviour	What happened next?
Danielle was playing with the fir cones and Bradley asked for one.	Danielle hit Bradley in the stomach.	Bradley cried and tipped all the cones on to the floor.

2   *Spider's web observation* (e.g. Henderson, 1994) can look at the adult-supported child's ability to sustain in depth play experiences. Activities provided are listed around the edge of a circle (the adult support is included as an activity); the observer can chart the movement of the child in the group (see Figure 8.1). The time spent at each activity can be noted at the perimeters of the circle. This type of observation can also highlight a child's particular interests or areas that are avoided.

3   *Tracking observations* can be useful in observing an unsupported child around the setting. They indicate the areas of play experience that may be targeted for the child. A rough plan of the layout is drawn and the movement of the child is recorded by arrowed lines, with numbers to indicate the length of time spent at each activity (see Figure 8.2).

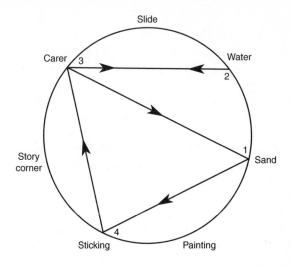

Figure 8.1: Example of a spider's web observation

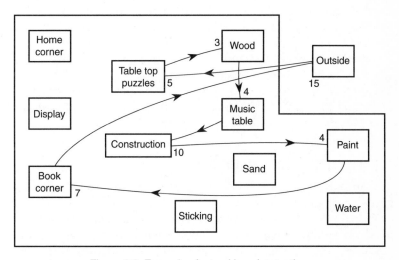

Figure 8.2: Example of a tracking observation

These detailed observations can provide a lot of information with regard to the child's level of skill, what the child gains from the activity, the social context and level of interaction, and the child's use of language. Any observation should run alongside the ongoing planning and assessment that will be done for all the children wherever possible.

ARE CHECKLISTS A GOOD IDEA?

Some checklists (such as the Portage checklist introduced on page 50) are highly detailed and become useful for a child with significant special needs who requires highly detailed planning and help, perhaps through a special support assistant. Even then, early years practitioners will have to carry out their own task analysis to break down the steps even more finely if they are to be used to inform planning and teaching. The Portage checklist is divided into six areas of behaviour: infant stimulation (for very early skills), socialization, self-help, cognitive, language and motor. There is now a Portage Classroom Curriculum (Brinckerhoff and the Portage Project Staff, 1987) to extend the Portage step-by-step teaching approach into an early years setting. However, this step-by-step approach to breaking down steps and making them accessible to a child whatever their individual needs, is an approach which can be applied to all linear curricula and checklists. Their main limitation is that we cannot assume that children learn in linear ways, but must be aware of the need to encourage and assist them in making links and connections in their learning, and in generalizing to new situations what they have learned.

Therefore, a checklist should only be used as a 'coat hanger' on which to hang the careful planning and teaching you will be doing across all areas. It does help the setting and the parents to keep a long-term goal for their child's development, and to highlight areas of strength and weakness that need working on.

THE PLAYLADDERS CHECKLIST

The author (Mortimer, 2000c) wanted to devise a developmental checklist based not on specific areas of development, but on early years activities themselves. What did we know about the typical ways in which children develop their play when playing with water, when learning to climb, when painting or gluing, or when pretending? Was it possible to draw together the milestones from existing developmental checklists, and divide these into areas of practical activity? As such, the checklist would seem immediately accessible to an early years educator without the time or resources to withdraw the child for individual assessment. Moreover, the teaching targets that it would suggest would make more practical sense to the class or group.

The developmental skills in the checklist were drawn from a number of sources. The *Portage Guide to Early Education* (Frohman and

Hilliard, 1976) provided the main starting point, taking items from a number of different skill areas, but re-sorting these into play activities. Kay Mogford's 'Play Repertoires' (in Newson and Newson, 1979) were most useful, and provided the idea of listing the playladder skills as repertoires of play, rather than as a chronological progression. Thus the need for approximate age levels is avoided, and the skills are arranged in three arbitrary stages, reflecting a growth in the complexity of play from a simple enjoyment of sensations, through greater exploration and experimentation, through to flexible and combining play which moves from one area of activity or interest to another. The play skills are arranged in three arbitrary steps, arranged in clusters as the steps of a ladder; hence the term, 'playladders'.

Other sources of items, often adapted to suit the activity area, included the Mary Sheridan (1975) checklists, approximations to the skills listed in the Griffiths Developmental Scales (Griffiths, 1970), and information from the general literature on the development of play including Piaget (e.g. in Donaldson, 1978), and on teaching developmental skills including the P.I.P. Developmental Charts (Jeffree and McConkey, 1976). These were supplemented by a year of placements and visits to nursery classes, reception classes and preschool playgroups, observing standard early years activities, recording the typical stages of play and collating these into an order which made sense.

Early years educators are encouraged to play alongside the child as part of their regular activities within a group of children. By observing how the child is playing, it becomes easy to visualize and record the stage on the playladder later, once the children have left. Play thus proceeds uninterrupted by the assessment and recording. Once the play behaviour is recorded on the checklist, a 'next step on the ladder' is suggested, and this new skill can be encouraged or taught at a future play session. This is helpful towards providing activities at a level appropriate to the child, or adapting an existing activity so that the child is always included. Criticisms have included the fact that the 'playladders' are not linked to the QCA Areas of Learning, and have not been tested for inter-observer reliability.

OTHER WAYS OF 'WRITING IT DOWN'

In their book *Making Assessment Work*, Drummond, Rouse and Pugh (1992) list various approaches to writing down the assessment record and encourage educators to develop their own approach which suits their setting, their curriculum and the particular children. One way is to use a checklist of behaviours or play activities (as in the Portage and playladders approaches above). Another is to assess under topics using flow charts and curriculum content (e.g. 'learning about travel', 'learning about water'). 'Schemas of learning' (e.g. in Nutbrown, 1999) can be used to record children's prevailing patterns of thinking or 'schemas', and yet other approaches might look at the processes through which children learn (such as collaborating, exploring, talking and sharing). The High/Scope Child Anecdotal Record (developed from Brickman and Taylor, 1991) is a method of gathering anecdotal evidence for each child in the nursery under their key experiences in social relations and initiative, music and movement, and cognitive development (creative representation, language and literacy, classification, seriation, number, space and time).

Yet other settings have developed checklists, record sheets or profiles based on the early years curriculum, usually relating to the six areas of learning defined by the QCA: language and literacy, knowledge and understanding of the world, personal social and emotional development, creative development, mathematical development and physical development (e.g. page 44).

PLAY-BASED ASSESSMENT

We introduced the idea of using play as a means of assessment when we were talking about adopting child-centred approaches, on page 65. Why does play offer such a useful medium for assessing children's progress and needs? It is a natural means of expression for most children and is something that almost every child can engage in at their own level. It therefore provides a relaxed and positive situation in which the child can show of his or her best and not be subject to 'failure' if he or she does not respond to the standardized wording or procedures of a psychometric test. Play is the activity within which young children explore and develop new concepts and can therefore provide a window of how a child is doing so. Vygotsky (in Butterworth and Harris, 1994) suggests that during play, children function 'above' their ages and their everyday behaviour. In this, he is referring to the fact that the child is frequently at the threshold of understanding new concepts whilst he or she is playing, developing new strategies and learning new skills. By assessing through play, we are therefore at a useful vantage point for observing the emergence of cognitive functions. We are also in a good position to actually intervene and promote that learning; when assessment and intervention are combined in this way, we speak of a 'dynamic assessment' (see below).

Newson and Newson (1979) were among the first to explore the use of play as a more flexible, yet still systematic, way of assessing young children with special needs and disabilities. With a comprehensively equipped playroom and a one-way viewing screen, they developed a semi-structured format for engaging children in natural play and assessing how they responded to the toys, the activities and the adult intervention. Parents and child psychologists would sit behind the screen as another adult played with the child in the assessment room. In this way, they were able to assess how the child joined in and imitated, how they responded socially and how they were able to 'turn-take' in their play. The toys would also provide evidence of how the child could move, balance and manipulate. The session would provide ample opportunity to assess the child's use of language and communication, their response to language and gesture, their imaginative play and their ability to problem-solve and work things out. The whole picture that was gathered during these sessions enabled parents and psychologists to draw together a 'picture' of the child and their needs that made sense to everyone involved.

The use of 'play-based assessment' gathered respect as a tool for use both in settings and at home. Newton (1988) argued that the richest information could be gathered by both observing a child at play and by participating as well. If we think back to the Code of Practice (DFE, 1994), we know that a child has 'special educational needs if he or she has a *learning difficulty* which calls for *special educational provision* to be made for him or her' (see page 109). In order to be helpful to us in assessing SEN, any assessment needs to have a structure (so that the assessor knows what to target during the assessment), and to be linked in some way to strengths and weaknesses for that child, based on what is known about child development and how children play. In other words, if we are to make sense of our observations when assessing special educational needs, then we need some idea of what is typical play and what might suggest an area of need.

Observation studies involving recording how children typically play have been invaluable here and have led to useful observation schedules (such as the 'Target Child Approach', in Sylva, Roy and Painter, 1990). Criterion-referenced approaches, easily accessible to parents and professionals, can take place in a natural context, be ongoing, and involve both observing the child as they play uninterrupted and observing the child as they play with the assessor. The PBA or play-based assessment (Sayeed and Guerin, 2000) is one example of this and is illustrated in the boxed section below. These approaches lent themselves to the development of more dynamic forms of assessment.

Play-based assessment

Sayeed and Guerin (2000) have developed a method of using play-based assessment to establish a child's strengths and weaknesses, working with parents and early years educators in Tower Hamlets, London. It is an approach that combines observation and adult participation, and regards parents as key partners in the assessment process. Whereas norm-referenced assessment would be biased on cultural and linguistic grounds, the authors have found their criterion-referenced approach to be more useful in outlining learning potential and empowering the child. The approach allows the child to play in their familiar setting, wherever that is. There is an initial observation phase in which the assessor records how the child plays in a number of areas of skill or ability within five developmental areas (physical, language, cognitive, social and emotional), both in solitary play and in groups of other children. A code of '1', '2' or '3' is allocated depending on whether the child's play still needs to be developed, whether there is room for improvement and encouragement, or whether the play has developed appropriately. In the second phase, the assessor interacts with the child in a play situation individually or as part of a group. The adult is directly and equally involved in the child's play and observations made in the first phase can be explored more fully. The assessment leads to further planning and target-setting, again using play as the method of intervention.

DYNAMIC ASSESSMENT

We have spoken of some of the dilemmas and doubts arising from using static psychometric assessments. Some practitioners are now looking towards more ongoing and dynamic methods of assessing children's learning. Dynamic approaches to assessment involve the assessor actually working with the child to encourage active participation in the learner (Lidz, 1991). The focus is on the process of learning and how a child arrived at a solution. An effort is made to modify the way a child approaches learning so that he or she can be helped to become a more effective learner.

The interactions between assessor and child which assist the child's cognitive development are known as 'mediation' and the aim is to understand through intervention what best supports the child's learning. Many people see this as a better measure of 'potential' than a psychometric score or IQ. 'When adults help children to accomplish things that they are unable to achieve alone, they are fostering the development of knowledge and ability . . . From this perspective, which places instruction at the heart of development, a child's potential for learning is revealed . . . '(Wood, 1988, p. 24)

The 'bunny bag'

This refers to a collection of toys used by the Newcastle upon Tyne Educational Psychology Service in a dynamic approach to the assessment of play described in Waters/Newcastle upon Tyne LEA (1999). Toys were selected on the basis of how attractive they were to the children, how flexible they were in allowing the children to demonstrate a range of play and learning, and how practicable they were to purchase and carry around. The assessor is encouraged to mediate the child's play by helping them feel at ease, focusing their attention, helping them to generalize, helping them to plan, helping them break down a task, and helping them feel successful. A practical guide gives examples of how this might be done during an assessment. The assessment guide lists typical repertoires of play and learning for each toy used in the assessment, and there are very approximate age norms for each. A second guide lists how children approach play and learning, what the assessor did to affect or improve the performance and what the outcome was in the child's response. The assessment therefore measures not only how the child plays with each toy, but also how adult support can be used to improve this.

INVOLVING PARENTS ACTIVELY IN THEIR CHILD'S ASSESSMENT

Some assessment schedules are designed to ensure parent participation. Challen (1997) describes an approach in which educational psychologists routinely visit parents of all preschool children who have been referred to the LEA as possibly requiring statutory assessment of their SEN. The Barking and Dagenham Preschool Assessment Schedule focuses on collecting developmental history and information about the child's current skills and areas of concern. It is done collaboratively with the family via a clear layout and structure, and with section summary boxes for joint completion by parents and psychologist.

The Portage checklist (Frohman and Hilliard, 1976) was also designed as a tool to be used both by Portage home visitors and parents. In order to make sure that the items are completed 'reliably', home visitors are trained to observe the child actually carrying out each skill and not to rely solely on parent report. This is to make sure that the checklist identifies areas that still require teaching. Those skills that a child can perform sometimes but not every time are suggestive of 'emerging' skills which might be the easiest ones to teach first.

Other checklists and schedules are designed solely for use by the family but the information they provide has proved useful in designing the individual teaching approach for the child. The ALL ABOUT ME materials (Wolfendale, 1998) introduced on page 63 were the first to become widely used.

Settings can design their own 'welcome profiles' for completion either by parents before their child enters an early years setting, or for joint completion during an introductory home visit. Gathering information in the early stages of a child's placement is not only essential for planning but is also an ideal time for asking questions. The 'welcome profile' in Figure 8.3 (pp. 132–3) was put together by a cluster of early years educators in Northallerton, North Yorkshire. They supplemented it with questions about the child's medical history. They decided not to word-process their profile in order to keep it friendly and to personalize it with drawings by the children.

About your child's health and needs

- Are there any medical problems we need to know about?
- Is your child on any regular medication?
- Does your child have any special needs?
- Are there other professionals who help your child?
- Has your child any allergies?
- Has your child received a tetanus injection recently?
- Are there any problems with hearing and seeing?

About any possible concerns

- Is there anything that is worrying your child about starting here?
- Do you yourself have any concerns about it?
- Is your child frightened by anything in particular?
- What does your child think about starting here?
- Is there anything else you would like to tell us about your child?

LINKING ASSESSMENT TO CURRICULUM PLANNING

'Curriculum' is sometimes seen as what is offered rather than what the child actually experiences. For a young child with SEN, settings need to consider how a child's learning difficulties or disabilities might actually interfere with his or her accessing the curriculum that has been planned. It is not sufficient to plan rich experiences and encourage children to 'learn on their own' (Wilson, 1998). No matter how enriching the environment and how many the opportunities for learning, the child who is deaf still cannot hear what the other children are saying, and children who have attention deficit hyperactivity disorder (ADHD) still cannot attend to what you are saying and ignore what they might be doing with their own hands. In order to meet needs inclusively, settings therefore need to think about both individual targets for the child with SEN and providing the best environment for learning for all the children.

Some settings have learned how to write carefully targeted individual education plans (IEPs) for children with SEN in their setting, but have been tempted to deliver most of the content of these in one-to-one or small group situations, running the IEP separately from the general planning of the whole group. In order to deliver the SEN curriculum inclusively, practitioners need to think about how activities can be planned for *all* the children that also meet children's *individual* needs.

We have already met 'Jonathan' who has a moderate hearing loss. He is introduced on page 162 where you will also find his Individual Education Programme and the play chart that was used by his family is shown on page 48. The example in Figure 8.4 (p. 134) shows how Jonathan's IEP was built into the setting's medium-term (say term by term) planning so that it became embedded into what was planned for the whole group.

In Jonathan's example, his individual targets were embedded within the early years curriculum which was planned to lead to the Early Learning Goals by the end of the children's foundation stage (QCA, 1999). There are also assessment procedures that help settings embed assessment and planning within particular areas of development, such as in language and communication. This is particularly useful for settings where many of the children have certain very specific needs. The Redway School approach is one example of an assessment of language and communication that happened to be developed in a special school setting.

Family and friends

- in our family, the grown-ups are called:
- names and ages of any brothers and sisters:
- any other people who help look after your child:
- pets:
- who will bring and collect your child?
- are there close friends or relatives already in school?
- has your child already spent time out of the home (e.g. at nursery, playgroup or childminder's)?

Is there anything else you would like us to know about your child's family life?

Favourite things

Please ask your child to tell us:
- a favourite toy:
- a favourite activity:
- favourite story:
- favourite rhyme or song:
- favourite family outing:
- favourite memory:

Figure 8.3: A welcome profile

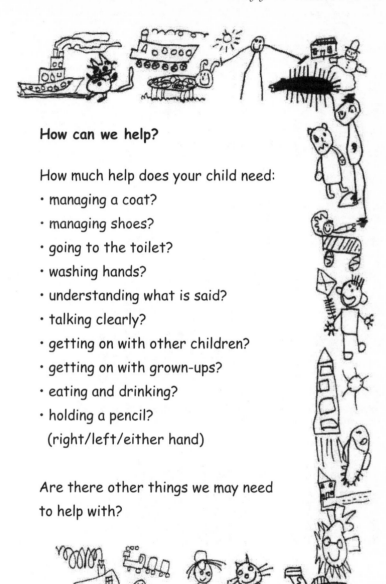

How can we help?

How much help does your child need:
- managing a coat?
- managing shoes?
- going to the toilet?
- washing hands?
- understanding what is said?
- talking clearly?
- getting on with other children?
- getting on with grown-ups?
- eating and drinking?
- holding a pencil?
  (right/left/either hand)

Are there other things we may need to help with?

Early Learning Goal	Area of skill	Activity	Arrangements for inclusion of SEN	Opportunities for assessment
• Children will enjoy listening to and using spoken language • Children will use language to imagine and re-create roles and experiences	• to use imagination • to co-operate • to take turns • to develop vocabulary skills	Build a snow palace together for role play Introduce dressing up clothes for cold weather	Use of radio aid for Jonathan Introduce new vocabulary for topic to Jonathan and others in small group session	Record of Achievement Profile (make observations) Anecdotal evidence of how the children are understanding new concepts
• Children will listen with enjoyment and respond to stories, songs and other music, rhymes and poems, and make up their own	• auditory discrimination • listening skills • attention skills	Stories, books, rhymes and songs about weather, clothing and shelter Offer a variety of materials for recording: stickers, chalk on black paper, collage, paints	Look for concrete practical opportunities for developing Jonathan's concepts	Record new vocabulary used and understood by Jonathan
• Children will know that print carries meaning • Children will attempt writing for various purposes	• looking and listening skills • understanding vocabulary linked to topic			Make weather books to keep for the children's portfolios
		Offer writing and recording opportunities: postcards, weather charts, etc.		

Figure 8.4: Medium-term planning, autumn term: topic – weather; area of learning – language and literacy

The Redway School approach to assessing communication

Latham and Miles (1997) show how assessment can be central to a curriculum for children with severe and profound learning difficulties. Working in a special school setting, they devised an assessment approach that looks at all areas of a child's communication up to level 1 of the National Curriculum. Starting with the child's first pre-intentional communications (like smiles, vocalizations, 'stilling' and gesturing), it invites the assessor to comment on the behaviour the child has developed. It moves through the stages of early intentional communication (like using sounds and gestures to request, to draw attention to things, to give information) and on to the use of first words and meanings. Practitioners are encouraged to use the information to build up a unique profile of a child's language and communication, and to use this to design a total communication system for that child which will lie at the centre of the child's whole curriculum. The approach has been designed to include assessment of children who use signing or symbols in their communication as well. All the assessment sheets are photocopiable.

POINTS TO CONSIDER WHEN THINKING ABOUT ASSESSMENT OF SEN

The questions in the box might help the early years professional to reflect on the ways in which they are assessing the needs of young children.

Reflecting on assessment

- Does your assessment have a clear purpose?
- Is it an ongoing process?
- How do you include parent(s) and carers?
- Does it reflect cultural and linguistic background?
- Does it involve how the child responds to teaching and intervention?
- Does it fit practically within the assessment and planning you do for all the children?

SUMMARY

Early years assessment

In this chapter, we looked at various approaches for assessing a child's progress and individual needs.

We talked about the need to assess a child's strengths as well as any weaknesses and of the need to link assessment into curriculum planning, intervention and monitoring.

Various ways of 'writing it down' were discussed and we looked at both static and dynamic ways of assessing children's performances.

The importance of assessing children in partnership with parents was emphasized and pointers given for good practice.

References were also made to Chapter 3 in which we discussed ways of involving children in their own assessments and planning.

9

Effective intervention in inclusive early years settings

> Rather than to make them outstanding and special, we need to give them something extra . . . to include them in the programme as much as we can. (Playgroup leader talking about children with SEN in her setting)

WHAT WORKS FOR CHILDREN WHO HAVE SEN IN THE EARLY YEARS?

In this chapter, we look at some of the interventions that have been used for young children who have special educational needs. We have met others throughout the book since effective intervention is inextricably combined with assessment, identification, monitoring and evaluating progress. You cannot intervene without being clear about with whom you are intervening and what you are intervening for. You cannot know whether your intervention is effective unless you know what has been achieved and what the effect of this was for the children, their learning and their families.

Early intervention typically has these main goals (Wolfendale, 2000c, p. 13–14):

- to support families to support their children's development;
- to promote children's development in key domains (cognitive, social, physical, emotional, linguistic) via early years curriculum and learning opportunities;
- to promote children's coping competence;
- to prevent the emergence of future problems.

Some of the recent interventions with *families and parents* have already been introduced in Chapter 3. There is also a single chapter, Chapter 11, given over to the issue of supporting children's *emotional development and behaviour* since this is felt to be such a crucial area. In this chapter, we focus on what interventions can be made in *early years settings* to meet individual needs by supporting children's learning and play.

> Effective intervention is purposeful and designed to effect as close a match as possible between a young child's identified special needs and that provision or resource which will meet his or her needs and best facilitate learning and development. The interventions should manifestly *make a difference*. (Wolfendale, 2000c, p. 14, original emphasis)

How do we define an 'effective' intervention that manifestly 'makes a difference'? Effective for whom and over what period of time? In order to show 'effectiveness', we need clear and well-researched evidence that the services we provide are achieving their stated aims. These services, or 'interventions', might be at a national level or local authority level (as in initiatives arising from political policy and legislation). The DfEE has now set up a unit on evidence-informed practice in education. Alternatively, 'interventions' might relate to a particular approach which a setting has adopted for a whole group of children (as in the I CAN evaluation study described on page 140) or to the individualized approach planned for a certain child (as recorded in an Individual Education Plan, page 163).

All early years practitioners are accountable for the work they do: accountable to parents, to employers, to inspectors and to funders. Without evaluation and evidence that what they do 'manifestly makes a difference', how can they account for their practice? Nowadays, we also have the issue of 'quality assurance' in which it is a professional duty to provide young children with provisions that meet quality standards. Therefore, continuous monitoring and evaluation is likely to play a role in all our professional lives. Within this chapter, there is an introduction to evaluation, and also some starting points for planning interventions for children with particular individual needs.

For some time now, researchers have been interested in looking at the capacity of educational interventions to redress inequality or offset the consequences of social disadvantage. A series of well-evaluated American studies showed that early intervention could indeed be effective in improving the outcomes for disadvantaged children. The best-known was the High/Scope Perry Preschool Project (in Sylva, 1994) which followed a cohort of students through to the age of 27. These adults had significantly higher monthly earnings if they had received the High/Scope education. They had a higher percentage of home ownership, a higher level of schooling completed, a lower percentage needing social services, and fewer arrests for drug-related crimes. A snapshot of 'High/Scope' in action appears in the description of the I CAN intervention on page 140. Sylva describes the curriculum in this way.

> In the High/Scope curriculum children learn to be self-critical, without shame, to set high goals while seeking objective feedback. There is a deliberate encouragement to reflect on efforts and agency, encouragement to develop persistence in the face of failure and calm acceptance of errors. (Sylva, 1994, p. 142).

The High/Scope curriculum is also characterized by the active and ongoing involvement of parents in their children's education, enhancing their interest and confidence and breaking down institutional barriers.

HAVE WE GOT IT RIGHT? AN INTRODUCTION TO EVALUATION

Throughout this book, we have seen examples of how early years practitioners, parents and SEN professionals have worked together to plan and develop effective services for young children who have SEN. But how do we know whether these are 'effective' and how do we define 'success'? In this era of bidding for provision and setting targets, we are increasingly expected not only to evaluate what we are doing but prove 'value for money' as well. Robson (2000) provides a very readable and comprehensive introduction to small-scale evaluation. There is a useful chapter on ethical and political considerations, including the issues of consent, privacy, ensuring that clients and children benefit from the evaluation.

Evaluations typically involve running an educational programme for a short period of time, perhaps for a few weeks or a term or two, and then looking for evidence of change in children's progress or in participants' attitudes. Perhaps the child's progress is measured against a set of targets as when monitoring an individual education plan (page 163). Perhaps sets of observations are kept before and after a behavioural intervention (page 122). Sometimes, parents, professionals or children themselves will be questioned about how they feel about the intervention and their progress. Sometimes the results of an intervention are followed through a year or many years later to see what the long-term effects might be, as in the High/Scope Perry research above.

Evaluative research is notoriously difficult. If we obtain a set of excellent 'evaluation forms' after a day's early years training event, can we assume that the training has actually been 'successful', or are trainees simply telling us that they had an enjoyable day? Do we measure the 'cost-effectiveness' of the training in terms of how helpful trainees thought the training event was at the time, or should we be looking for changes in how they practise several months later? Even if we did so, how do we spot the crucial part of the training that led to that change? If an early years practitioner evaluates her own practice by carrying out a piece of 'action research', will the very fact that she is involved not only in the action but the research bias the findings?

The box below contains one case study in which a combination of both quantitative (measuring changes in children's attainments) and qualitative (looking at how the adults and children were behaving and learning together in the setting) methods were used to evaluate an early years provision (Mortimer, Law and Ladd, 2000). It was the evaluation of an integrated speech and language nursery in which the authors found all sorts of pitfalls in trying to identify by quantitative techniques whether children's language skills improved spontaneously or as a result of intervention. However, they discovered that the *qualitative* findings (how adults were interacting to support the young children's learning) were far more productive.

Any evaluative research must start by defining the provision to be evaluated.

What was the provision to be evaluated?

I CAN, the national educational charity for children with speech and language difficulties, has been responsible for helping to set up and fund a number of nurseries for children with language disorder throughout the UK. In one such nursery in the north of England, children attended sessions at an integrated nursery where they also received support from a team of teacher, nursery nurse and speech and language therapist. There was also outreach support for children attending outlying nursery schools and preschools or to their homes, and a consultation/training service for parents and professionals. All children attending the integrated nursery followed the High/Scope curriculum (e.g. in Drummond, Rouse and Pugh, 1992, section 7.8). A typical nursery session would follow the format of: greeting (plenary group), language group, planning (small group), activity time (with adult support), talk-about (small group), language group, outdoor play, small group work, rhyme time, story, home. The 'time to play' session involved outdoor as well as indoor free play. There was also a structured refreshment time part way through the session when the children sat in mixed groups for a snack and a drink. Choices were offered and conversations fostered.

In addition, the children with speech and language difficulties were withdrawn into a small group twice per session, and also had individual sessions. During the language group sessions, all the I CAN children would be involved in language work differentiated to the level of each individual child. Such sessions involved teaching or reinforcing new topic vocabulary and concepts, comprehension work, listening and interacting in a structured group setting, the social use of language, re-enacting and illustrating stories, and discrimination and production of speech sounds. In addition, each child received one-to-one therapy specifically targeting their individual needs approximately two or three times a week. The session would last ten to fifteen minutes and would be delivered in a quiet room or in the integrated nursery, depending on the child's needs and the activity involved.

HOW COULD YOU EVALUATE SUCH A PROVISION?

There are key questions to answer. Even if we can see the children attending this kind of integrated speech and language nursery making great strides in their progress, how do we know that they would not have made spontaneous improvements anyway, and how can we be sure that the provision is more effective and 'better value for money' than community speech and language therapy alone? We begin to see the need for a comparison or control group, and are immediately faced with the challenge of finding a comparable group of children, with similar difficulties, from a similar area, and with similar cognitive ability.

All evaluative research calls for the researcher to define the provision to be evaluated clearly, and to be absolutely clear about the researcher's own values which might impinge on the results. The researcher must also consider the methodology of the study: whether to be actively involved in the intervention and the evaluation (as in the 'action research' model of research), and whether to gather numerical data which might or might not show significant change with each kind of intervention, or to look in a more qualitative way at any changes. In quantitative measures, much detailed information might be lost in the act of number-crunching. In qualitative methods, the researcher must nevertheless follow a rigorous approach in which others might replicate the results.

How was the I CAN provision evaluated?

The provision was independently evaluated by speech and language therapists and an educational psychologist (Mortimer, Law and Ladd, 2000). They decided to use both quantitative and qualitative measures. Children attending the unit were assessed before and after their intervention on a number of measures. They demonstrated highly significant improvements in language expression and comprehension. The authors also wanted to gather qualitative information about how the children learned to use their language in social situations. A pragmatic checklist was designed to analyse video transcripts of children's communication when playing at home before and after the I CAN intervention, and this again demonstrated positive change across all areas rated.

Parental questionnaires were used to tap parents' views. Parents reported that the I CAN service had helped them to understand better their child's communication difficulty, had made them feel more involved in therapy and had left them feeling less concerned about their child's progress. They also saw their children as becoming less frustrated with themselves, better able to communicate and better able to cope with the transfer into school.

A small control group of children receiving community speech and language therapy services was also followed through. Though these children also showed positive changes in their language skills, parents did not feel so involved and the pragmatic checklist analysis demonstrated less positive changes in the children's communication skills in a play context. Obtaining a comparative control sample, so important in evaluative research, was extremely difficult. The study relied on referrals of children for the control group from community workers in another catchment area who found it hard to ask parental permission for a study of what might be considered a 'Rolls Royce' provision in another area of the county. There were many other reasons why the control sample was difficult to gather and these are discussed in the study.

What else did the study tell the authors? In the I CAN evaluation study outlined above, children were observed continually throughout their session to record their experiences and opportunities for learning. What was it that made this speech and language provision 'specialist', and what experiences did the children receive which differed qualitatively from mainstream early years provision?

Certain themes emerged from the detailed observations and careful analysis (using the 'grounded theory' approach, e.g. Strauss and Corbin, 1990) suggesting that the quality of experiences related to three factors. First, the adult–child ratio was sufficiently high to enable certain learning experiences to happen. Second, the adult support was itself specialist enough to target those experiences precisely for the child with specific speech and language disorder. Third, the very presence of the large group of mainstream children without such difficulties afforded opportunities for modelling and interaction that might not have been possible in a segregated setting. These themes were interesting because of their practical implications, and might well have been overlooked in a purely quantitative study. What did the adults do that was specialist in nature, and what learning experiences resulted for the children observed?

How did the adults support the children with language and communication difficulties within their setting?

1 Interpretation of needs. For children who have difficulty in making their needs known, the adult was able to interpret their actions and act on them consistently, thereby ensuring any signalling of need becomes meaningful and intentional.

2 Verbal commentary. The adult was able to play alongside the child with speech and language difficulty and provide a simple spoken commentary of the child's play. This afforded opportunities for the child to link action with word.

3 Non-verbal modelling. For a child with a limited repertoire of play, the adult is able to model and extend the child's play.

4 Reciprocal play. The adult is able to encourage the development of reciprocal play for a child who lacks the pre-verbal skills of social turn-taking.

5 Facilitating joining in. The adult is able to facilitate the child with communication difficulties joining in with other children.

6 Supporting turn-taking and sharing. The adult is able to consistently encourage turn-taking and sharing for those children who would find these skills particularly difficult.

7 Supporting receptive language skills. The adult is able to provide language at the correct level for the child with language difficulties to understand and respond to.

8 Providing continual reassurance. The adult is able to provide a higher level of reassurance to a child whose language difficulties make them

more likely to lack confidence and feel insecure in a social setting.

9   Social skills teaching. The adult is able to encourage appropriate social skills and behaviour for children likely to be experiencing difficulties in understanding social situations.

10 Assisting pragmatic skills. Some children had 'pragmatic difficulties' in using language and communication in a social context. The adult is able to help these children see the other point of view and maintain a flow to their interaction.

What opportunities did the inclusive setting provide for the children with speech and language disorder, which might not have been available from a specialist and segregated setting?

11 Supporting large-group play. The children had opportunities to play within a large group of other children whose language skills were more proficient.

12 Extending imaginative play. The children had opportunities to play imaginatively and develop symbolic skills, with either an adult or another child facilitating.

13 Supporting expressive language. The children had opportunities to develop expressive language with others more proficient than themselves, thereby benefiting from both their models and their responses.

14 Supporting the children's planning and persistence. The children had opportunities to plan future activities and to see them through (a particular feature of the High/Scope approach), having the advantage of a full range of activities.

SUPPORTING CHILDREN WITH PARTICULAR DIFFICULTIES

The results of the I CAN study suggested some of the ways in which adults usefully intervened to support the children with speech and language difficulties within their care. The boxed sections below provide 'starting points' for practitioners to consider in other areas of need, general difficulties in learning or development and autistic spectrum difficulties. There are also 'starting points' to consider when working with children who have attention difficulties (page 179) and who have experienced family breakdown (page 182) in Chapter 11. These 'starting points' have been kept deliberately general so that early years practitioners can adapt and develop them to include their setting and the particular needs being met. The 'Inclusion ' publication from the Preschool Learning Alliance (Chizea, Henderson and Jones, 1999, and see page 26) takes these ideas further and is a practical resource where a child's SEN have already been identified.

Starting points: including children who have learning difficulties

Do you have children with these needs in your setting?

- Some children's development appears to be progressing normally, but more slowly, than most children their age.
- Some children find it difficult to understand instructions that contain more than one or two pieces of information at a time.
- Some children tend to play very fleetingly with the toys and activities.
- Some children enjoy feeling and manipulating the toys and equipment rather than playing with them constructively or imaginatively.
- Some children are still at the stage of playing alone, or in parallel to, other children and have not yet reached the stage of playing socially.
- Some children find it difficult to control their fingers in fine movements, or to climb, balance and run smoothly.
- If these children's skills appear to be out of line with their age, then it could be that they are mildly delayed in their development and need your careful planning, teaching and support to learn the 'next steps'.

What you can do

- Observe the child carefully using an observational checklist, or using your own early years curriculum. Work out what the child can already do and make a note of all their strengths, interests and areas of difficulty.
- Discuss your findings with parents, saying that you are keen to encourage their child in their learning. Find out how they are managing with simple skills at home: getting dressed, eating their food, playing and talking.
- Then work out together what you would really like the child to be able to do in the next term. Use your existing knowledge and experience of the child to select a few developmental steps which you feel could reasonably be achieved in that time. Again, use your early years curriculum and planning as a 'coat hanger' to hang these steps on (e.g. page 44).
- If you are monitoring the child's needs on the Code of Practice for Special Educational Needs, use these goals as the targets you will write into an 'Individual Education Plan', stating what the child's difficulties are, what action you will take to help, what targets you aim to teach, how parents

will help, and how you will monitor progress (page 161).

- Once you have decided on a reasonable long-term goal, break this down into manageable steps which the child can achieve week by week. Plan how you will achieve each step, perhaps working alongside the child in a small group or using some individual time. Use your strong praise and your help and encouragement to make sure each step is achieved.
- Plan with parents how you will keep closely in touch with each other, so that each of you can be supporting the work the other is doing.
- Keep records of your achievements, examples of work and creations, and diary notes of the child's learning so that you can share this at another review session in a term's time. (From Mortimer, 2000h)

THE EARLYBIRD PROGRAMME

The EarlyBird Programme was originally set up by the National Autistic Society in 1997 to develop and evaluate a model of early intervention for children with autism using a parent programme. It is a three-month programme that combines group-training sessions for parents with individual home visits. Video feedback is used to help parents apply what they have learned on the course to their child at home. It aims to support parents in the period between diagnosis and the start of school, to empower parents and help them facilitate their child's communication and appropriate behaviour at home, and to help parents develop good practice in handling their child. At the time of writing, the first evaluation results had yet to be published, though parents' reports were very positive. The approach used incorporates elements from the Hanen Program, the SPELL approach, techniques from the TEACHH approach and the Picture Exchange Communication System (PECS). All these approaches may be of interest to early years practitioners working with young children who have autism, and further information can be obtained through the National Autistic Society (see page 204). The society also has information about the various interventions which have been used to work with children with autism, though not all have been fully evaluated.

Starting points: including children who have autistic spectrum difficulties

Do you have children with these needs in your setting?

* Some children appear indifferent to other people and behave as if they are 'in a world of their own'.
* They may not play with other children, and join in activities only if an adult insists and assists.
* They might indicate their needs by taking an adult's hand and leading him or her to what they want.
* They might have very little language, they might echo what is said to them or they might talk a lot about topics of great interest to them.
* Sometimes, they might become absorbed in arranging toys in a certain way, collecting certain objects, or spinning or turning toys repeatedly to watch them move.
* Their eye contact might be very poor and they might be unable to play imaginatively, unless it is in a very stereotyped way.
* Their behaviour might be bizarre or very fearful, especially if familiar routines are disturbed.
* They might be extremely good at some things, such as doing puzzles, identifying numbers, making music or drawing.
* They might have been diagnosed as having 'autism', 'autistic features' or 'Asperger Syndrome'. All these conditions have some overlap. Children with 'semantic pragmatic language difficulties' can also behave in similar ways.

What you can do

* Start by helping the child feel settled when playing one-to-one with a key-worker. Gradually involve one or more other child in the play, staying close to support and assist. If the child understands language, use this time to talk about sharing, taking turns and understanding what other children might be thinking.
* For children who are severely affected, try this approach. Spend ten minutes a session playing alongside them with another of the same toy or piece of equipment. Copy what they are doing. When they begin to notice what you are doing, move in to play with them, sharing the same toy. Again, copy their actions. The idea is to encourage them to see that their behaviour is resulting in your behaviour. You can then begin to play turn-taking games.

- Useful turn-taking games include blowing bubbles for the child to burst, shaking a 'slinky toy' between you so you can each feel its movement, rolling a musical ball to and fro, setting up and knocking down skittles. The idea here is that the child will begin to see your company as useful and fun.
- Try to keep to a familiar and structured routine. Show the child pictures or symbols about what is happening next.
- Provide a simple commentary about what the child is doing: 'John is building.'
- Provide plenty of encouragement whenever the child communicates with you, whether they have done so with their voice or their actions.
- Try to be interested in their interests but introduce new things too. Try to support their activities, and to distract them gently if they become too absorbed or obsessed with them.
- Give very clear and simple messages, showing the child as well as telling.
- Provide a quiet 'safe base' where the child can go to if they are feeling 'overloaded' or stressed. (From Mortimer, 2000i)

PROVIDING AN INCLUSIVE AND DIFFERENTIATED EARLY YEARS CURRICULUM

These boxed 'starting points' provide examples of how differentiated approaches might be planned, depending on the particular setting and the needs being met there. How can we intervene effectively to enable a child to learn, whatever their special or 'additional' educational needs? And how can this be done in such a way that we are including them in the early years curriculum available for all children? The most important and essential feature of differentiation is good planning.

For example, when early years educators draw up an individual education plan (page 161) for a child who has SEN, they can then show how that plan will sit within their short-, medium-, and long-term planning of the early years curriculum for the whole group, and how it will be 'differentiated' to enable the individual child to learn. Through careful monitoring and evaluation of effectiveness, it becomes possible to ensure that planning for inclusion and differentiation helps the child with SEN to achieve success in learning. Each child has unique learning needs and experiences. Here are some of the ways in which the special needs of a child can be included within a setting's planning:

1   *Content.* It is important to build on children's strengths if they are
    to cope with the content of what is on offer more successfully. The
    content of the story, for example, may be at a level appropriate to
    the child's stage of language or may include concrete props to hold
    attention, emphasize meaning and allow a child to participate
    with more than one sense at once.

2   *Pace.* Allowing the child extra time to respond, or ensuring oppor-
    tunities to get there first, are ways of building confidence.
    Activities may be presented at a slower pace to ensure under-
    standing or a succession of materials presented to maintain
    interest during a discussion. Some children need to 'sandwich'
    short periods of structured activity with periods of free play or
    quiet. Some children take a long time to process information, and
    need longer silences than usual if they are to answer a question or
    fulfil a request. Others may find it hard to remember more than
    the last piece of information given them and therefore need sup-
    porting and prompting at each step, taking longer to carry out
    structured activities.

3   *Level.* All planning for the Early Learning Goals will include a
    degree of planning for different levels of children's ability. Within
    this, it might be that some children need the learning steps broken
    down finer, and it may be necessary to give value to a smaller and
    less obvious learning outcome or 'stepping stone'. On page 44,
    there is an example of how Early Learning Goals can be divided
    into stepping stones that may be two or three steps along the way.
    In practice, early years practitioners working with young children
    who have SEN usually find themselves having to break down
    steps into much finer stages so that even a child with considerable
    learning difficulties has a chance of succeeding and learning.

4   *Access.* This involves the way in which materials and resources are
    presented. Some children may need adapted scissors to cut out a
    picture, or require photographs rather than line drawings in order
    to name objects. Some might need toys and playthings which are
    easy to handle (such as form-boards with knobs on the pieces).
    Others might need table tops at a suitable height for them to access
    when in a standing frame. Some might need radio hearing aids to
    hear, or to sit close up to large picture books to see.

5   *Response.* This involves the outcome produced by the child and
    may be linked to the level at which the activity is presented. Some
    children may be able to show they have learned through actions
    rather than words, and any response that the child is able to give
    needs to be valued. For example, some rely on sign language to

make their sounds clear. Others may not be able to tell you their wishes, but can demonstrate by their smiles or their choices where they would like to play.

6　*Sequence.* Some children need to have opportunities provided at different times, or need to cover different aspects of a topic at separate sessions. If attention is short, it might be necessary to revisit an activity at another time in order to ensure success. Some children find it harder to settle and to concentrate after they have been very active. Others need to 'let off steam' for a while in order to return more attentively to an activity.

7　*Structure.* Some children learn best when they are playing in a highly structured setting, led and supported by an adult. Others seem to respond best when provided with free play and supported in developing their own agendas. Every child needs opportunities to play and to learn both on their own terms and in groups with other adults and children. The play-based assessment and intervention approach introduced on page 126 provides an example of how both can be assessed and worked on.

8　*Teacher time.* Some children need more individual adult support and time. This can include some one-to-one work or withdrawal into a small group, but mainly refers to supporting the child with additional encouragement and prompting within the regular group. Simply having a heightened awareness of the child's individual needs can affect teacher involvement. In an inclusive setting, any time spent relating individually to an adult would take place in the nursery room itself, with opportunities for involving other children as well.

9　*Grouping.* The group structure may afford opportunities to allow the child to respond or for other members of the group to provide good models which can reinforce the child's learning. Sometimes meeting the needs of individual children with SEN has led to children working alone on individual materials but arrangements to include the child's IEP within planning for the whole group can overcome this and lead to a more purposeful and supportive way of meeting SEN.

All these approaches to differentiation are common sense and arise from the practitioner's personal knowledge and experience of the child and his or her needs. Taking time in the early stages to closely observe and monitor the child can help practitioners 'tune in' to the way in which children are experiencing their session and allow for more practical differentiation where opportunities are lacking.

DEVELOPING A FLOW BETWEEN ASSESSMENT, PLANNING, INTERVENTION AND MONITORING OF SEN

Early years practitioners need to look for systems of assessment, planning, intervention and monitoring that 'work' for their setting and the needs of their particular group of children. They find it most helpful if these systems 'flow' readily from discovery and identification of SEN through to intervention and measuring whether or not this has been effective.

One example of how this can be achieved is given in the 'Quality Play' training materials introduced on page 79 (White and Parry, 1997). There is a helpful illustration taken from a real-life playgroup setting showing how an individual intervention for a child whose behaviour was particularly challenging in playgroup can be designed and monitored. The setting, St John's Playgroup in Winchester, found it helpful to adopt a 'jig-saw' pattern to present their initial findings for the child. A jig-saw relationship implies that each new skill or piece of learning interlocks with others and does not lead in a line or ladder along a typical and discrete path. On each 'jig-saw piece' of their recording sheet, they wrote a 'strength' of the child they had observed in the setting or parents had noted at home. Examples might include 'can share a toy', 'can play independently', 'can help clear away' or 'can join in regular routines'.

Playleaders who followed the process of the 'Quality Play' course were then supported as they learned how this initial 'jig-saw' assessment (their 'starting points') and observations could lead easily into an individual education plan for the child with agreed targets. These could then be monitored carefully and reviewed with parents six weeks later. On their individual education plan, they listed the nature of their concerns:

'Social Development

- Children are intimidated by 'N.'s behaviour
- She uses physical force to take toys, push in, and generally direct events
- Children avoid her and she is often playing alone
- Very demanding of adults
- Flits between activities
- Loses interest in toys/tools as soon as she has control of them.'

Most importantly, they went on to list the child's strengths.

- 'Enthusiasm and energy
- Desire to "help" (on her terms)
- Enjoys craft and painting
- Understands concept taking turns despite difficulty in doing so
- Enjoys being with other children despite problems of interaction.'

This flowed into their proposals for the action to be taken.

'1. Check N.'s starting points in all play experiences
   Talk to mother about her play at home
   Observe her closely in group time – when does she join in?
2. Set up adult led activities involving N. and one other child
   Model appropriate behaviour EVERY TIME N. grabs, etc.
   e.g. 'requesting' rather than grabbing
   Give N. responsibilities for clearing away – preparing drinks with adult
   Praise N.'s help in front of group
   Use N.'s preferred songs in group time
   Share N.'s progress with mother.'

This led in turn to the targets they hoped to see the child ('N') achieve before the next review meeting in six week's time.

- 'N. to join in play with other children without physical force to control the play
- N. to take responsibility for specific activities
- N. to make contributions to group time on a turn-taking basis.'

(Quotes taken from White and Parry, 1997, p. S6.17.)

Because the staff had observed the child carefully in each area of play, the training approach enabled them to draw up a play plan, linking starting points at both home and school, and the action they would take to develop these further. The box offers one example.

Sand/water play

Home: Enjoys playing in bath with brother – occasionally plays with earth and containers.

Group: Likes filling and emptying pots in sand occasionally playing happily alongside another child – enjoys washing up cups in soapy water.

Action:

- Involve another child in emptying filling game – prepare pots for seeds.
- Let N. find materials for second child.
- Remind N. to request equipment in sand play.
- Play lotto with one other child – praise turntaking.
- Praise ALL positive behaviour. (From White and Parry, 1997, p. S6.17)

An essential part of the Quality Play training is to help trainees recognize the need for ongoing monitoring and review of the child's individual progress. This is done through regular weekly review meetings between parents and providers, and a termly review to consider the child's progress in more depth and make joint decisions about future plans for play. The child's individual play plans are also linked in to the Code of Practice monitoring and assessment (DFE, 1994; DfEE, 2000a).

SUMMARY

Effective intervention in inclusive early years settings

In this chapter, we asked what works for children in the early years who have SEN. What should effective intervention aim to achieve and how can we know whether it is effective?

We looked at some of the problems associated with 'evaluation' and met one example of an evaluation study using both quantitative and qualitative methods.

Perhaps the most useful outcome of this study was the examples of what practitioners could do to support children with SEN in their setting. We looked at practical 'starting points' for adult intervention in other areas of special educational need as well.

We looked at the process of 'differentiating' the curriculum and how this might be achieved in an inclusive early years setting.

Examples were given of how a flow can be developed between assessment, planning, intervention and monitoring of SEN, looking at the 'Quality Play' training approach.

10

Monitoring special educational needs: the Code of Practice

We have only our own experience and minimal training to call on. Changes in SEN procedures, if they are to be the right ones, must be made with guidance and more training (Playleader in response to training survey, 1997)

HOW AWARE ARE EARLY YEARS PRACTITIONERS ABOUT THEIR DUTIES TOWARDS CHILDREN WITH SEN?

We have seen how all early years providers registered to provide government-funded education are now required to both identify and meet any SEN of children within their settings. Just how confident do they feel about doing so? The author approached many leaders of preschool playgroups and private nurseries in a rural area and found that they felt that much further training was needed. Their main training requests were for practical 'how to do it' approaches (Mortimer, 1997a).

Most groups felt the need for further training in these aspects of SEN. They wanted to know about the requirements of the national framework (such as the SEN Code of Practice). They wanted to develop skills in the assessment of children and they wanted to be able to write individual education plans for early years children with SEN. They also needed to feel more confident in involving parents and families, and they needed to know how to plan activities for children with SEN in early years. Finally, they wanted guidance and practical suggestions about how to combine paperwork on early years curriculum and SEN.

What was their current understanding of the Code of Practice on which any training approach would need to be built? About half the 46 groups contacted were already catering for the needs of at least one child with SEN. Most had a copy of the Code of Practice but few felt familiar with its contents or translated these into action. Less than half had an appointed member of staff who acted as a contact for SEN. Only a third of groups knew who to contact for further help and advice concerning their special needs children if they needed to. Any training package which aims to be tailor-made to the specific context of an early years setting *must* start with 'where the trainees are at' in terms of their present understanding and knowledge base (page 73).

CHALLENGES AND SOLUTIONS IN REGARDING THE SEN CODE OF PRACTICE IN EARLY YEARS SETTINGS

Because early years settings have requested more accessible information about the Code of Practice, the remainder of this chapter relates to the DfEE (2000a) *SEN Code of Practice on the Identification and Assessment of Pupils with SEN in England.* It aims to make the guidance accessible to early years settings who might not have had the same experiences in meeting SEN that larger school settings have. This Code of Practice is being updated for implementation in September 2001. The general guidance in this chapter on monitoring and setting targets should be of interest to those living and working outside England as well.

WHAT IS THE SEN CODE OF PRACTICE?

The SEN Code of Practice is a guide for school governors, registered early years providers and LEAs about the practical help they can give to children with special educational needs. It recommends that schools and early years providers should identify children's needs and take action to meet those needs as early as possible, working with parents. The aim is to enable all pupils with SEN to reach their full potential, to be included fully in their school communities and make a successful transition to adulthood. The Code gives guidance to schools and early years providers, but it does not tell them what they must do in every case.

In 1996, the DfEE stated that all preschool providers in the voluntary and non-maintained sectors who registered to redeem vouchers should also have regard to the Code of Practice. This continues to be the case for groups registering with the LEA under the Early Years and Childcare Development Plan.

WHAT ARE THE UNDERLYING PRINCIPLES FOR EARLY YEARS SETTINGS?

All children have a right to a broad and balanced curriculum which enables them to make maximum progress towards the Early Learning Goals. Early years practitioners *must* recognize, identify and meet SEN within their setting. There will be a range of need and a range of provision to meet that need. Most children with SEN will be in a local mainstream early years group or class, even those who have 'statements of SEN' (page 169). Parents, children, early years settings, and support services should work as partners in planning for and meeting SEN.

HOW DOES THE CODE OF PRACTICE WORK TO HELP THESE CHILDREN?

The Code of Practice is designed to enable SEN to be identified early and addressed. These SEN will normally be met in the local mainstream setting, though some children may need extra consideration or help to be able to access fully the early years curriculum.

It is recognized that good practice can take many forms and early years providers are encouraged to adopt a flexible and a graduated response to the SEN of individual children. This approach recognizes that there is a continuum of SEN and, where necessary, brings increasing specialist expertise on board if the child is experiencing continuing difficulties. Once a child's SEN have been identified, the providers should intervene through 'Early Years Action'. When reviewing the child's progress and the help they are receiving, the provider might decide to seek alternative approaches to learning through the support of the outside support services. These interventions are known as 'Early Years Action Plus'.

This does not mean that assessment should be seen as a linear process, moving from 'Early Years Action' to 'Early Years Action Plus'. Instead, assessment and intervention should be appropriate to a child's individual needs at any particular time, each review of the process informing and feeding back to the next. This graduated approach is firmly based within the setting. Very few children will be considered by the LEA as having the kind of long-term needs that would benefit from a statutory assessment, perhaps leading to a statement of SEN.

WHAT DOES THE CODE OF PRACTICE REQUIRE FROM OUR SETTING, EVEN IF WE DO NOT HAVE A CHILD WITH SEN ATTENDING?

The Code of Practice also requires all providers to do the following, whether or not they have a child with SEN currently attending. They should have a clear policy about how they will meet SEN in their setting put together by the setting's management group and with the involvement of all its practitioners. This is also a requirement of nursery inspection. This policy must be made available to parents. They should also be able to demonstrate that they have regard to the SEN Code of Practice and that systems are in place for identifying any child who might have SEN.

They should appoint one member of staff who is familiar with the requirements of the Code of Practice and who can act as a point of contact for parents, staff and the LEA. For small settings, the special educational needs co-ordinator, or 'SENCO', might also be the playleader or one member of staff with a particular training or knowledge of special needs. The SENCO works closely with the head of the setting and colleagues, and has responsibility for the day-to-day operation of the setting's SEN policy.

WHAT SHOULD THE SEN POLICY CONTAIN?

For nursery schools and classes, an SEN policy will already be in place approved by the governing body. Other settings should have written an SEN policy based on information provided within the Code of Practice and available to parents. This policy should contain the following information.

Policy for special educational needs

Summary statement
The policy should begin with a short summary of the beliefs shared by staff regarding pupils with SEN. These might include:

- the intention to ensure an entitlement for all children, including those with SEN, to a broad, balanced and purposeful early years curriculum;
- the commitment to a partnership with parents;
- the development of collaborative working with other agencies;
- that the policy adopted be part of a whole-group approach to SEN, in con-

sultation with parents and other agencies;
- how the policy relates to the SEN Code of Practice.

Arrangements for SEN provision
The policy should identify arrangements made to:

- ensure the entitlement for all children to the curriculum;
- monitor, record and evaluate all children's progress;
- identify, assess and review individual needs within the Code of Practice;
- provide additional resources for children under the Code of Practice;
- share responsibility for meeting SEN with parents;
- work with LEAs, health services, social services and other parties on any matter to do with the group's SEN work;
- ensure that the SEN policy is known, agreed and implemented by all staff;
- publish admissions arrangements with relation to SEN;
- regularly evaluate the arrangements for SEN and regularly review the SEN policy;
- consider complaints about SEN provision within the setting.

Implementation of the SEN policy
Consideration should be given within the policy to the practice and procedure required to implement the policy, providing information on:

- the name of the setting's member of staff with responsibility for the day-to-day operation of the SEN policy (the 'SENCO');
- a description of the expertise and qualification of the staff within the setting in relation to SEN;
- in-service training arrangements to update the knowledge and understanding of staff on how to identify early indications of SEN, how to take early action to meet these needs within the normal work of the setting, monitoring and recording the child's progress and obtaining advice where necessary;
- involving parents in sharing information, using community languages where necessary;
- responding to parental concerns and sharing information at all stages – identifying resources available within the setting;
- recent and relevant information about the support services available, and the way in which your setting would access this;
- the sharing of information with other settings, mainstream and special schools.

WHAT ARE THE RESPONSIBILITIES OF THE SENCO?

Special educational needs co-ordinators should act as a contact for other members of staff on interpreting the Code of Practice and training. They should support them in identifying and meeting the SEN of children within the setting. They must oversee records kept on SEN for individual children. They should act as a first point of contact for the LEA, health services, social services and others on SEN. They should seek outside advice and support if needed, for children in the setting or about to join it. They should ensure that parents of children with SEN are kept informed and consulted throughout. They should put other members of staff in touch with relevant SEN training so that they can identify and plan for any SEN early. The *SENCO Guide* is a useful document produced by the DfEE (1997b) that covers the role of the SENCO as well as the writing and monitoring of individual education plans (page 161).

DO SETTINGS NEED TO KEEP INDIVIDUAL RECORDS OF CHILDREN WITH SEN?

As well as the information that all settings will record for all children, the pupil record or profile for a child who has SEN should include information about the child's progress and behaviour from the early years providers, from the parents and from health and social services. What are the child's own perceptions of his or her difficulties? What strategies have been used to ensure that the child has access to the early years curriculum? How have these worked? What are the child's strengths and weaknesses?

Usually, the child would be allowed time to settle in before supposing that their needs might be special and 'significant'. The process of identifying young children's SEN is discussed in Chapter 7. However, sometimes a physical or congenital difficulty makes it clear immediately that a child may have long-standing and significant needs. Most needs respond to help and change in time. Some pointers towards deciding whether or not a child might be considered to have SEN are given on page 108.

WHAT IS MEANT BY 'EARLY YEARS ACTION'?

Perhaps an early years practitioner has just begun to have concerns that a child might have special educational needs. Perhaps the child has made little or no progress even when the teaching has been carefully targeted towards their needs. Perhaps the child continues to work and play at a level significantly below what might be expected for that age. Perhaps there are persistent emotional or behavioural difficulties that have not improved despite the setting's usual strategies. Possibly the child has physical or sensory difficulties, or there are particular problems with communication or interaction which require special individual interventions.

The early years practitioner should gather information about the child from any other professionals involved and make the play and early learning activities more accessible to the child by breaking them into smaller steps or making them easier. This is called 'differentiation' and examples of differentiating the early years curriculum are given on page 149. The practitioner should also speak with parents; this becomes easier if they have shared progress from the beginning and have developed a welcoming and positive atmosphere for the families who attend. They should ask parents for further information about the child's health, development or behaviour at home as well as in the setting, and tell their group's SENCO who should be able to share ideas and approaches.

The SENCO and the early years practitioner will then be in a position to consult with parents and agree an Early Years Action aimed at enabling the young child with SEN to reach maximum potential. This usually involves individualized teaching by the practitioners and individualized learning on the part of the child. It will not necessarily mean one-to-one teaching, and this might not be appropriate if the child is to be included fully in the curriculum. Staff can then work closely with the child, following the plan that has been agreed, observe and record the child's progress, and meet with parents and SENCO to review progress. Parents must always be kept fully informed of their child's progress.

WHAT IS MEANT BY AN 'INDIVIDUAL EDUCATION PLAN'?

Another characteristic of Early Years Action for the child with SEN is the writing of the individual education plan or 'IEP'. This is a plan which should lead to the child making progress. This plan should be reviewed regularly with the parents. The plan should be seen as an integrated aspect of the curriculum planning for the whole group. It should only include that which is additional to or different from the differentiated early years curriculum that is in place for all the children. Differentiation of the activities planned will make the curriculum accessible to those children who have SEN.

The individual education plan

1   Nature of the child's difficulties.
2   Three or four targets to be achieved in a given time.
3   Action
   • the special educational provision
   • staff involved, including frequency of support
   • specific programmes/activities/materials/equipment
   (included in the curriculum planning).
4   Help from parents at home.
5   Any pastoral care or medical requirements.
6   Monitoring and assessment arrangements.
7   Review arrangements and date.

There are various ways of writing an 'IEP' and practitioners need to develop a style that suits their situation and meets the requirements above. An example of an IEP is shown following Jonathan's pen picture.

Pen picture:
supporting children with hearing difficulties – introducing Jonathan

Jonathan is nearly five years old. When he was a baby, his family suspected that he was not responding when they spoke to him. He was beginning to babble, but his range of sounds was limited and no clear words developed. He was also having frequent infections with fevers and what appeared to be earaches.

He was assessed by the community paediatrician who found Jonathan to have a moderate to severe hearing loss. The ear, nose and throat consultant carried out investigations and found that his deafness was due to a mixture of conductive loss (the sound vibrations were not being conducted through his middle ear due to a build up of glue-like fluid) and central neurological damage (the sound signals were not all being received from ear to brain). Jonathan had grommets inserted to help to drain his middle ear, and hearing aids to help him make best use of his remaining hearing.

These investigations took time, and Jonathan's hearing was affected at a vital stage for learning language. He has therefore missed valuable opportunities to learn to speak clearly and to link actions and words in a way that helps him understand abstract concepts. The teacher for children with hearing impairment has advised that Jonathan should stay in nursery as long as possible to make up for these missed opportunities in his play and communication. He is also receiving regular speech and language therapy.

His needs are being monitored and supported within the setting, with outside professional advice and an ongoing assessment of how much specialist support he might need once he is in school. His nursery school must therefore draw up an individual education plan at least every term with advice from their SENCO, and meet with parents and outside professionals regularly to review it. They will keep careful records of all their planning, assessment and reviews so that, if necessary, they can present these to the LEA for consideration of a statutory assessment of his special needs in the future.

Individual education plan

Name: Jonathan

Nature of difficulty: Jonathan has a moderate to severe hearing loss. He has been fitted with a radio hearing aid, through which his helpers can communicate clearly with him from any distance, allowing him to hear more clearly against the background noise.

Jonathan still tends to play in a solitary manner and has difficulty in identifying abstract concepts such as 'bigger', 'more than', 'longer'. He speaks in short phrases that are still not clear, and other children cannot always understand what he says.

Action:
1 Become familiar with the special equipment.
We will take turns to wear the radio aid microphone, with the advice of the teacher for the hearing impaired, so that we each become used to using it, and Jonathan relates to each one of us in turn.

2 Seeking training
The speech and language therapist has suggested a programme of activities for encouraging speech for Jonathan. We will contact the therapist to liaise regularly on this.

3 Assessing Jonathan
The teacher for children with hearing impairment will visit the nursery once a fortnight to check on his equipment, work individually with him, advise on

helpful approaches and materials, assess how he is responding to his aids, and help the staff with their planning, assessment and monitoring.

We will use a range of practical play opportunities to see which words Jonathan understands, and we will note down those he does not, planning practical opportunities for building them in. Initially, we will use sand and water play, and play with the train set which he really enjoys.

4 Creating the right environment
We will approach the Head Teacher and governors about carpeting and curtains for the nursery area in order to absorb background noise.

Help from parents:
A diary will run between nursery, speech and language therapist and home, so that everyone can work on the same language activities and goals.

Targets for this term:
1   Jonathan will play for ten minutes with the train set with another child, with a grown up repeating and developing what he is saying to help the conversation.
2   Jonathan will be able to converse in phrases of at least four words that can be clearly understood by an adult.
3   Jonathan will look and listen within a large group, when the leader wears the radio aid.
4   Jonathan will show which of two objects is 'bigger', 'smaller', 'longer', 'shorter', 'more than', 'less than', 'faster', 'slower', and also show that he understands ordinal numbers to four.

Review meeting with parents: In six weeks' time. Invite the speech and language therapist, teacher for children with hearing impairment and the SENCO for our school. If we feel that Jonathan might need a statement of special educational needs in the future, we will need to involve the educational psychologist.

GUIDELINES WHEN WRITING AN IEP

The 'nature of difficulty' should give a clear statement about what the difficulty is in terms of what the child can or cannot do, e.g. 'Can only speak using single words', 'Runs out of the playroom several times each session', 'Cries for half an hour when joining the group even after half-a-term's settling in'. This is far clearer than vague or medical statements such as 'is very aggressive', 'is hyperactive' or 'has cerebral palsy'.

The targets set should be specific and measurable, and written in terms of what the child will be able to do following an intervention (see below). They should give a clear and practical statement about what is going to be done about this difficulty: by whom/when/how long or often/with what (any special equipment involved). The 'help from parents' section must be negotiated and agreed with parents. Any suggestions or difficulties expressed should be noted.

WHAT IS MEANT BY A 'TARGET'?

The target should be clear to everyone who reads it and should be a realistic statement of what the child is expected to be able to do, say, in six to eight weeks' time.

Some statements are vague and give you no clear idea of what the child is doing now and what they *will* be doing when the target is achieved, e.g. 'Tariq will be less aggressive to her peers', 'Hyacinth's self-help skills will be more age-appropriate'.

Instead, aim for targets that are clear and measurable, e.g. 'Suzy will play alongside another child for ten minutes without attempting to pinch or bite', 'Nergis will put his shoes and socks on and off without help'.

Aim for between one and six targets depending on how wide the child's difficulties are. Each difficulty mentioned should have at least one target set against which to measure the effectiveness of any help. Targets should be manageable and practical so that they actually lead to changes in what is done and positive progress for the child.

Targets can usually be broken down into smaller steps for the child to achieve step by small step, week by week. This breaking down into steps is called *task analysis*, and the process of making the whole early years curriculum easier and in smaller steps is called the process of *differentiation*, e.g.:

Step 1: Suzy will play alongside an adult without attempting to bite another child for ten minutes.
Step 2: Suzy will play alongside an adult in a small group of other children without attempting to bite for five minutes.
Step 3: Suzy will play with a small group of children and separate toys for five minutes without biting, watched closely by an adult.

WHAT IS MEANT BY 'EARLY YEARS ACTION PLUS'?

When assessing and working with a young child who has SEN, it might be that an outside professional is involved in helping the setting monitor and meet the child's needs. Some children entering an early years setting may already be at this stage. The kinds of advice and support available will vary with local policies and practices.

Usually, a request for help from outside agencies is likely to follow a decision taken by SENCO, colleagues and parents when reviewing a child's progress in the setting. Has progress been made? What do parents feel? Do we need more information and advice on the child's needs from outside?

Early Years Action Plus is characterized by the involvement of specialists from outside the setting. The SENCO continues to take a leading role, working closely with the member of staff responsible for the child, and

- draws on the advice from outside specialists, for example early years support teachers, sensory support teachers, speech and language therapists and educational psychologists;
- ensures that the child and his or her parents are consulted and kept informed;
- ensures that an IEP is drawn up, incorporating the specialist advice, and that it is incorporated within the curriculum planning for the whole setting;
- with outside specialists, monitors and reviews the child's progress;
- keeps the head of the setting informed.

HOW IS STATUTORY ASSESSMENT REQUESTED?

For a very few children, the help provided by Early Years Action Plus will still not be sufficient to ensure satisfactory progress, even when it has run over several review periods. The provider, external professional and parents may then decide to ask the LEA to consider carrying out a statutory assessment of the child's SEN. In most LEAs, the SENCO needs to consult a support teacher or educational psychologist from the LEA support services. They will advise on completing the necessary forms and ensure that all the relevant evidence in support of a request is attached. A special form is usually needed countersigned by parents. Sometimes it is parents themselves who write to the LEA and request them to consider initiating a statutory assessment. Parents can seek further information about this from the LEA's Parent Partnership Service if they need to, or by sending for information from the DfEE (page 203).

It is helpful if SENCOs attach this information to any request to an LEA for statutory assessment: copies of IEPs and evidence of the implementation of the IEP within the curriculum planning for the setting and whether it was effective, a report concerning the child's general development and health, perhaps from the health visitor or school nurse, the notes from review meetings, reports from any outside specialists and any written views of the parents.

WHAT IS MEANT BY A 'STATUTORY ASSESSMENT OF SEN'?

The LEA must decide quickly whether or not it has the 'evidence' to indicate that a statutory assessment is necessary for a child. It is then responsible for co-ordinating a statutory assessment and will call for the various reports that it requires, from the early years teacher (usually a support teacher, early years practitioner or LEA nursery teacher), an educational psychologist, a doctor, and the social services department if involved, and will ask parents to submit their own views and 'evidence'. The doctor (usually a school doctor or community paediatrician) collects together any reports and 'evidence' from other health service professionals involved such as a speech and language therapist or physiotherapist.

During this time, parents will receive a number of formal letters from the LEA. The LEA is required by law to send these, and it is often helpful if practitioners can reassure parents about their contents and put them in touch with the independent parental supporter (page 168) or parent partnership officer (page 46) if they need explanations or have concerns or queries.

The statutory assessment follows strict time guidelines, and if the early years setting is approached for a report, then a strict time for returning it to the LEA will be given. The whole procedure must not take longer than six months unless there are exceptional circumstances which are again defined clearly in the full text of the Code of Practice. The role of any outside support service becomes one of continuing to meet and monitor the child's needs in the interim, to help support the parents through the process where appropriate, to support the 'setting' and to submit any useful assessment information as part of the process.

The statutory assessment may or may not lead to a statement of special educational needs. When it has gathered all the evidence, the

LEA might feel that a statement is necessary because of the special educational provision required. Parents have various rights of appeal to an SEN tribunal if they are not happy with the statutory assessment procedures, and these are also fully covered in the SEN Code of Practice.

WHAT NEEDS TO BE DONE WHILST A CHILD IS BEING 'STATUTORILY ASSESSED'?

Early years practitioners need to gather the assessment information which they have for the child; each setting is in a unique position to provide information about how the child is learning and developing over a continuous period of time. They may be asked to submit a report directly to the LEA and, if so, they will be informed if a particular form is necessary. This is likely if a setting is the main provider for the child or if it is an LEA nursery school, assessment nursery or nursery class.

If a setting is part of a split placement for the child, or if an early years support teacher (rather than early years educator from a setting) is submitting the main educational report, then it will be helpful if each practitioner involved passes a report to the teacher completing the assessment report, so that it can be incorporated.

WHO ARE 'INDEPENDENT PARENTAL SUPPORTERS' AND WHAT DO THEY DO?

An 'independent parental supporter' is somebody who can support parents through their child's statutory assessment and afterwards. When the LEA issues a child's statement, they must inform the parents of somebody who can give advice and information as well as telling them the name of the 'named officer' of the LEA from whom further information can be obtained.

If a parent would like an independent parental supporter from the start of the statutory assessment process, they can contact the parent partnership officer (page 46) to discuss this. It may also be possible to be introduced to an independent parental supporter through a parents' support group or through a local volunteer centre. Many of these independent parental supporters are themselves parents of children with special needs who have volunteered to support other families.

Many parents feel that they already have enough help and support from family members and friends, and do not feel they need an independent parental supporter. If this is the case, many LEAs will give the name of local and national support groups and the parent partnership officer should be available as their supporter for as long as the parents wish.

WHAT IS MEANT BY 'STATEMENT' OF SEN?

Once a child's SEN have been statutorily assessed, the LEA might decide to issue a statement of SEN. This states what the child's special needs are, what provision will be made for them, how the needs will be monitored and where the child will be placed. It is the responsibility of the LEA to name the setting which the child should attend, taking parents' views into account.

If an early years setting is named as the child's placement, then it will need to see a copy of the child's statement which sets out what the child's special educational needs are, what should be done to meet them, what special educational provision will be made to do so, and what the monitoring and reviewing arrangements should be. If a setting is part of a split placement for the child, then each setting needs to keep closely in touch with each other to share planning, progress and expertise, working closely with parents at all times.

WHAT NEEDS TO BE DONE BY THE SETTING IF A CHILD IS 'STATEMENTED'?

If a setting is named on the statement, it remains their role to continue to meet and monitor the child's special educational needs as they did before, though with the support and provision named on the statement. Usually this will involve regular contact with a member of the support services, helping them to set the child's IEPs and review progress. Sometimes, there is additional equipment or perhaps additional hours of support provided to help the child in the setting or to help staff with curriculum planning.

If a setting is the provider named on the statement, the LEA will ask the SENCO to call regular (usually six-monthly) reviews to monitor whether the child's needs are being met. A six-monthly review cycle (or even less) is recommended for children under 5 because their needs change so rapidly at this stage. The SENCO needs to invite parents, and any support staff, community doctor, therapists or social worker involved with the child. It is also helpful, with parents' permission, to invite any potential future school prior to possible transfer. The main early years educator, any personal support assistant and the setting's SENCO should also be there.

Meetings should be called six weeks in advance, and all professionals involved should be invited to submit a written report if they feel it appropriate. Settings need to ask for these reports to be made available to them at least two weeks before the review so that they can be circulated to everyone attending. Not all professionals will actually produce a report, but the Code of Practice requires that they be invited to.

WHAT HAPPENS AT A STATEMENT REVIEW MEETING?

A member of staff from the setting, usually the SENCO, will normally chair these reviews. After the statement review meeting, information should be gathered on a special review form and sent to the LEA and all others involved in the review. Certain sections ask the question of whether the child still needs a statement, what changes in provision are suggested, and what are the main targets that the child should work towards over the next review period.

Points to consider when thinking about monitoring SEN

- Are you familiar with your national framework and Code of Practice for identifying and assessing SEN?
- Have you procedures and action plans in place to both identify and assess a child with SEN in your setting?
- Have you thought carefully about how to share the process with parents?
- Have you considered ways in which you can establish the child's own views and feelings about the education they are receiving? (Chapter 4)
- Have you thought about how to dovetail your SEN procedures with your approaches for monitoring all the children's needs and progress in your setting?
- Have you considered how to transfer information about SEN to the next school or setting?

SUMMARY

Monitoring special educational needs: the Code of Practice

In this chapter, we noted how many early years practitioners feel the need for support and guidance when meeting the needs of children with SEN. Therefore the chapter gave a simple outline of the SEN Code of Practice (England) and how it works to support these children.

The role of the special needs co-ordinator or 'SENCO' was introduced, and examples given for drawing up an individual education plan which can then be monitored and reviewed with parents.

The statutory assessment procedures and 'statement' of SEN were explained, and pointers given for good practice when monitoring the needs of a child under the SEN Code of Practice.

—11

Emotional climates for confidence and learning

I am a nettle. A growing weed that makes things look scruffy. I have rare things on me but most people want to cut me down. When I try and show them it goes wrong and I have to do it again and again and again to get it wright [sic]. Those people that want to cut me down should. I'm worthless. (Eight-year-old who was feeling very sad – quoted with permission)

LINKS BETWEEN CONFIDENCE, SELF-ESTEEM AND LEARNING

When a child tries anything new, be it a new learning task or behaving in a certain way, and this is met with success and praise, that child is more likely to try that thing again. We talk about a growth of 'confidence' and 'positive self-esteem', meaning that this child is likely to feel more positive about himself or herself as a learner and as a person. When a child is met with failure or criticism, their confidence and self-esteem shrink and they are less likely to try, or they might even 'give up'. Confidence, self-esteem and learning are so inextricably bound together (just as they are in the quotation above) that it becomes essential for us to provide the right emotional climate for learning. For a child with special needs, the very fact that they have been identified as having 'learning difficulties' means that their chances of meeting failure are much greater. Therefore, the risks of suffering low self-esteem and poor confidence are magnified.

Here is one example of a centre of excellence where the emotional welfare and self-esteem of the children, particularly those who are vulnerable, is paramount.

The Pen Green Centre

Many life events affect the families of children attending the community nursery at the Pen Green Centre of Excellence in Corby, Northamptonshire. By using semi-structured interviews with the parents, the staff has been able to keep up with these. For example, about a third of the children's families have been affected by change of job, major illness, separation or divorce. The children respond in many different ways to these changes. Some of them may appear withdrawn or full of grief, some may be angry and aggressive, some may be distractible or find it hard to relate to others, many find it hard to concentrate, and many become needful of constant attention. The staff work hard to enhance these children's emotional well-being. They encourage close attachments to a key worker in the centre. They are also seeking to work creatively to support children through these changes and to evaluate the effectiveness of their interventions. (Whalley, 1999)

It is possible to observe the child whose self-esteem is low. Quite often you will notice certain characteristics and patterns of behaviour, which are listed below. Children who have high self-esteem also have their characteristics and, though they are not a fixed rule, these are also illustrated. Of course, we all feel 'up' and 'down' on particular days depending on recent events, our general sense of well-being, our health and our moods. Children, too, have their 'good days' and their 'bad days'.

Children who have low self-esteem may:

- have a strong need for reassurance;
- appear to feel insecure;
- seem to feel safer if they 'take control';
- seem to have no faith in their own capabilities;
- sometimes have problems learning;
- be reluctant to express their opinions;
- find it hard to accept correction;
- find it hard to make decisions;
- tend to overreact to failure;
- have a low opinion of themselves;
- tend to hurt or bully others.

Children who have high self-esteem may:

- behave more appropriately;
- learn faster;
- be more willing to take risks when learning new things;
- be more confident;
- be better motivated to try;
- make friends more easily;
- view other people positively;
- be able to accept correction or suggestion without giving up;
- develop a good sense of their strengths and weaknesses.

We have seen how confidence and learning seem to be bound together. That is why it is so important that the approaches we design for helping children's behaviour to change should remain positive and should leave the children feeling good about themselves. Negative approaches (such as 'tellings off' or negative sanctions used *on their own*) might control a situation in the short term, but can only leave the child feeling worse in the longer term.

Children with a positive self-image are likely to be more independent, better socially adjusted and more likely to achieve academically (Hall and Delaney, 1989). They are also more likely to view others positively (Lawrence, 1988). Linking this to what we know about attachments (see page 180), children with warm, affectionate relationships with their parents are more likely to have high self-esteem (Flowers, 1991).

PUTTING BEHAVIOUR DIFFICULTIES INTO PERSPECTIVE IN EARLY YEARS SETTINGS

Early years educators know better than anyone that young children arrive in their settings at many different stages of development and understanding, and with many various experiences. In particular, they arrive with many different behaviours and levels of confidence. Sometimes, their behaviour becomes particularly challenging or difficult to manage. We speak of 'difficult behaviours' and not 'difficult children' since, if there is a 'problem behaviour', it does not follow that there is a 'problem child'. The child's behaviour will be influenced by many factors: how the early years setting is organized, family circumstances, factors within the child and also the early years educator's own particular experiences, outside influences and stresses which will affect how the behaviour is handled.

Even for factors which seem to lie 'within the child', behaviour will depend on the developmental stage the child has reached and the particular experiences they have had. Perhaps they are still at a very early stage in learning to concentrate, to look and listen, and this is why they do not do as they are asked. Perhaps they do not understand abstract words like 'still' or 'gentle'. Perhaps your very words and instructions are 'overloading' them with language that they cannot comprehend. For some children, the whole business of separating from home might still be traumatic for them, or they lack experience and confidence when having to adjust to new people or places. Perhaps they are still at a stage of needing to explore and to touch, and this is why they appear to 'fiddle' with everything. Perhaps the very idea of 'rules' is very new to them and they have yet to learn that 'no' means 'no' or that playing socially involves a degree of turn-taking and sharing. In this light, behaviour that might at first seem 'inappropriate' can be understood differently. Suddenly the adult's task becomes one of teaching new skills and inspiring new confidence, rather than just 'getting rid of' an inappropriate behaviour.

What behaviour are we hoping to encourage in the early years setting? If we were going to speak of 'difficult' behaviours, it would be helpful to be clear about the appropriate behaviours we are hoping to encourage in early years settings. It is also helpful if we can define these appropriate behaviours in terms of clear teaching objectives so that we can 'know when we have got there' in our teaching. Here are some examples. We would like children to be able to

- feel motivated and confident enough to develop to their best potential, e.g. *Dana will join in a familiar action song in a group of 12 to 15 children;*
- respect themselves and other people, e.g. *Carly will make room for another child to sit beside her at story time without pushing them;*
- make friends and gain affection, e.g. *Liam will play co-operatively with Ross on the car mat for ten minutes;*
- express their feelings in appropriate ways, e.g. *Hayley will use the words 'sad' or 'cross' whilst explaining why she is crying;*
- 'do as they are nicely asked', e.g. *Robbie will do as he is asked 50 per cent of the time, with one reminder;*
- make a useful contribution to the group, e.g. *Sultan will join in a small group discussion (up to five children) about the Fire Station visit;*
- and develop a positive self-esteem, e.g. *Darren will look pleased when praised for his appropriate behaviour.*

How do we need to order the environment to make this likely? Experience tells us that appropriate behaviour is most likely if children know what is expected of them. Some children may be coming to your setting with the idea that 'play' is synonymous with 'rough and tumble' or chasing each other around. They may need to be shown how to play appropriately, and helped to understand the right and wrong times for more physical behaviour. They respond best to a familiar structure with a calm and purposeful atmosphere, but it may take them a while to become familiar with your routines and to understand that play can be purposeful and intrinsically rewarding.

Children also respond best where there is mutual courtesy, kindness and respect, making it easier for people to work and play together. Again, this might need to be learned in the context of your setting with the adults constantly modelling courteous and kind behaviour to each other and to the children. 'Pleases' and 'thank yous' come much more easily when they are part of the daily exchange rather than when children are confronted with constant demands to 'say the magic word'.

Where the children are behaving appropriately towards each other, each individual enjoys maximum freedom without threatening the freedom or enjoyment of others. This is best achieved when there are observant and interested adults ensuring that each child's needs are met, and where children are encouraged and supported while they learn self-discipline (Henderson, 1995).

Appropriate behaviour is also more likely if positive approaches are used to raise and maintain children's self-esteem. Children who are 'nagged' constantly with 'don't . . . ' and 'no', tend to stop listening or trying after a while, and come to see themselves as 'naughty'. Children whose appropriate behaviour is noticed and praised, are more likely to repeat the behaviours which are attracting your admiration and to see themselves as helpful and kind: *'Good to see you sharing the tractors, James!'*

Practitioners also need to be aware of their own behaviour. If they use stern or loud voices to 'tell children off', and adopt certain expressions on their faces or certain postures with their bodies, children soon begin to copy. A child behaving in this way would soon be seen as 'aggressive' or 'bossy' and this can lead to further difficulties. In other words, practitioners need to beware of any inappropriate modelling.

What skills do the children need to develop appropriate behaviour? We have listed above many of the behaviours we would like to see from children in early years settings. It is usually helpful when designing approaches to change inappropriate behaviour to teach another behaviour in its place. That way, the child not only learns what *not* to do, but what they could be doing instead. This is another feature of positive behavioural teaching; we show or teach the child what they should be doing as well as design approaches to reduce the behaviour that is inappropriate.

For example, instead of telling a child not to slam a door, teach them how to close it gently and quietly. When teaching a child to stop kicking or biting another child, teach them how to play alongside that child happily instead. For most negative behaviours, you will be able to think of an opposite or competing positive behaviour that you can teach or praise in its place.

Pen picture: Ashley

Ashley was four and had just joined her local nursery. She was very excited about it all. Happy and clearly delighted to be there, Ashley would tend to run everywhere, move quickly from activity to activity, begin to 'rough and tumble' her neighbour whenever on the story mat, and to grab for whatever toy she wanted. All this appeared to be done in good humour and with no intention to hurt.

The staff sat down together to formulate how they could help Ashley to behave more calmly and with more consideration. They considered that her main difficulties were her short concentration span, her inability to see other children's points of view, and her difficulty in sharing and turn-taking. Having given her a few weeks to settle, they set up an individual education or 'behaviour' plan to help Ashley:

- to concentrate for five minutes with a short picture book and one adult;
- to take it in turns to share a glue stick when doing craft activities;
- to talk with a ' keyworker' about how another child might be thinking whenever she unintentionally upset them.

By focusing on these positive skills, Ashley soon began to think more carefully before racing into action, and the staff met with parents and withdrew the individual behaviour plan after a term.

Bearing all this in mind, it is clear that the definition of a 'behaviour difficulty' cannot be black and white. Difficult behaviours can arise from many different sources: from the way your setting is organized, from your own experiences or stresses in managing behaviour, from family factors and from factors linked to the child themselves. Perhaps their social skills are still very immature, perhaps 'play' means 'fighting' to them, perhaps they are not yet used to playing and learning with other children or away from home. It is clear that, before deciding that a child 'has' behaviour or emotional difficulties, you will need to give them every chance to settle in and to learn about your rules and boundaries first.

At what stage do you describe a child exhibiting challenging or withdrawn behaviour as 'having special educational needs'? The SEN Code of Practice (DfEE, 2000a) guides us to use the same graduated assessment and intervention as for any other area of learning difficulty (Chapter 10). Consider carefully before you decide on whether there might be the need for 'special' approaches; perhaps you need to follow the approaches for managing *all* behaviour within your setting but with more structure and more consistency?

Has the child had time to settle into your group? Some children take longer than others to settle into new routines, so the behaviour might settle once the child is used to your setting. Talk with parents; they know their child inside-out and can contribute useful information and ideas. What they say might allay your fears; perhaps there are changes at home that will inevitably leave the child unsettled for a while. What they say might also lead you to feel that you need to use more special approaches or to work in a closer partnership with them.

Have you considered that poor self-esteem and confidence might be at the root of things? If so, use a keyworker to befriend and support the child, using positive encouragement and support to enable them to feel more confident and 'tuned in' to you all. Has the child not yet learned to play calmly and socially? This might not be a 'behaviour problem', but more a case of teaching the child another way to play and behave. Look for strategies to make play extra fun, and to make rules clear. Play alongside the child with one or two other children showing that playing socially can be 'safe' and enjoyable. Is the child at a developmental stage yet where he or she has learned sharing, turn-taking and asking for things, etc.? It might be that the 'behaviour problem' is related to the fact that the child is still at a young stage of development.

Choose a few clear rules that the children have contributed to. Talk about them in 'Circle time' (Bliss, Robinson and Maines, 1995; Mosley, 1993; Mortimer, 1998b). Look for opportunities to praise children specifically (*'Thank you for sharing that train'*) for following the rules. Help children who do not follow the rules by *showing* them what to do instead and then praising it. If the child has had time to settle with you, and still is not responding to your usual encouragement and boundary setting, despite all the approaches above, then you might consider talking to parents about more special approaches. Consider entering the child's name on your special needs register and putting together a within-setting individual behaviour plan (e.g. Mortimer, 2000b).

Another way in which children's behaviour can become particularly challenging for the early years educator is when the child has significant attention difficulties. Sometimes children are diagnosed as having an actual disorder and sometimes it is simply that the practitioner knows that attention and concentration need developing and supporting. Here are some general 'starting points' for planning interventions with children whose attention and concentration are particularly short. A similar format is used for children who have experienced recent family breakdown on page 182.

Starting points: including children who have attention difficulties

Do you have children with these needs in your setting?

- Some children find it very hard to attend. Their behaviour tends to be impulsive and poorly controlled to a degree far beyond what you would expect from most three- or four-year-olds.
- They may also be extremely active (attention deficit/hyperactivity disorder or 'ADHD') but not always so (attention deficit disorder or 'ADD'). These are medical diagnoses and it is thought that the condition is caused by a neurological dysfunction in the brain.
- Or it might be that staff members have realized that the child's concentration and attention need working on.
- These children cannot help their short and changing attentions; even if they really try, they still seem to experience difficulties.
- The behaviour of children with ADHD tends to be very inconsistent; it varies greatly from day to day and this might have baffled you.
- Perhaps the child is 'always on the go', cannot settle to look at a picture book with you, rushes into new activities without thinking ahead, disrupts other children constantly and stumbles through obstacles as if they have not been seen.
- On the other hand, the child might be sluggish and slow, often in a daydream and presenting as 'deaf' even when you know that hearing is normal.
- All will find it hard to deal with distractions, to respond to instructions given

to the group, and to remember what you have just said. This is not their fault, but it might sometimes seem to you as if they are misbehaving 'on purpose'.
• Some children receive medication to help with their condition but this is usually when they are older. In the early years, the main help is through positive behaviour management.

What you can do

• Have a small distraction-free area where you and the child can withdraw to sometimes in order to look through picture books or play quietly.
• Keep instructions simple and brief. Make sure the child is attending fully before you speak by using their name and a light shoulder touch.
• Warn the child that you are about to speak to the whole group, and check afterwards that they have 'registered'.
• Use a familiar routine and structure to the day, perhaps using a series of pictures or symbols to help the child predict what happens next.
• Break new activities down into small manageable steps so that the child can concentrate and complete each part of the task successfully.
• 'Sandwich' short structured activity with periods of free play, gradually building up the concentration, step by small step.
• Use frequent rewards and praise to reassure the child.
• Work in small groups, supporting and praising the child's attempts at inter-action, sharing and turn-taking.
• Patiently repeat instructions that the child has forgotten.
• Target your comments carefully; avoid words like 'good' and 'naughty', but use words that describe what you would like the child to do: 'thank you for giving that to Michael', 'please sit down'.
• Try to form a positive and supportive relationship with the family; they are likely to be finding life difficult at home. (From Mortimer, 2000f)

PRACTICAL IMPLICATIONS OF WHAT WE CAN LEARN FROM 'ATTACHMENT THEORY'

There are some children whose behaviour is very resistant to change, though they can settle better if given a 'secure attachment figure' to relate to in the nursery or playgroup: an interested keyworker who can support, offer consistency of handling, and be there to reassure and to encourage. 'Attachment theory' argues that children develop a style of relating to important attachment figures in their lives, which secures for them the best parenting available under the circumstances.

Where attachment is working securely, an infant's cries and demands will be met reliably with sensitivity and warmth by the carer, and the growing child develops in confidence and independence (e.g. Bowlby, 1988). If a parent is unresponsive or rejecting of their cries of distress, that child may act as if they are independent long before they are emotionally ready to be. They may pay little attention when their parent leaves them at nursery, and seldom look at their parent or try to involve them in their play. This is known as a pattern of 'anxious-avoidant' attachment.

If a parent is inconsistent in their responses, perhaps because of periods of depression, or frequent absences, the child learns to cry or shout louder with their demands, producing a pattern of 'ambivalent' attachment. There is also a pattern of 'disorganized' or 'controlling' attachment in which children develop a very controlling style over their parent in order to maintain some degree of predictability or structure in their lives. This pattern is common with parents who might themselves have suffered loss, trauma or abuse, or lack a 'secure base' of their own from which to provide nurture and care to others in their lives.

PIPPIN

The PIPPIN project (Parents in Partnership – Parent Infant Network) is based in Hertfordshire and brings together mothers and fathers during the third trimester of pregnancy, seeking to provide the 'secure base' that was not sufficiently available to them during their own childhoods and is not present for them in their current relationships. They meet in a non-judgemental setting in which they can explore their feelings, deal with issues and learn more about their own relationships and patterns of behaviour. Though this can be a painful process, it can help them to understand better what are appropriate responses to their children in a particular situation (Pound, 1990). Parents who have attended the PIPPIN classes say that they are less anxious, less vulnerable to depression, enjoy their babies more, develop better relationships with their partner, and generally feel more confident, child centred and skilled in coping with the ups and downs of family life.

The study of attachments has opened up a whole new way of assessing family relationships and providing therapeutic support. The patterns of attachment remain remarkably consistent over time until the child is about 6, and so can be observed, identified and worked with. Many of these parents find that their preschool children are difficult to control, extremely angry and aggressive, or highly anxious and 'clingy'. Therapists might have tried to teach them behavioural management techniques, but where there is an attachment difficulty, the behaviour tends to persist, partly because the emotional climate and the relationships are not conducive to change.

Hugs and tugs

This relationship playgroup is run regularly by a Child and Family Service and a local Social Services Family Support Team in a large garrison town. It is based on the work of Binney, McKnight and Broughton (1994). Six mothers and children under 6 who have been identified as having attachment difficulties join a weekly group for twelve sessions. For the first hour, the mothers join a supportive counselling group with a clinical psychologist, a family support worker and a second psychologist (myself) who observes and provides feedback to the counsellors. Whilst this is happening, the children play in a crèche. After sharing a drink together, everyone joins a circle for a series of finely graded relationship play activities that aim to gradually build up mother and child physical contact and enjoyment of each other. Mothers reported that the group had helped them feel closer to their children and more in control of things. They were able to share more pleasure and fun with their child and did not have to 'nag' all the time.

'Attachment theory' also provides helpful pointers for early years educators in their work with children who have emotional and behavioural difficulties. If a child is to feel settled and confident enough to behave and to learn in a setting, educators need to invest time in building up trust, security, routine and consistency so that the setting becomes a 'secure base' for the child. It is also helpful to provide an 'attachment figure' for the child in the form of a warm, supportive and consistent keyworker.

Starting points: including children who have experienced recent family breakdown

Do you have children with these needs in your setting?

- At least one in four families in the UK has one parent absent for whatever reason, and in 90 per cent of these families, it is the father. About one child in eight is likely to experience family divorce before the age of ten, and about a third of these children are under five.

- For some children, a family breakdown may have become a fact of life. For others, feelings will still be raw and sensitive, and you will need to plan how you are going to support that child best through the next few months.

What you can do

- Try to understand what family breakdown means from the child's point of view. A family breakdown can take them utterly by surprise and cause misery and bewilderment. Coming just at a time when the parents will be absorbed in their own conflicts and emotions, this can leave the child feeling isolated, and even in some way responsible for the split.
- Make sure that your setting is an important 'constant' at a time when home life might be confusing and unsettled. Keep to your familiar routines and make allowances if the child wants to play with very familiar or less demanding activities for a while.
- Some children may be feeling very miserable or cross. Others may behave as if nothing is wrong, but may show a delayed reaction later or may show you through their atypical behaviour that they are unsettled. Make allowances for difficult behaviour and stay calm and reassuring as you handle it firmly and consistently, but lovingly too.
- Sometimes you may be approached by parents for advice and it is helpful to be aware of research findings in this area. Children adjust best to the change if they continue to feel loved and valued by both parents, even though they live apart. Children whose parents discuss with them what is going on appear to cope better. They need clear information in a way that they can understand. Where is everyone going to live? When will I see Mummy or Daddy next? Is he still my Daddy? Was it because I was naughty? What about Grandma and Grandad?
- It is important that parents do not expect the child to support one against another, no matter how rejected, angry or guilty the remaining parent feels. Children must feel 'allowed' to talk about the missing parent, even if this is distressing for the partner remaining. A photograph album of their previous and present life can be a useful talking point for the child to reach for whenever they feel a need to talk about things.
- As a carer, it will be helpful for you to gather the facts from the parent, and establish what the child knows. If you feel you have to, share what you know about ways to help children through recent family breakdown. Agree the factual information you may need to give the child, and agree one carer in your setting who is going to be giving particular support to the child.

- Concentrate on making the child feel secure and comforted during the session. Help to find words to express what the child is feeling, even if these feelings are coming out as challenging behaviour or particular quietness. Do not force the child to talk, but just be there, close by, as an extra comforter and listener as needed.
- If you are also able to offer a listening and impartial ear and practical help to the parents themselves, you may be helping them find the emotional resources to help their children through this difficult time in their lives. (From Mortimer, 2000g)

CHILDREN WHO ARE VULNERABLE TO EMOTIONAL AND BEHAVIOURAL DIFFICULTIES

What factors will determine whether there are likely to be difficulties in a child's emotional development or behaviour? As children develop, their behaviour and their emotional development are going to be influenced in different ways. They will inherit a certain pattern of genes that will affect their behaviour and personality to a certain extent. They will have certain experiences both within the family and in their social groups. Research has shown that positive behaviours, such as empathy and nurturing behaviour, are influenced both by genes and environment. However, anti-social behaviour is most strongly affected by the child's environment and particular experiences (e.g. Rushton et al., 1986; Stevenson, 1997).

Nurture groups

These were developed 30 years ago in the Hackney area of London by psychologist Marjorie Boxall. There were many such groups in London in the 1980s, but then they fell into decline. Now they are being revived in many local education authorities as a means to help some of their more vulnerable children. As an approach, it has been shown to reduce the number of children excluded from schools on account of their behaviour. The groups attempt to replicate a form of 'family life' based on intense personal interest and positive support from the teacher or classroom assistant. Each child is helped to feel special and valued. There are shared meals, and an emphasis on early sensory play and familiarity. Outings are arranged with parents and there are 'coffee days' for parents to come in and share notes about their children. The teachers and assistants are trained by the School of Education at the University of Cambridge. (See Bennathan and Boxall, 2000)

Becoming anti-social or becoming withdrawn is often a learned reaction to frustrating or hurtful experiences. It might be the product of repeated losses or changes in their lives. It therefore makes sense to offer these children support and coping strategies, as well as making sure they receive as many positive experiences as possible in their setting, rather than 'punishment'. Meeting their needs thus involves helping them to manage their own behaviour, using positive praise and encouragement, boosting self-esteem and actually teaching those social skills which are lacking. This is the challenge for the early years educator.

Are boys seen to be more aggressive than girls are? Many research studies have suggested that boys and girls are no different to each other in the amount of anti-social behaviour they show in their preschool years (Loeber and Hay, 1997). Others suggest that girls are more skilful at communicating and co-operating then boys, and this is partly due to girls being socialized at an early age into a nurturing role (Hall and Delaney, 1989). Boys are found by their teachers to have more problems on entry into infant school and at follow-up, several weeks later (Hughes, Pinkerton and Plewis, 1979). Girls are more likely to work quietly in small groups whilst boys engage in more boisterous, aggressive play in larger groups (Tizard, Mortimore and Burchell, 1981). Certainly, after a few years, there are three times as many anti-social and aggressive boys reported as girls. Because these behaviours are linked to poor school progress, it makes sense for schools and early years settings to see what can be done to ensure that the boys keep up with the girls in both learning and behaviour. There are various national and local initiatives to research this further.

Though much can be achieved for early years children within the mainstream curriculum, there will continue to be a need for more therapeutic help for those children with emotional and behavioural difficulties who have suffered abuse or repeated losses over time. This is likely to need more effective inter-agency working and also more training for educators in how to meet their needs. What therapeutic interventions have been developed? Here is one example of an intervention aimed at supporting children with emotional difficulties by preventing patterns of destructive family behaviour through early supportive intervention.

NEWPIN

NEWPIN is a national voluntary organization that helps parents under stress break the cycle of destructive family behaviour. Through a network of local centres, expectant mothers, parents, carers and children are offered a unique opportunity to achieve positive changes in their lives and relationships based on respect, support, equality and empathy. There are training programmes in parenting skills, family play, attachment and befriending skills and learning for life. There is support for mothers with depression and other forms of mental distress. One of the principle aims is to prevent emotional abuse.

Families can refer themselves in or be encouraged to attend by professionals. For the adults, NEWPIN offers an initial home visit, befriending, a 24-hour telephone support network, play sessions with the children, training for personal development, and therapeutic group or individual work. For the children, there is a safe, caring and stimulating environment away from family turmoil, with opportunities for developing play and learning with their parent or carer, perhaps for the first time. Some centres are now developing fathers' groups too. The national contact address is given on page 204.

With the introduction of 'Parenting Orders' through the court system, there is likely to be a rapid growth in parenting programmes and, at the same time, a need for careful evaluation of what seems to work both for parents and for children in the longer term.

CIRCLE-TIME APPROACHES

There appear to be positive benefits for all children, and particularly those experiencing emotional and behavioural difficulties, associated with working in circles (e.g. Ballard, 1982; Bliss, Robinson and Maines, 1995). Authors such as Lawrence (1988), Mosley (1993) and Curry and Bromfield (1994) encourage 'circle time' as a process that enhances the self-esteem of the participants. The process of 'circle time', states Ballard (1982), involves key skills required of any individual belonging to a social group: awareness (knowing who I am), mastery (knowing what I can do) and social interaction (knowing how I function in the world of others).

Jenny Mosley (1993) has designed a whole-school Quality Circle Time model which encompasses regular circle times with all the children, circles for encouraging staff self-esteem and morale, and smaller therapeutic circle times for 'children beyond' (those who are beyond being able to respond to or benefit from the usual approaches). The present author (Mortimer, 1998b) has borrowed from the benefits of 'circle time' and has written about using circles to deliver the early years curriculum across all areas of learning.

EMOTIONAL INTELLIGENCE

For many years, psychologists have debated the controversy surrounding the term 'intelligence'. Does 'intelligence' exist as a concept, or is it simply a measure of how a child performed on a certain assessment on a certain day? Can 'intelligence' be measured in a reliable way and is it a valid predictor of future achievement and ability? Is intelligence 'fixed' by genetic make-up, or does it alter with life's experiences and by what is learned and practised? Over time, environmental influences have been seen as having a significant impact on an individual's intellectual development. Also, there is now a school of thought which claims that there are many different kinds of intelligences, all of which affect our abilities (Gardner, 1983).

From these debates, the term 'emotional intelligence' began to emerge. Mayer and Salovey (1993) defined this as a type of social intelligence that involves the ability to monitor one's own and other people's emotions, to discriminate among them, and to use the information to guide one's thinking and actions. Emotional intelligence was seen as encompassing self-awareness, the ability to manage emotions, self-motivation, empathy and relationship skills.

Some would argue that these 'intelligences' are no more than 'social skills' that can be taught or learned through experience. Others have argued that they are ways to perceive and regulate emotional thought, and some are better endowed than others. This led to a definition of emotional intelligence as the ability to perceive accurately, appraise and express emotion, the ability to access and/or generate feelings when they facilitate thought, the ability to understand emotion and emotional knowledge, the ability to regulate emotions to promote emotional and intellectual growth (Salovey and Sluyter, 1997).

It is likely that we will begin to see a growing market of tools and assessments for measuring and for intervening in children's emotional intelligence if these views are further researched and gain credence. We already have entire industries of websites, consultants, trainers, foundations and partnerships, all seeking to assess and improve the emotional and social climate of the workplace, the school or the home. We may be on the brink of a revolution in the way we view children's intelligence, challenging any traditional views we might still hold that children have fixed 'potentials' and can be selected and divided on the basis of their academic 'intelligence'.

When intelligence and early learning is seen in this much wider context, there is a strong argument for using play-based approaches to early learning. The Early Learning Goals issued in 1999 (QCA) and now subsumed within the QCA Curriculum Guidance pack (QCA, 2000) have emphasized the need for children to learn through play, and state that 'practitioners need to ensure that all children feel included, secure and valued'. This would move towards the vulnerable child being nurtured and supported by their teachers and settings, rather than being rejected or excluded in any sense.

THE PERSONAL, SOCIAL AND EMOTIONAL EARLY LEARNING GOALS

In order to meet the special needs of children with behavioural and emotional needs inclusively we need to embed our approaches within an early years curriculum available for all. The *Early Learning Goals* published by the QCA in 1999 provide a framework for working with early years children in all areas of the curriculum. It is helpful to look at the section of the framework which looks at children's personal, social and emotional learning because we can then be encouraged to see children's behaviour as a matter of what needs to be taught and learned rather than of potential 'difficulty'. These goals are written in terms of what most children will be able to achieve by the end of the foundation stage of learning, that is, by the end of their 'reception' year in school.

Most children will be developing confidence and friendships. They will be confident to try new activities, initiate ideas and speak in a familiar group, and form good relationships with adults and peers. Most will also be settling into learning by working as part of a group or class, and maintaining attention, concentrating, and sitting quietly when appropriate. Most children will continue to be interested, excited and motivated to learn, selecting and using activities and resources independently.

They will be becoming independent in other ways too, dressing and undressing independently, and managing their own personal hygiene. Their awareness of themselves and others will be developing, with a developing awareness of their own needs, views and feelings, and a growing sensitivity to the needs, views and feelings of others. They will understand that people have different needs, views, cultures and beliefs, which need to be treated with respect. In turn, they will have a developing respect for their own cultures and beliefs and those of other people, and understand that they can expect others to treat their needs, views, cultures and beliefs with respect as well.

Most children will also be developing appropriate social behaviour by this time. They will take turns and share fairly, understanding that there need to be agreed values and codes of behaviour for groups, including adults and children, to work together harmoniously. They will also respond to significant experiences, showing a range of feelings when appropriate. By now, most will be able to consider the consequences of their words and actions for themselves and others, understanding what is right, what is wrong, and why.

The author (Mortimer, 1998a; 1998c) has written activity books to serve as ideas and resources for early years educators seeking to teach inclusively towards the early learning goals for personal, social and emotional development. The curriculum profile map shown on page 44 chose one section of the early learning goals for personal and social development and showed how the stepping stones which feed towards these skills can be differentiated into finer or earlier steps in order to help a child develop those skills.

Points to consider when thinking about the emotional climate for early learning

- Does your setting provide an ethos in which each child can feel secure, valued and respected, whatever their ethnicity, religion or special needs?
- Does your setting provide clear and consistent guidelines for behaviour, and follow positive approaches for managing this?
- Does your setting work hard to ensure that each child develops positive esteem and confidence?
- Does each child know whom to turn to for support?

SUMMARY

Emotional climates for confidence and learning

In this chapter, we looked at the importance of positive self-esteem if the young child is to develop as a confident learner and being.

Difficult behaviours were discussed in this light and strategies introduced for helping the child feel emotionally secure and to develop appropriate behaviours.

Some useful strategies for working with groups of young children were introduced, along with larger projects and interventions.

Research into children's attachments and patterns of behaviour has influenced many of these approaches and 'attachment theory' was introduced. We also examined findings from recent work on 'emotional intelligence' and discussed how these might influence provision in the future.

We looked at examples of interventions for children who are vulnerable or who have particular needs in the area of personal, social and emotional development. Pointers were shared for good practice in creating the best emotional climate for all children's learning and development.

—Part Four

Conclusions and Visions

−12

Journey into the future

All young children have needs. (Chapter title in Goodall, 1997)

OVERVIEW

'The inclusion of all young children' has been a recurring theme throughout this book. There are more and more publications on inclusion, many recent examples of joint-working towards inclusion and a government commitment to promoting the inclusion of children with special needs into education (Wolfendale, 2000a). As we noted in the Introduction, we live and work in exciting times.

It is worth remembering that inclusive education for young children is still a comparatively recent phenomenon and that the pathway from philosophy through policy to practice is still being laid down in many areas. The signposts are in place; we know the direction we should go in, but some of us at many levels have still to take the leap of faith which will set us firmly on that journey. We still have to evaluate the best routes for getting there so that we can provide better maps and light the way for others. In this book, we have read the signposts and explored some of those routes. This final chapter explores where these routes might be leading us as we journey into the future.

You will have read many practical suggestions for making inclusion in the early years realistic and practical. There is a useful guide of practical approaches in Dickins and Denziloe (1998; and see page 24). Yet, as we reflect, we begin to see 'inclusion' as more than a list of 'what to do' and come to see it as a whole process and 'way of life'. Widdows expresses inclusion in this way:

> it embraces the functioning of families and of societies. In the context of families with disabled children, especially young

children, it covers such everyday but important issues as the role of families and friends, and the assistance and support they provide; the impact of disability and non-disabled siblings; the practicality of getting out and about on family outings; the way in which intervention is organized; and the impact of attitudes held by the general public. (Widdows, 1997, p. 12)

Whilst 'inclusion' has been one theme which has permeated each chapter of this book, it is true to say that 'change' has been a second. We have seen in Part 1 how recent policy change has brought with it a new era of partnership, 'joined-up' working and moves towards a higher status for family and community learning. In Part 2, we met the key players in the early education. We met the parents, first educators of their children, and discovered new directions for status, partnership and support. We met the children, and noted new efforts to involve children more actively in their own early education and assessment and in decisions affecting their futures. When we turned our attention to the early years educators, we saw how their role was in a state of change and development, with new responsibilities and accountabilities, and also new opportunities for training and professional development. We examined methods of 'engendering reflective practice', so that children's needs could be met flexibly and individually as well as collectively.

As we considered work within multidisciplinary teams, we noted moves to encourage closer teamwork and collaboration, and we looked at how this could be achieved on a local level as well as between services. In all these key players, we saw moves towards change and development, but we also noted that, in practice, educators were still finding themselves working at different points along the continuum of change.

In Part 3 of the book, we moved on to look at the processes involved in assessing and intervening with young children who had special educational needs. We began to see, in this new era of inclusion, that 'special educational needs' could be defined more widely and more pragmatically than we might have done before. We found that, in inclusive settings, we could redefine 'special needs' as 'individual' or 'additional' needs and, in so doing, see that early years expertise could be applied to *all* children. We found that 'assessment' was developing into a more dynamic and interactive tool in which parents and practitioners could participate actively in gathering the fullest picture of the child's needs in a range of settings and situations. We saw how the early years curriculum itself could form a basis for assessment, intervention and monitoring, and how, in 'good practice', all of these were inextricably linked. We also met the proposed revisions in the SEN Code of Practice and began to visualize what these might look like in practice. We recognized that many of us still had a long way to go to feel confident enough to meet all kinds of special educational need within our settings, and saw the importance of more training and professional support for parents and practitioners so that we could all develop competencies and skills.

Finally, because children's emotional development and confidence were felt to be such crucial foundations for successful learning, we took time to look at ways of developing warm emotional climates for early learning. We had been introduced to the Reggio-Emilia approach earlier on page 27. The perspective and practice of this approach shows us how a courageous and reflexive shift in the way we think about young children learning can lead us to new and creative approaches which are child centred, inspire self-confidence and are inclusive. The developers of the approach (and particularly Loris Malaguzzi, the first head of the early childhood service who died in 1993) are commended by Moss as:

> choosing to adopt a social constructive approach; challenging and deconstructing dominant discourses, realizing the power of these discourses in shaping our thoughts and actions, including the field of early childhood pedagogy; rejecting the prescription of rules, goals, methods and standards, and in so doing risking uncertainty and complexity; having the courage to think for themselves in constructing new discourses, and in so doing daring to make the choice of understanding the child as a rich child, a child of infinite capabilities, a child born with a hundred languages; building a new pedagogical project, fore-grounding relationships and encounters, dialogue and confrontation, reflexion and critical thinking; border crossing disciplines and perspectives, replacing 'either/or' positions with a 'both/and' openness; and an active and enquiring relationship to the major issues of our times – childhood, the environment, peace and human coexistence – as well as to developments in science and philosophy. (Moss, 1999, p. 86)

This concept of the child as being born with 'a hundred languages' fits with what we saw to be new moves in the description of intelligence. Children can be seen as having multiple intelligences, which challenges our traditional view of cognitive ability. If we understand 'intelligence' in a much broader sense, then each individual child may have a chance to shine in their own very unique way.

ENTITLEMENT AND PROVISION FOR *ALL* CHILDREN

So what could a 'good' entitlement and provision look like from the perspective of the child? In their document *Quality in Diversity in Early Learning*, members of the Early Childhood Education Forum and National Children's Bureau (1998) have looked at the existing expertise and experience of people working in a wide range of settings in order to draw together and consolidate what might be seen as 'good practice'. They make the point that it is meaningless to look at 'early learning goals' without also elaborating on the role that adults will play in helping children achieve those goals. This led them to summarize what children's entitlements might be when learning in the early years, and what practitioners might do to ensure these. They are written in inclusive terms, and the reader can equally substitute 'children *with special needs*' or, indeed, '*all* children' to each statement:

Belonging and connecting . . .
Children are entitled to be cared for by a small number of familiar and consistent practitioners who understand and are sympathetic to their needs
and to be supported in their learning by practitioners who work with parents/carers or other family members in a partnership of trust, respecting each other's concerns, circumstances, practices and traditions.

Children are entitled to opportunities to form mutually respectful relationships with a range of other people, families and communities
and to be supported in their learning by practitioners who act respectfully and with equal concern towards all the members of the community in which they work.

Being and becoming . . .
Children are entitled to be well-fed, rested, physically active and mentally stimulated, safe from emotional and physical harm
and to be supported in their learning by practitioners who are respectful of differences between individual children and who provide an environment, indoors and outdoors, that is healthy, interesting, involving, safe, enjoyable.

Children are entitled to a sense of well-being, to feelings of self-worth and identity, and confidence in themselves as learners

and to be supported in their learning by practitioners who have high expectations of all children's developing capabilities, giving them opportunities to take risks, to experience success and failure, and to reflect on their learning and achievement.

Contributing and participating . . .
Children are entitled to contribute their individual and unique thoughts, feelings and ideas, and to be respected for the choices and decisions they make
and to be supported in their learning by practitioners who value them for their religious, ethnic / racial, cultural, linguistic and sex / gender identities, and for their special needs, aptitudes and interests.

Children are entitled to opportunities to take on a range of responsibilities in the setting, progressively becoming more aware of what is involved in being a member of a group
and to be supported in their learning by practitioners who welcome their contributions to shared endeavours, and to the tasks of caring for others, and who sensitively extend the range of each child's responsibilities.

Being active and expressing . . .
Children are entitled to opportunities to learn through their senses and physical activity, through active involvement in first hand experiences and play
and to be supported in their learning by practitioners who plan and organize an environment, indoors and outdoors, for active learning, physical movement, first hand experiences, creativity and play.

Children are entitled to express their feelings and emotional needs
and to be supported in their learning by practitioners who are well informed, sensitive and responsive to children's feelings and the full range of their emotional needs.

Thinking, imagining and understanding . . .
Children are entitled to opportunities to think, to understand, to ask questions, to learn skills and processes, and to pursue their own interests and concerns
and to be supported in their learning by practitioners who listen,

watch, take time to understand, welcome children's curiosity, follow where children lead, and provide time, space and opportunities for extending children's thinking, imagining and understanding.

Children are entitled to opportunities to learn about themselves and others, to become critically aware, and to grow to recognize and challenge bias, stereotypes and discriminatory behaviour **and to be supported in their learning by practitioners who** treat everyone with respect and equal concern, who are committed to challenging prejudice and bias and who are aware of strategies for counteracting all forms of discrimination. (Early Childhood Education Forum and National Children's Bureau, 1998, pp. 43–5, reproduced with permission)

ARE WE GETTING IT RIGHT?

In a *Dispatches* programme for Channel 4 television on 'the early years' (Mills and Mills, 1998), much interest was raised in the differing standards of educational attainment across the world and how this related to differing patterns of early years provision. The programme reported on three major international research projects: the International Assessment of Educational Progress, the International Association for Evaluation and Achievement and the Third International Mathematics and Science Study. These studies had already identified important differences in curricular methods across countries, but there was also an increasing awareness of the importance on preschool education in explaining later success. In particular, the preschool approaches used in Hungary, German Switzerland and Flemish Belgium were found to be almost identical, once cultural differences had been accounted for, and to relate to high school achievement in later years. Remarkably similar methods were used in all three countries.

In almost identical ways, children are taught attention, listening and memory skills, appropriate group behaviour, conceptual understanding and phonological and motor skills. The preschool teaching is highly structured and aims to slowly consolidate knowledge and confidence through concrete concepts before moving on to the abstract. The teaching is dominated by an oral linguistic approach and through methods that protect children from failing, or even the perception that they might be failing. Attention, listening and memory skills are taught through eye-contact games during circle time, with each child being 'signed on' and 'signed off' the group activity using an eye-contact greeting and farewell. Listening skills are taught by 'stop/go' games in which children must listen for a specific signal, such as a drum beat, in order to pursue different activities. These skills are developed particularly in whole group music and language activities, which also provide a useful vehicle for teaching memory skills, particularly on the auditory side.

Appropriate group behaviour is also encouraged using whole-class activities at an early age, targeting in particular early linguistic skills and confidence. Music sessions are also seen as a key time for developing phonological awareness as a precursor to later literacy learning. Though formal education begins comparatively late in these countries, the evidence was that children soon catch up their academic learning and indeed overtake other countries in their performance. Mills and Mills (1998) bewailed the fact that no such approaches exist in Britain for engendering these aspects of 'learning to learn' in the preschool years and note that the tendency has been to introduce formal academic skills at the earliest stage instead.

The new curriculum guidance (QCA, 2000) moves away from this emphasis on early academic attainment and introduces a much broader and play-centred approach. We also saw an example of this group-based 'learning to learn' approach embodied in the Music Makers (page 29). Are we beginning to 'get it right' now? We can be sure that there will still be changes to be made, debates to be continued and provisions to be evaluated over the short and long term. We learn in early years to be flexible and creative practitioners, and we can be sure that these skills will continue to be called on in the future.

AN INDEX OF INCLUSIVE EARLY YEARS EDUCATION

Following the impetus of the UNESCO conference in Salamanca which advocated inclusion in education, an 'Index for Inclusion' team of teachers, parents, governors, researchers and a representative of disability groups, developed a programme of research and trials in English schools. This led to the development of an 'Index of Inclusive Education' built on existing good practice and on ideas from other countries. The index allows schools to travel through a process in which they consider how those involved perform at present, and how they might like to perform in the future in order to be more inclusive. It is an aid to reflecting on inclusion and on considering how to develop inclusive practices, policies and cultures starting from 'where you are' at present. The final version (Booth et al., 2000) was financially supported by the DfEE with free distribution to all primary, secondary and special schools and LEAs in England.

Readers are encouraged to gain sight of the publication and to use the index in a variety of ways. The authors welcome any ways of using the materials which help to promote greater reflection about inclusion and lead to greater participation of children in the cultures, curricula and communities of their settings. Here are some examples of what such an index might look like for an early years setting, based on the index but adapted so as to be appropriate to early years provision. Early years practitioners might wish to use this to consider and discuss their own inclusive practice. A version to use or adapt with early years children themselves is given later in this chapter.

Our organization
- Our setting welcomes all early years children from its local community.
- We work together to plan and deliver the early years curriculum.
- We support each other in dealing with difficulties.
- Support assistants work with all the children.
- Parents are partners in their child's learning.
- Our setting seeks to enrol an increasingly diverse population.

Our communication
- We all take part in major decision-making.
- Everybody's views are listened to.
- We listen to the children's views and give them real choices.
- We keep parents, governors and management committees well informed about our policies and practices.
- Our setting is well thought of in our local community.

The experiences we offer
- Each child is entitled to take part in everything we offer.
- Teaching, learning and play are planned with all the children in mind.
- Our early years curriculum develops understanding and respect for differences and for different cultures.
- Each child experiences success in their learning and play.
- We use child-centred assessment methods.
- Difficulties in learning are seen as opportunities for developing our practice further.

Our social climate
- New children are offered particular support and encouragement.
- All children feel equally valued and respected.
- All children are encouraged to work and play together.
- Each child knows what to do if they feel in need of help or comfort.
- We tackle challenging behaviour by using positive teaching.
- Exclusion from and within our setting is minimized.

Our relationships
- There is a sense of teamwork among staff.
- The children approach us readily for help.
- The adults are helpful and supportive to one another.
- We address each other in ways that confirm our value of each other as individuals.
- Our external support services support us in our efforts to increase the children's participation.
- Our visitors always feel welcome. (Adapted from Booth et al., 2000)

This checklist seems to draw together very aptly the various con-clusions reached in this book. Following the 'Index for Inclusion' process could lead to real and solid change in an educational setting, and a change which reflects not only its policy and practice but the culture beyond it as well. It serves as a most appropriate beacon to light the way of early years travellers as they journey inclusively into the future.

CONCLUDING COMMENTS FROM CHILDREN'S VOICES

What might 'inclusion' feel like from the voices of the children them-selves? In the spirit of including children, here is a possible questionnaire which can be talked through with early years children as one measure of whether the provision is approaching 'inclusion'. This is again adapted from the *Index for Inclusion* (Booth et al., 2000). Children can be asked whether they agree with these statements, adapting them so that each child can understand.

- All children my age can come here if they want.
- There is more than one teacher to help me.
- The teachers help each other too.
- Teachers ask me what I would like to do next.

- Teachers listen to me.
- My Mum/Dad/parents/carers know a lot about what I do here.
- Children like coming here.
- I can have a go at everything.
- There are lots of different things to do.
- The teachers show you what to do if you don't know.
- Sometimes I work and play with other children.
- I know who to go to if I am not happy here.
- The teachers are nice and friendly. (Adapted from Booth et al., 2000)

The voices of children bring a fitting end to a book which has concerned itself with including them all. Here are the voices of two five-year-olds reflecting on their early years experiences (quoted in Hutchin, 1999; and Sherman, 1997).

So, why do you come to nursery and school?

If you go to school you'll do good things otherwise you don't know what to do.

I enjoyed coming to my nursery. I liked playing with my friends . . . Best of all I like drawing and pretend in the house and dancing and singing. I like reading books and finding out about minibeasts
        and . . .
                and . . .
                        and . . .

Useful contacts and resources

ADHD Family Support Group, 1A High Street, Dilton Marsh, Westbury, Wiltshire BA14 4DL.

The Centre for Studies on Inclusive Education, 1 Redland Close, Elm Lane, Redland, Bristol BS6 6UE (for copies of the *Index for Inclusion*).

Children in Scotland (courses in early years including SEN), Princes House, 5 Shandwick Place, Edinburgh EH2 4RG.

The 'CaF Directory of specific conditions and rare syndromes in children with their family support networks' can be obtained on subscription from 'Contact a Family', 170 Tottenham Court Road, London W1P 0HA.

The Council for Awards in Children's Care and Education (CACHE) (for Professional Development Award on SEN), 8 Chequer Street, St Albans, Herts AL1 3XZ.

The Department for Education and Employment (DfEE) (for parent information and for government circulars and advice including the SEN Code of Practice). http://www.dfee.gov.uk.

The High/Scope Institute UK, 190–192 Maple Road, London SE20 8HT.

I CAN Training Centre (for day courses for those working with language-impaired children from early years up), 4 Dyers Building, Holborn, London EC1N 2QP.

KCS (specialist tools for making computer equipment accessible to all children) FREEPOST, Southampton SO17 1YA.

National Association for Special Educational Needs (NASEN) (for publications and workshops on all aspects of SEN), 4–5 Amber Business Village, Amber Close, Amington, Tamworth, Staffordshire B77 4RP.

National Association of Toy and Leisure Libraries (send s.a.e. to find out where the nearest toy library is), 68 Churchway, London NW1 1LT.

The National Autistic Society can be contacted at Willesden Lane, London NW2 5RB (Helpline telephone 0171 903 3555). http://www.oneworld.org/autism_uk/nas

National Children's Bureau (many seminars and workshops on children and on SEN), 8 Wakley Street, London EC1V 7QE.

National Early Years Network (for customized in-house training), 77 Holloway Road, London N7 8JZ.

National Portage Association (for Portage parents and workers, and for training in Portage and for information on the 'Quality Play' training), Administrator, 127 Monks Dale, Yeovil, Somerset BA21 3JE.

National Society for the Prevention of Cruelty to Children (NSPCC) (for training on SEN, Child Protection and family work), National Training Centre, 3 Gilmour Close, Beaumont Leys, Leicester LE4 1EZ.

National NEWPIN, Sutherland House, 35 Sutherland Square, Walworth, London SE17 3EE.

Nursery World (for weekly early years magazine, plus six-monthly training supplements covering current early years and SEN courses), Admiral House, 66–68 East Smithfield, London E1 9XY.

The Nurture Group Project, University of Cambridge, School of Education, Shaftesbury Road, Cambridge CB2 2BX.

The Parent Network, 44–46 Caversham Road, London NW5 2DS.

PIPPIN (Parents in Partnership – Parent Infant Network) Registered Office: Derwood, Todds Green, Stevenage SG1 2JE. www.pippin.org.uk

Preschool Learning Alliance National Centre, 69 Kings Cross Road, London WC1X 9LL (information on DPP courses and their special needs certificate, also send for free catalogue, order form and price list of publications).

Rowland Hill Centre for Childhood, White Hart Lane, London N17 7LT.

Royal National Institute for the Blind (RNIB) (for short training courses designed for those who work with children who have visual impairment and their families), Head Office, First Floor, 206 Great Portland street, London W1N 6AA.

The Sarah Duffen Centre (for workshops and courses on young children with Down's syndrome), Belmont Street, Southsea, Hampshire PO5 1NA.

Wales Preschool Learning Alliance (early years SEN courses), 2A Chester Street, Wrexham LL13 8BD.

The Writers' Press, USA (http:www.writerspress.com) publish a number of books for young children about a range of SEN.

References

Abbott, L. and Pugh, G. (1998) 'Training to work in the early years: the way ahead', in L. Abbott and G. Pugh (eds) *Training to Work in the Early Years: Developing the Climbing Frame*, pp. 147–63. Buckingham: Open University Press.

ACCAC (1996) *Desirable Outcomes for Children's Learning on Entering Compulsory School (Wales)*. Wales: ACCAC.

Ainscow, M. (1999) *Understanding the Development of Inclusive Schools*. London: Falmer Press.

Alderson, P. (ed.) (1999) *Learning and Inclusion: The Cleves School Experience*. London: David Fulton.

Bacon, H. (1991) Ch. 6 in S. Richardson and H. Bacon (eds) *Child Sexual Abuse: Whose Problem?* Birmingham: Venture Press, pp. 81–118.

Bagnato, S. J. and Neisworth, J. T. (1991) *Assessment for Early Intervention: Best Practices for Professionals*. London: Guilford Press.

Ballard, J. (1982) *Circlebook*. New York: Irvington.

Balshaw, M. (1991) *Help in the Classroom*. London: David Fulton.

Barnard, C. and Melidis, S. (2000) *Playsense: A Guide and Resource for Play for Babies and Young Children*. London: National Association of Toy and Leisure Libraries (see page 204).

Baskett, H. K. (1983) 'Continuing professional education in social work – an examination of knowledge utilisation from a field perspective'. D.Phil. thesis. University of Sussex.

Bender, M. and Henderson, A. (1996) *Nursery Vouchers: Preparing for Inspection*. London: Preschool Learning Alliance.

Bennathan, M. and Boxall, M. (2000) *Effective Intervention in Primary Schools – Nurture Groups*, 2nd edn. London: David Fulton.

Beveridge, S. (1997) 'Implementing partnership with parents in schools', in S. Wolfendale (ed.) *Working with Parents of SEN Children after the Code of Practice*, pp. 55–68. London: David Fulton.

Binney, V., McKnight, I. and Broughton, S. (1994) 'Relationship play therapy for attachment disturbances in four to seven year old children', *The Clinical Application of Ethology and Attachment Theory*, Occasional Papers No 9, Association for Child Psychology and Psychiatry.

Blamires, M., Robertson, C. and Blamires, J. (1997) *Parent–Teacher Part-nership: Practical Approaches to Meet Special Educational Needs*. London: David Fulton.

Bliss, T., Robinson, G. and Maines, B. (1995) *Developing Circle Time*. Bristol: Lucky Duck.

Booth, T. and Ainscow, M. (1998) *From Them to Us: An International Study of Inclusion in Education*. London: Routledge.

Booth, T., Ainscow, M., Black-Hawkins, K., Vaughan, M. and Shaw, L. (2000) *Index for Inclusion: Developing Learning and Participation in Schools*. Bristol: CSIE (Centre for Studies on Inclusive Education) in collaboration with Centre for Educational Needs, University of Man-chester and Centre for Educational Research, Canterbury Christ Church University College (see page 203).

Bowlby, J. (1998) *A Secure Base: Clinical Implications of Attachment Theory*. London: Routledge.

Bowyer, R. (1970) *The Lowenfeld World Technique*. London: Pergamon.

Boxer, R. (1999) 'Educational psychology service perspective', *Rethinking Support for More Inclusive Schooling*, in SEN Policy Options Steering Group, Policy Paper 1, ch. 6. Tamworth: NASEN.

Brickman, N. A. and Taylor, L. S. (eds) (1991) *Supporting Young Learners*. Ypsilanti, MI: High/Scope Press.

Brinckerhoff, J. and the Portage Project Staff (1987) *The Portage Classroom Curriculum*. Cooperative Educational Service Agency 5, Portage Project, USA (available through NFER-Nelson).

British Psychological Society Division of Educational and Child Psychol-ogy (undated, issued 1999) *The Professional Practice of Educational Psychologists*. Leicester: British Psychological Society.

Bruner, J. S. (1964) 'The course of cognitive growth', *American Psycholo-gist*, **19**, 1–15.

Bruner, J. S. (1966) *Towards a Theory of Instruction*. New York: Norton.

Butterworth, G. and Harris, M. (1994) *Principles of Developmental Psychol-ogy*. Hove: Lawrence Erlbaum.

Challen, M. (1997) 'A pre-school assessment model', in S. Wolfendale (ed.) *Meeting Special Needs in the Early Years*, pp. 14–29. London: David Fulton.

Chizea, C., Henderson, A. and Jones, G. (1999) *Inclusion in Pre-school Settings – Support for Children with Special Needs and their Families*. London: Preschool Learning Alliance.

Clayton, T. and Wiltshire Education Department (1989) *SAINTS – Special Assistants In-service Training Scheme*. Wiltshire Education Department.

Cline, T., Frederickson, N. and Wright, A. (1990) *Effective Inservice Training Resource Pack*. London: University College.

Clinton, H. R. (1996) *It Takes a Village*. New York: Simon & Schuster.

Court, S. D. M. (Chair) (1976) *Fit for the Future: The Report of the Committee on Child Health Services, Volume 1*. London: HMSO.

Cunningham, C. C. and Davis, H. (1985) *Working with Parents: Frameworks for Collaboration*. Milton Keynes: Open University Press.

Curry, M. and Bromfield, C. (1994) *Personal and Social Education for Primary Schools through Circle Time*. Tamworth: NASEN.

Dale, N. (1996) *Working with Families of Children with Special Needs*. London: Routledge.

Dalton P. (1989) 'Working with mothers and children: a personal construct approach', *Clinical Psychology Forum*, **23**.

DENI (Department of Education Northern Ireland) (1998) *Code of Practice on the Identification and Assessment of Special Educational Needs*. Bangor: DENI Special Education Branch.

Department of Health (1991) *The Children Act 1989: Guidance and Regulations; Volume 6, Children with Disabilities*. London: HMSO.

Department of Health and Social Security (Chair: Prof. D. Court) (1976) *Fit for the Future: the Report of the Committee on Child Health Services, Vol 1*. London: HMSO.

Desforges, M. and Lindsay, G. (1995) *The Infant Index*. London: Hodder and Stoughton.

DES (Department of Education and Science) (1990) *Starting with Quality* (The Rumbold Report). London: HMSO.

DFE (Department for Education) (1994) *Code of Practice on the Identification and Assessment of Special Educational Needs*. Nottingham: DFE Publications.

DfEE (Department for Education and Employment) (1996a) *Code of Practice on the Identification and Assessment of Special Educational Needs – Nursery Education Voucher Scheme*. Nottingham: DfEE Publications.

DfEE (Department for Education and Employment) (1996b) *Nursery Education, The Next Steps*. Nottingham: DfEE Publications.

DfEE (Department for Education and Employment) (1997a) *Excellence for All*, Green Paper. Nottingham: DfEE Publications.

DfEE (Department for Education and Employment) (1997b) *SENCO Guide*. Nottingham: DfEE Publications.

DfEE (Department for Education and Employment) (1998a) *Meeting SEN, a Programme for Action*. Nottingham: DfEE Publications.

DfEE (Department for Education and Employment) (1998b) *Early Years Development and Childcare Partnership, Planning Guidance, 1999–2000*. Nottingham: DfEE Publications.

DfEE (Department for Education and Employment) (1998c) *Meeting the Childcare Challenge: A Summary*. Nottingham: DfEE Publications, ref. MCCA5.

DfEE (Department for Education and Employment) (1998d) *Self-Appraisal Schedule: Nursery Education Provision*. Nottingham: DfEE Publications, ref. PP 80/D14/32849/298/253.

DfEE (Department for Education and Employment) (1998e) *Home School*

Agreements, Guidance for Schools, Nottingham: DfEE Publications, ref. PPY984.

DfEE (Department for Education and Employment) (2000a) (draft) *SEN Code of Practice on the Identification and Assessment of Pupils with SEN* and *SEN Thresholds: Good Practice Guidance on Identification and Provision for Pupils with SEN.* Nottingham: DfEE Publications, ref. 0120/2000, July.

DfEE (Department for Education and Employment) (2000b) *Educational Psychology Services (England): Current Role, Good Practice and Future Directions, Report of the Working Group.* Annesley, Notts: DfEE Publications, ref. 0132/2000.

DfEE (Department for Education and Employment) (2000c) *Consultation Pack* (regulation of day care). Nottingham: DfEE Publications, ref. 142/2000.

Dickins, M. and Denziloe, J. (1998) *All Together: How to Create Inclusive Services for Disabled Children and their Families.* London: National Early Years Network.

Donaldson, M. (1978) *Children's Minds.* London: Fontana/Collins.

Drummond, M. J., Rouse, D. and Pugh, G. (1992) *Making Assessment Work: Values and Principles in Assessing Young Children's Learning.* London: National Children's Bureau; and Nottingham: NES Arnold.

Early Childhood Education Forum and National Children's Bureau (1998) *Quality in Diversity in Early Learning.* London: National Children's Bureau.

Farrell, P. (ed.) (1985) *EDY: Its Impact on Staff Training in Mental Handicap.* Manchester: Manchester University Press.

Flowers, J. V. (1991) 'A behavioural method of increasing self-confidence in elementary school children – treatment and modelling resource', *British Journal of Educational Psychology,* **61**, 13–18.

Freud, A. (1928) *Introduction to the Technique of Child Analysis* (L. P. Clark, trans.). New York: Nervous and Mental Disease Publishing.

Frohman, A. H. and Hilliard, J. M. (1976) *Portage Guide to Early Education.* Windsor: NFER-Nelson.

Gardner, H. (1983) *Frames of Mind: The Theory of Multiple Intelligences.* New York: Basic Books.

Gersch, I., Holgate, A. and Sigston, A. (1993) 'Valuing the child's perspective: a revised student report and other practical initiatives' *Educational Psychology in Practice,* **9**(1), 36–45.

Gillham, B. (1978) 'The failure of psychometrics', in B. Gillham (ed.) *Reconstructing Educational Psychology.* Beckenham: Croom Helm.

Goodall, J. (1997) 'All young children have needs', in S. Wolfendale (ed.) *Meeting Special Needs in the Early Years,* ch. 14. London: David Fulton.

Gray, P. (1999) 'Policy issues raised by rethinking support', in *Rethinking Support for More Inclusive Schooling,* SEN Policy Options Steering Group, Policy Paper 1, ch. 2. Tamworth: NASEN.

Grenier, J. (1999) 'New possibilities', *Nursery World*, 18 November, 12–13.

Grennan, T. (1996) *Checklist for the Identification of Children with Special Educational Needs*. Stockport: Hollywood Park Combined Nursery Centre.

Griffey, H. (1999) 'Come to your senses', *Nursery World*, 19 August, 14–15.

Griffiths, R. (1970) *The Abilities of Young Children*. London: Child Development Research Centre.

Hall, C. and Delaney, J. (1989) 'How a personal and social education programme can promote friendship in the infant class', *Research in Education*, **47**.

Hamer, C. (1997) 'STAR Children's Centre – comprehensive working with young children with special needs', in S. Wolfendale (ed.) *Meeting Special Needs in the Early Years*, pp. 30–44. London: David Fulton.

Hanko, G. (1985) *Special Needs in Ordinary Classrooms: Supporting Teachers*. Oxford: Blackwell.

Henderson, A. (1994) *Observation and Record Keeping*. London: Preschool Learning Alliance.

Henderson, A. (1995) *Behaviour in Pre-school Groups*. London: Preschool Learning Alliance.

Henderson, A., Allez, A., Arnott, J. and Toff, M. (1991) *Equal Chances: Eliminating Discrimination and Ensuring Equality in Pre-schools*. London: Preschool Learning Alliance.

Hertfordshire County Council (undated) *Pre-school Pack for Achieving Progress for Children with Special Educational Needs*. St Albans: Area Education Office (West), Hertfordshire House, Civic Close, St Albans AL1 3JZ.

Hinton, S. (1993) 'Assessing for special educational needs and supporting learning in the early years and nursery education', in S. Wolfendale (ed.) *Assessing Special Educational Needs*, ch. 3. London: Cassell.

Home Office (1998) *Supporting Families, A Consultation Paper*. London: Stationery Office.

Howard, V. F., Williams, B. F., Port, P. D. and Lepper, C. (1997) *Very Young Children with Special Needs*. Columbus, OH: Merrill.

Hug-Hellmuth, H. (1921) 'On the technique of child-analysis', *International Journal of Psycho-Analysis*, **2**, 287–305.

Hughes, M., Pinkerton, G. and Plewis, I. (1979) 'Children's difficulties in starting infant school', *Journal of Child Psychology and Psychiatry*, **20**, 187–96.

Hutchin, V. (1999) *Right from the Start: Effective Planning and Assessment in the Early Years*. London: Hodder & Stoughton.

Jeffree, D. M. and McConkey, R. (1976) *P.I.P. Developmental Charts*. Manchester: Hester Adrian Research Centre, University of Manchester.

Kenyon, P. (1998) *Learning in the Early Years: Ready for Inspection*. Leamington Spa: Scholastic.

Klein, M. (1932) *The Psycho-analysis of Children*. London: Hogarth Press.

Latham, C. and Miles, A. (1997) *Assessing Communication*. London: David Fulton.

Lawrence, D. (1988) *Enhancing Self-esteem in the Classroom* London: Paul Chapman.

Leach, P. (1994) *Children First*. London: Michael Joseph.

Lidz, C. S. (1991) *Practitioner's Guide to Dynamic Assessment*. New York: Guilford Press.

Lindsay, G. (1998) in 'Baseline assessment: a positive or malign initiative?', pp. 8–40 in NASEN *Baseline Assessment: Benefits and Pitfalls*. Special Educational Needs Policy Options Steering Group, Policy Paper 3. Tamworth: NASEN.

Loeber, R. and Hay, D. (1997) 'Key issues in the development of aggression and violence from childhood to early adulthood', *Annual Review of Psychology*, **48**, 371–410.

Lorenz, S. (1992) 'Supporting special needs assistants in mainstream schools', *Educational and Child Psychology*, **9**(4), 25–33.

McCarthy, M. (1992) 'Human resource development: issues facing EPs in times of changing needs', in S. Wolfendale, T. Bryans, M. Fox, A. Labram and A. Sigston (eds) *The Profession and Practice of Educational Psychology*, pp. 86–99. London: Cassell.

McIntyre, D. and Duthie, J. (1977) 'Students' reactions to microteaching', in D. McIntyre, G. McLeod and R. Griffiths (eds) *Investigations of Microteaching*. London: Croom Helm.

Malchiodi, C. (1998) *Understanding Children's Drawings*. London: Jessica Kingsley.

Mayer, J. S. and Salovey, P. (1993) 'The intelligence of emotional intelligence', *Intelligence*, **17**, 433–42.

Miller, J. (1996) *Never Too Young*. London: National Early Years Network and Save the Children.

Mills, C. and Mills, D. (1998) *Dispatches: The Early Years*. (Supporting material to their Channel 4 documentary, 4 January 1998). London: Channel 4 Television.

Mortimer, H. (1995) 'Welcoming young children with special needs into mainstream education', *Support for Learning*, **10**(4), 20–5. Tamworth: NASEN.

Mortimer, H. (1997a) *How Ready and Able are Non-maintained Pre-schools and Nurseries to 'have regard to' the Code of Practice?* Research Design and Pilot Study Implementation Module, Ed.D. (Educational Psychology) programme, University of Sheffield.

Mortimer, H. (1997b) 'Surveying professional practice in the early years; multi-disciplinary assessment teams', in S. Wolfendale (ed.) *Meeting Special Needs in the Early Years*, pp. 136–46. London: David Fulton.

Mortimer, H. (1997c) 'Dovetailing: developing professional roles and sharing skills in a multi-disciplinary pre-school setting', in *Proceed-*

ings of the National Portage Conference 1997, pp. 25–33. Yeovil: National Portage Association.

Mortimer, H. (1998a) *Personal and Social Development*. Leamington Spa: Scholastic.

Mortimer, H. (1998b) *Learning through Play: Circle Time*. Leamington Spa: Scholastic.

Mortimer, H. (1998c) *Photocopiable Activities for Personal and Social Development*. Leamington Spa: Scholastic.

Mortimer, H. (2000a) 'A study to evaluate how the Music Makers approach can be used as a training method to develop reflective practice in pre-school workers in the voluntary and private sectors'. Doctorate in Education (Educational Psychology) thesis, University of Sheffield.

Mortimer, H. (2000b) *Developing Individual Behaviour Plans in Early Years Settings*. Tamworth: NASEN.

Mortimer, H. (2000c) *Playladders*. Lichfield: Q.Ed.

Mortimer, H. (2000d) *Starting Out*. Lichfield: Q.Ed.

Mortimer, H. (2000e) *Taking Part*. Lichfield: Q.Ed.

Mortimer, H. (2000f) 'Including children with AD/HD', *Nursery Projects*, June, p. 17. Leamington Spa: Scholastic.

Mortimer, H. (2000g) 'Including children who are experiencing family breakdown', *Nursery Projects*, July, p. 19. Leamington Spa: Scholastic.

Mortimer, H. (2000h) 'Including children who have learning difficulties', *Nursery Projects*, August, p. 19. Leamington Spa: Scholastic.

Mortimer, H. (2000i) 'Including children who have autistic difficulties', *Nursery Projects*, September, p. 19. Leamington Spa: Scholastic.

Mortimer, H. (2000j) *The Music Makers Approach: Inclusive Activities for Young Children with Special Educational Needs*. Tamworth: NASEN.

Mortimer, H. (2001 to 2002) *Special Needs in the Early Years Series* (provisional title: series of eight books on meeting SEN in early years settings). Leamington Spa: Scholastic.

Mortimer, H., Law, R. and Ladd, J. (2000) *An Evaluation of the I CAN Speech, Language and Communication Unit, Northallerton*. London: I CAN Central Office, 4 Dyers Buildings, Holborn, London EC1N 2QP.

Mosley, J. (1993) *Turn Your School Around*. Cambridge: LDA.

Moss, P. (1999) 'Going critical: childhood, parenthood and the labour market', in S. Wolfendale and H. Einzig (eds) *Parenting Education and Support: New Opportunities*. London: David Fulton.

National Children's Bureau (1997) *Statistics: Under Fives and Pre-school Services 1995*. London: National Children's Bureau, Early Childhood Unit.

Newell P. (1991) *The UN Convention and Children's Rights in the UK*. London: National Children's Bureau.

Newson, E. and Hipgrave, T. (1982) *Getting Through to your Handicapped Child*. Cambridge: Cambridge University Press.

Newson, J. and Newson, E. (1979) *Toys and Playthings*. London: Penguin.

Newton, C. (1988) 'Who knows me best: assessing pre-school children. Levels of participation in a child's world', *Educational Psychology in Practice*, **3**(4), 35–9.

NICCEA (Northern Ireland Council for the Curriculum, Examinations and Assessment) (1997) *Curriculum Guidance for Pre-school Education*. Belfast: NICCEA.

Nutbrown, C. (1999) *Threads of Thinking*, 2nd edn. London: Paul Chapman.

O'Connor, K. J. (1991) *The Play Therapy Primer*. Chichester: John Wiley & Sons.

Open Business School (1983) *Choosing and Developing your Team*, Book 6 of 'The Effective Manager'. Milton Keynes: Open University Press.

OPTIS (1988) *Working Together*. Oxfordshire Programme for Training, Instruction and Supervision.

Peterson, N. L. (1987) *Early Intervention for Handicapped and At-risk Children*. London: Love.

Pound, A. (1990) 'The development of attachment in adult life – the NEWPIN experiment', *British Journal of Psychotherapy*, **7**(1), Autumn, 77–85.

Pugh, G. (1998a) 'Early years training in context', in L. Abbott and G. Pugh (eds) *Training to Work in the Early Years: Developing the Climbing Frame*, pp. 1–15. Buckingham: Open University Press.

Pugh, G. (1998b) 'Children at risk of becoming socially excluded'. Treasury Seminar, 21 January.

Pugh, G. (1999) 'Parenting education and the social policy agenda' , in S. Wolfendale and H. Einzig (eds) *Parenting Education and Support: New Opportunities*, ch. 1. London: David Fulton.

QCA (Qualifications and Curriculum Authority) (1998) *The National Framework for Baseline Assessment: Criteria and Procedures for the Accreditation of Baseline Assessment Schemes*. Hayes: QCA Publications.

QCA (Qualifications and Curriculum Authority) (1999) *Early Learning Goals*. Hayes: QCA Publications, ref. QCA/99/436.

QCA (Qualifications and Curriculum Authority) (2000) *Curriculum Guidance for the Foundation Stage*. Hayes: QCA Publications.

Robson, C. (2000) *Small-Scale Evaluation*. London: Sage.

Rodger, R. (1999) *Planning an Appropriate Curriculum for the Under Fives*. London: David Fulton.

Roffey, S. (1999) *Special Needs in the Early Years: Collaboration, Communication and Co-ordination*. London: David Fulton.

Rosenthal, T. (1978) 'Psychological modelling – theory and practice', in S. Garfield and L. Bergin (eds) *Handbook of Psychology and Behaviour Change*, 2nd edn. Chichester: Wiley.

Rushton, J. P., Fulker, D. W., Neale, M. C., Nias, D. K. and Eysenck, H. J. (1986) 'Altruism and aggression: the heritability of individual differences', *Journal of Personality and Social Psychology*, **50**, 192–8.

Russell, P. (1997) 'Parents as partners: some early impressions of the impact of the Code of Practice', in S. Wolfendale (ed.) *Working With Parents of SEN Children After the Code of Practice*, pp. 69–81. London: David Fulton.

Salovey, P. and Sluyter, D. J. (1997) *Emotional Development and Emotional Intelligence*. New York: Basic Books.

Samra, B. (1999) 'Supporting parents though parenting programmes', in S. Wolfendale and H. Einzig (eds) *Parenting Education and Support, New Opportunities*, ch. 8. London: David Fulton.

Sayeed, Z. and Guerin, E. (2000) *Early Years Play: A Happy Medium for Assessment and Intervention*. London: David Fulton.

SCAA (School Curriculum and Assessment Authority) (1996) *Nursery Education Desirable Outcomes for Children's Learning on Entering Compulsory Education*. London: DfEE.

SCCC (Scottish Consultative Council on the Curriculum) (1999) *A Curriculum Framework for Children 3 to 5*. Dundee: Scottish Consultative Council on the Curriculum and The Scottish Office.

Schon, D. (1995) *The Reflective Practitioner: How Professionals Think in Action*. Aldershot: Arena.

Sebba, J. and Sachdev, D. (1997) *What Works in Inclusive Education?* Ilford: Barnardo's.

Self, L. (1977) *Nadia: A Case of Exceptional Drawing Ability in an Autistic Child*. London: Academic Press.

Sheridan, M. (1975) *From Birth to Five Years: Children's Developmental Progress*. Windsor: NFER-Nelson

Sherman, A. (1997) 'Five-year-olds' perceptions of why we go to school', *Children and Society*, **11**, 117–27.

Siraj-Blatchford, I. (1994) *The Early Years: Laying the Foundations for Racial Equality*. Stoke-on-Trent: Trentham Books.

Smith, R. (1983) *Learning How to Learn: Applied Theory for Adults*. Milton Keynes: Open University Press.

Social Services Inspectorate (1998) *Removing Barriers for Disabled Children: Inspection of Services to Disabled Children and Their Families*. Wetherby: Department of Health.

SOEID (1996) *Children and Young Persons with Special Educational Need: Assessment and Recording*, Circular 4/96. Edinburgh: SOEID.

Stevenson, J. (1997) 'The genetic basis of personality', in C. Cooper and V. Varma (eds) *Processes in Individual Differences*. London: Routledge.

Strauss, A. and Corbin, J. (1990) *Basics of Qualitative Research: Grounded Theory Procedures and Techniques*. London: Sage.

Sylva, K. (1994) 'School influences on children's development', *Journal of Child Psychology and Psychiatry and Allied Professions*, **35**(1), 135–70.

Sylva, K., Roy, C. and Painter, M. (1990) *Childwatching at Playgroup and Nursery School (Oxford Pre-school Research Project)*. Oxford: Grant McIntyre Blackwell.

Tizard, B., Mortimore, J. and Burchell, B. (1981) *Involving Parents in Nursery and Infant Schools – a Source Book for Teachers*. London: Grant McIntyre.

UNESCO (1994) *The Salamanca Statement and Framework for Action on Special Needs Education*. Paris: UNESCO.

Wade, B. and Moore, M. (1993) *Bookstart*. London: Book Trust.

Wade, B. and Moore, M. (2000) 'Starting early with books', in S. Wolfendale and J. Bastiani (eds) *The Contribution of Parents to School Effectiveness*, ch. 8. London: David Fulton.

Warnock, M. (Chair) (1978) *Special Educational Needs: The Report of the Committee of Enquiry into the Education of Handicapped Children and Young People*. London: HMSO.

Waters, J./Newcastle upon Tyne LEA (1999) *Let's Play: A Guide to Interactive Assessment with Young Children*. Newcastle upon Tyne: Educational Psychology Service, Education and Libraries Directorate, The College Street Centre, Newcastle upon Tyne NE1 8DX.

Whalley, M. (1999) 'Unsettled Times', *Nursery World*, 16 September, 10–11.

White, M. (1997) 'A review of the influence and effects of Portage', in S. Wolfendale (ed.) *Working With Parents of SEN Children after the Code of Practice*. London: David Fulton.

White, M. and Parry, J. (1997) *Quality Play: A Response to Special Needs in the Group Setting*. Yeovil: National Portage Association (see page 204).

Widdows, J. (1997) *A Special Need for Inclusion*. London: Children's Society.

Wilson, R. A. (1998) *Special Educational Needs in the Early Years*. London and New York: Routledge.

Wolery, M. and Wilbers, J. S. (eds) (1994) *Including Children with Special Needs in Early Childhood Programs*. Washington, DC: National Association for the Education of Young Children.

Wolfendale, S. (ed.) (1993) *Assessing Special Educational Needs*. London: Cassell.

Wolfendale, S. (1997) 'The state and status of special educational needs in the early years', in S. Wolfendale (ed.) *Meeting Special Needs in the Early Years: Directions in Policy and Practice*, pp. 1–13. London: David Fulton.

Wolfendale, S., (1998) *ALL ABOUT ME*, 2nd edn. Nottingham: NES Arnold.

Wolfendale, S. (1999) 'Parents as key determinants in planning and delivering parenting education and support programmes: an inclusive ideology', in S. Wolfendale and H. Einzig (eds) *Parenting Education and Support, New Opportunities*, ch. 4. London: David Fulton.

Wolfendale, S. (ed.) (2000a) *Special Needs in the Early Years – Snapshots of Practice*. London: Routledge, in association with OMEP.

Wolfendale, S. (2000b) 'Effective schools for the future: incorporating the parental and family dimension', in S. Wolfendale and J. Bastiani (eds) *The Contribution of Parents to School Effectiveness*, ch. 1. London: David Fulton.

Wolfendale, S. (2000c) 'Special needs in the early years: policy options and practice prospects', in *Early Years Development and Special Educational Needs*, SEN Policy Options Steering Group, Policy Paper 2, ch. 2. Tamworth: NASEN.

Wolfendale, S. and Bryans, T. (1979) *Identification of Learning Difficulties: A Model for Implementation*. London: National Association for Remedial Education.

Wolfendale, S. and Cook, G. (1997) *Evaluation of Special Educational Needs Parent Partnership Schemes*, Research Report No. 34. Suffolk: DfEE.

Wood, D. (1988) *How Children Think and Learn*. Oxford: Basil Blackwell.

Name index

Abbott, L. 80
Ainscow, M. xii, xiii, 19, 20
Alderson, P. 22

Bacon, H. 61
Bagnato, S. J. 90
Ballard, J. 186
Balshaw, M. 74
Barnard, C. 51
Baskett, H. K. 75
Bender, M. 10
Bennathan, M. 184
Beveridge, S. 38
Binney, V. 182
Blamires, J. 49
Blamires, M. 49
Bliss, T. 178, 186
Booth, T. xii, xiii, 20, 199, 201, 202
Bowlby, J. 181
Bowyer, R. 60
Boxall, M. 184
Boxer, R. 29
Brickman, N. A. 126
Brinckerhoff, J. 124
Bromfield, C. 186
Broughton, S. 182
Bruner, J. S. 75
Bryans, T. 13
Burchell, B. 185
Butterworth, G. 126

Challen, M. 129
Chizea, C. 25, 27, 102, 145

Clayton, T. 74
Cline, T. 73
Clinton, H. R. 55
Cook, G. 47
Corbin, J. 76, 143
Court, S. D. M. 83
Cunningham, C. C. 88, 89
Curry, M. 186

Dale, N. 83
Dalton, P. 59, 61
Davis, H. 88, 89
Delaney, J. 174, 185
Denziloe, J. 24, 25, 193
Desforges, M. 14
Dickins, M. 24, 25, 193
Donaldson, M. 125
Drummond, M. J. 55, 118, 125, 140
Duthie, J. 76

Farrell, P. 75
Flowers, J. V. 174
Frederickson, N. 73
Freud, A. 64
Frohman, A. H. 129

Gardner, H. 187
Gersch, I. 57
Gillham, B. 121
Gray, P. 29
Grenier, J. 31
Griffey, H. 25
Griffiths, R. 125
Guerin, E. 127, 128

Hall, C. 174, 185
Hamer, C. 91
Hanko, G. 61
Harris, M. 126
Hay, D. 185
Henderson, A. 10, 25, 27, 46, 102, 122, 145, 176
Hilliard, J. M. 129
Hinton, S. 119
Hipgrave, T. 41
Holgate, A. 57
Howard, V. F. 19
Hug-Hellmuth, H. 64
Hughes, M. 185
Hutchin, V. 54, 61, 119, 202

James, W. 73
Jeffree, D. M. 125
Jones, G. 25, 27, 102, 145

Kenyon, P. 10
Kingsley, E. P. 41
Klein, M. 64

Ladd, J. 140, 142
Latham, C. 135
Law, R. 140, 142
Lawrence, D. 174, 186
Leach, P. 57
Lepper, C. 19
Lidz, C. S. 128
Lindsay, G. 13, 14
Loeber, R. 185
Lorenz, S. 74, 75

Subject index